Praise for *The Art*

W. Paul Jones knows well "the wild and wonderful foolishness that awaits any-one who dares to receive and give spiritual direction." We are sure to make fools of ourselves in the process. But this book provides solid guidance for making fools of ourselves not foolishly but wisely. It proves that the art of spiritual direc-tion can indeed be a wild and wonderful adventure in the Spirit.

—DAVID STEINDL-RAST
Benedictine monk, author, lecturer, and
mentor of www.gratefulness.org

Brimful of insights for one-with-one and group spiritual direction contexts, Paul Jones draws from his Wesleyan roots and now from his Catholic monastic prac-tice to provide a map for experienced guides and those just beginning.

—KENT IRA GROFF
Founder and director, Oasis Ministries for Spiritual
Development and author of *The Soul of Tomorrow's Church*

Paul Jones has written a book that will be generously underlined, have numer-ous notes jotted in the margin, and will be read again and again. *The Art of Spiritual Direction* is an encyclopedic resource on the history, theology, and practice of spir-itual direction. The chapter on church renewal through spiritual direction should be required reading for every pastor and priest serving a congregation.

This book is the careful harvest of a lifetime of study, experience, and prac-tice of a mature mind and a warm heart. Simply put, this is a splendid book!

—RUEBEN P. JOB
Retired United Methodist bishop
and coauthor, *A Guide to Prayer for All God's People*

Shortly after The Church of the Saviour learned that *The Recovery of Life's Meaning* was out of print, we made a call to Dr. Jones, whom we had never met, to ask that the book be reprinted, for it had been determinative in the formation of our little church. Since that time, we have awaited eagerly each new book he has written. *The Art of Spiritual Direction* is a helpful resource for those hoping to understand and practice this ancient but ever-new gift to the body of Christ.

—GORDON AND MARY COSBY
Founders, The Church of the Saviour
Washington, DC

The Art of Spiritual Direction argues that guidance is essential to Christian life and distinguishes between spiritual direction, counseling, and therapy. Eight ways of providing direction are suggested, as well as a listing of situations that cause people to ask for spiritual direction.

One of the best chapters is the one that suggests exercises and resources for each of nine dimensions of spiritual life. There is even a chapter that presents a plan for using spiritual direction to renew a local church. What we have been given here is a wonderful reference book on spiritual direction.

—SUSAN RUACH
Director of Spiritual Leadership Development
General Board of Discipleship
The United Methodist Church

The Art of
Spiritual
Direction

*Giving and
Receiving
Spiritual
Guidance*

W. PAUL JONES

UPPER
ROOM BOOKS®
NASHVILLE

THE ART OF SPIRITUAL DIRECTION: Giving and Receiving Spiritual Guidance
© Copyright 2002 by W. Paul Jones
All rights reserved.

No part of this book may be used or reproduced in any manner whatsoever without written permission of the publisher except for brief quotations in critical articles or reviews. For information, write Upper Room Books®, 1908 Grand Avenue, Nashville, TN 37212.

The Upper Room Web site: www.upperroom.org

UPPER ROOM®, UPPER ROOM BOOKS®, and design logos are trademarks owned by Upper Room Ministries, Nashville, Tennessee. All rights reserved.

Unless otherwise noted, Scripture quotations are from the New Revised Standard Version Bible, copyright © 1989, Division of Christian Education of the National Council of the Churches of Christ in the United States of America. Used by permission. All rights reserved.

Scriptures marked NIV are from the HOLY BIBLE, NEW INTERNATIONAL VERSION (NIV). Copyright 1973, 1978, 1984 by International Bible Society. Used by permission of Zondervan Publishing House. All rights reserved.

Scriptures marked RSV are from the Revised Standard Version of the Bible, copyright 1952 (2nd edition, 1971) by the Division of Christian Education of the National Council of the Churches of Christ in the United States of America. Used by permission. All rights reserved.

Scriptures marked KJV are from the King James Version of the Bible.

See page 297 for an extension of this page.

Cover design: Bruce Gore
Interior design and layout: Lori Lynch and Nancy J. Cole
First printing: 2002
Printed in the United States of America

Library of Congress Cataloging-in-Publication Data
Jones, W. Paul (William Paul)
The art of spiritual direction: giving and receiving spiritual guidance / W. Paul Jones.
     p. cm.
ISBN 0-8358-0983-8 (alk. paper)
1. Spiritual direction. I. Title.
BV5053 .J66 2002
253.5'3—dc21   2002002056

To
Susan Ruach, Kathy Sage, and Rich Burns,
my companions in mutual spiritual direction
through these many years
and
to the many with whom I have done
spiritual direction
and the many from whom I have received it

CONTENTS

Appendixes

INTRODUCTION

Over the past decade, a number of books on spirituality have appeared that reflect a growing awareness of spiritual direction as being essential to Christian life. Helpful as these books are, they lack a volume that is not only about spiritual direction but can also function as a text for spiritual direction. Such a book needs to be written for both clergy and laity, especially for those persons who might be called to spiritual direction as a ministry. The concern would be to provide an "informed how" for both giving and receiving direction—whether in a group, with a director, or as self-direction. This book aims to meet that need.

This book does the following:

- Clarifies the nature of spiritual direction—its types (what), purposes (why), and methods (how).

- Describes the eight major types of spiritual direction.

- Identifies basic characteristics one can expect in a spiritual director and tells how to find a suitable director.

- Explores the Christian faith as a process of redemption, and details how direction based on spiritual diversity individualizes this healing for each person.

- Offers guidance for doing communal direction (based on the Wesleyan model) and one-with-one direction (describing potential issues, levels, and types). Gives concrete steps from presession preparations to assignments and accountability, providing case studies for understanding concrete applications.

- Draws upon a trinitarian understanding of God as a basis for offering more than one hundred exercises and disciplines as resources for spiritual direction.

- Provides concise statements of principles that can be used in personal spiritual direction.

- Includes appendixes that provide inventories, instructions, and sample rules, as well as information about such tools as the Myers-Briggs Type Indicator, the Enneagram, the Twelve-Step Program, the TDF Personality Interpretation, Family Systems, and the Jo-hari Window.

Throughout, I will distinguish among therapy, counseling, and spiritual direction, while at the same time illustrating the creative interplay of these three disciplines. Perhaps most important of all will be learning the dynamic of creative listening. While it may well be true that spiritual direction is a gift more than a learned behavior, in either case, knowing how to listen is essential.

CHAPTER 1

SPIRITUAL DIRECTION:
ITS TYPES, PURPOSES, AND METHODS

O f all religions, Christianity is perhaps the most social. One cannot be a Christian alone. Even Christian hermits carry with them into their aloneness the liturgy, scripture, and formation of the church. Furthermore, they are traditionally under the spiritual direction of a person or group, which they regard as necessary lest their pilgrimages succumb to personal whim and defensive avoidance.

While scripture clearly states that all human beings are created in the image of God, even at best this image is badly tarnished. One thing is clear: Deep within our souls, actually as proof that we have a soul, is a profound something that will not be quieted. Experienced negatively, this something seems to be an emptiness, an ache, an anguish, an incompleteness, accompanied by an innate cry for it to go away. Experienced positively, it is a yearning, a craving, a desire, a hope. Karl Barth speaks of this active longing as our "universal homesickness."[1] All my experience and reading convince me that such feelings exist embedded deeply within each of us.

Even country-western music provides a secular version of this yearning or emptiness. There the inevitable sadness is always for what has been lost or is unavailable. We try all kinds of ways to fill this rumbling lack. Many of us are driven to be workaholics, staying so busy that we do not feel the void. Or we become obsessed with accomplishments and status in an effort to insulate ourselves from how we truly feel about ourselves. We may cram the hollowness full of goodies, developing an insatiable appetite for possessions. Perhaps we try to sedate the ache, whether through drugs, overeating, voyeurism, TV, or sports—almost anything, as long as we are "claimed." Yet the Christian knows that none of these universal scramblings that define our daily lives will be effective, at least not for long.

In spite of such denial or avoidance or compensation or sublimation, our craving is incredibly social, for at its heart the craving is for God. This is no arbitrary matter. Our unrecognized obsession with God is rooted objectively in the way things are—for literally it is in God that "we live and move and have our being" (Acts 17:28). And so the lethal teddy bears of our human condition are a collection of surrogate gods, each inviting us to "taste and see," competing as to which particular lord "is good." Competitively, Israel insists, "The LORD is a great God, and a great King above all gods" (Ps. 95:3).

Yet deep within us are more than the negativities of this hungering incompleteness. There are moments when we experience this lack positively—as a yearning that somehow life does have meaning, a meaning that is "not yet." Saint Thérèse of the Child Jesus, in the final year of her young life, was so ravaged by tuberculosis that she was taunted by thoughts that on death's other side there would be nothing. "Unthinkable," she insisted, yet the thought persisted—until with her last breaths the positive passion of her yearning prevailed.

The heart of our homesickness is that somewhere, somehow, there is something or someone through which meaning can flow back over the whole. Lincoln appealed to a divided nation at Gettysburg to live in such a manner that the "dead shall not have died in vain." This imploring echoes the innate call within us to live in such a way that our lives deny death's claim to finality. In truth, it is impossible for any human being to live if he or she becomes convinced that life has no meaning. Without the yearning that births hope, we will commit suicide, physically or emotionally. The thought of an end without proper closure is frightening.

Even Broadway musicals sing of this human condition. *Carousel's* "You'll Never Walk Alone" is a way of coping with the negative. In *West Side Story,* the positive yearning is that "There's a place for us, somewhere. . . ." In *The Wizard of Oz,* the longing is for "somewhere over the rainbow." Beyond suffering and tragedy and death, there must be more. The name behind such yearning is God.

So it has been for me. My own story begins with the emptiness of being an only child. I was claimed increasingly by the *why* questions, which the answers of an Appalachian coal mining town somehow did not touch. This yearning was invaded by a strange drivenness to succeed, causing me to scramble for scholarships to the best universities. Then one lonely, middle-age night, illumination came: All along, my drivenness was in order to earn the only thing I really wanted—four simple words from my mother: "Paul, I love you!" But since these words were unavailable to me, my pilgrimage went deeper. On the other side of degrees and promotions, this craving led by "chance" (which I later recognized as Providence) to a Trappist monastery. There, in the booming contemplative silence, I sensed what it might mean to be filled, to become lost in God, by giving myself away.

There was another dimension to this quest. In graduate school I abandoned the Christian faith of my birth. The New Testament had become clear: Without the Resurrection, there would be no Christianity, only heartbroken fishermen. But there was no conceivable way I could believe then that a dead person got up and walked through doors! Yet one spring morning, I awoke with a strangely new thought: *What would life look like if the resurrection of Jesus Christ were indeed God's promise for the cosmos?* For thirty years now, the vision that emerged that morning has so grasped me that my life is a wager based upon it. Everything exists because God holds it in being over an abyss of nothingness. Not only is each of us gifted by the miracle of being so held, but also we are created in God's image. And what is that? The image of the *Creator*—the One who is creating an awesome cosmos, inconceivable in its unending expanse of billions of billions of light-years, intersecting with the bottomless imagination of our own self-consciousness. By our very nature, then, we are *cocreators* in the completion of creation. Resurrection provides the eyes to see this divine promise of the fullness of time, which we are invited to accomplish together. Heaven and earth are the theater of God's glory, rendering each person and history itself as the kingdom in the making.

The call to become a priest was like giving liturgy to what my daily life had become. Each day is a eucharistic lifting up of the works of our hands, the ponderings of our minds, and the yearnings of our souls—lifting everything, throbbing with resurrection's promise, into God. Then, blessed and returned, the world is graciously fed, drinking in foretaste a toast to the vision of the Sabbath completion of all things. Resurrection is the only thing that makes sense of our yearning—giving us the confidence that God will indeed wipe away every tear from our eyes, and death shall be no more (Rev. 21:1-5).

This version of the Christian faith will not, of course, be the one able to grasp everyone. It is the one that has claimed me, no doubt in part because I am an extrovert, thinker, theologian, writer, monk, priest, and builder. But whatever the particular version, it will appeal as a proposed answer for each person's universal experience—the soul's emptiness within and the yearning for fullness without.

Now to the point not always recognized: Discovering and experiencing the version of the Christian faith that can lay such claim to a person requires spiritual direction. In this book we will explore three major types of spiritual direction: *communal, one-with-one,* and *personal.* All three modes of direction are ways in which a person is helped to discern what God is doing in, to, and with his or her life. We especially need such discernment today, in a society with little consciousness of the absence of the Presence and few viable names for the presence of the Absence. My pilgrimage has depended upon those who have functioned—unconsciously or consciously—as my "spiritual directors."

For better or worse, there is no exception to this need for any of us. I remember a comment by my professor H. Richard Niebuhr, one I now understand as summarizing his life and writings: "None of us are Christians without those who became Christ for us." Some of those folks I remember gratefully. They continue to "sit on my shoulders" as supportive and accountable friends. Others come to mind only at fleeting moments. It was this awareness that convinced me to enter into *self-conscious* spiritual direction. It first took the form of *corporate* direction, in a covenant discipleship group modeled on the class structure of the Wesleyan movement. Later, I felt pulled into serious *personal* spiritual direction. That is, my hunger seemed best fed by serious reading, disciplined praying, and visiting monasteries. The thread of continuity through this personal direction was journaling. This discipline held me accountable for using the spiritual methods I was learning, and it kept before me the model of several saints who knew my path before I did.

But there came a point when my mind, satiated by reading and thinking, craved some form of *mutual* spiritual direction. I found a person who seemed to be on a parallel pilgrimage. Our regularly scheduled sharing disclosed indeed that we were climbing the same mountain, our ascents within hailing distance of each other. This experience prepared me for an invitation by three friends from around the country to meet at least yearly for an intense three days of mutual direction, a strenuous practice that continues to the present.

Finally I knew that it was time for a more intense one-with-one direction, as remains the case now. In uncanny fashion, the Holy

Spirit chose for me the former abbot of the monastery to which I now belong. His own pilgrimage led him to become a hermit. While what he knows and practices is totally natural to his disposition and personality, ironically it is the opposite of mine. He is quiet; I am enthusiastic. He is gentle; I am energetic. He is solitary; I am gregarious. Yet I learn best by walking into my "shadow." Thus, to learn what he knows and to practice what he does were ways of learning who I am. He goes to bed early and arises at 1:30 A.M.; I am a night person. His waking hours, and probably his dreaming ones as well, are spent practicing the Presence. He does this basically in two ways: (1) by abandoning himself contemplatively in God, and (2) eucharistically. He celebrates the Eucharist in the morning as a sacrament of thanksgiving, receiving each new day as gift. I celebrate mine at twilight, lifting up the whole of a painful creation before the face of God, thereby redeeming it and then receiving it back as gift. His abandonment is internal, losing himself in the God of mystery within. My abandonment is external, losing myself ecstatically in the God incarnate in all of creation. We need each other. He teaches me the serenity of silence. I teach him the joy of nature's music.

Recently I have come to appreciate yet another form of spiritual direction in which I participate. I am spiritual director for a number of persons. Through this experience, I am discovering what John Wesley knew—that in directing others, the director is directed as well. Looking from within another person in a oneness of Spirit is mutually feeding. In many ways "it is more blessed to give than to receive," but in giving direction, the blessing is abundantly in the receiving. Thus, at their best, all types of spiritual direction are mutual.

My personal experience confirms the wisdom of the church in coming to this conclusion: *Spiritual direction is not optional.* Along each person's pilgrimage are persons who can make one's journey accountable and whose hospitality makes it possible. The only choice, then, is whether or not to make one's direction conscious and intentional, willing to be held faithful to the map that the Spirit discloses step-by-step. That is the reason for this book—to render conscious the art of giving and receiving spiritual direction. To do this, we need to explore the *what*, *why*, and *how* of direction.

THE *WHAT* OF SPIRITUAL DIRECTION
Toward a Definition

Some situations calling for spiritual direction are straightforward and thus not difficult. These may be as simple as responding to the question: "Would you help me with my prayer life?" And in a few cases the director may be able to keep the sessions on this level, providing disciplines with which the person being directed can experiment, and establishing an arrangement for accountability. The spiritual director can usually determine the level of direction needed. Factors important in discerning how deep to go are the director's training and comfort level, the directee's ability and readiness for depth, and the time available. But in most spiritual direction, when the above factors are in place, some deeper form of transformation will be involved.

In giving and receiving direction, two things need to be initially clear. First, the real director is the Holy Spirit, for simply to live is to be pursued by the divine Presence. According to Saint John of the Cross, a spiritual director is the Christian who watches in amazement the marvels of God as they unfold in another's heart. This implies, secondly, that both giver and receiver are fundamentally called to listen. That for which they are to listen is best imaged not as the "will of God," as if life were codified behavior, the discovery of which involves a guessing game with God. Rather, our listening is a participation in the divine yearning. Thus, directors must take care not to project their own spiritual perspectives upon the pilgrimages of others. The director needs to be transparent to the Spirit, for the more invisible one is in the functioning, the more authentic the direction is likely to be. This requires experience in placing oneself in the position of another, looking together at the person's backyard through the same window—or "walking a mile in their moccasins," as the saying goes.

It follows that an appropriate theological model for spiritual direction is the Incarnation. Thus, the techniques to be used are variations on the theme of creative listening, discerning together the incarnate luring of the Spirit's moving Presence toward fullness of being. Thomas Oden calls this kind of listening "empathy." He defines it as

> the process of placing oneself in the frame of reference of another, perceiving the world as the other perceives it, sharing his or her world imaginatively. Incarnation means that God assumes our frame of reference, entering into our human situation of finitude and estrangement, sharing our human condition even unto death.[2]

This Christian approach to direction touches on the Socratic method in education, where true learning entails midwifery so that each person can become "fully born."

When spiritual direction is understood as a birthing process, one might rightly question the terminology of *director* and *direction*. There have been times in the church's history when such names have been apt. Yet from the church's earliest days, spiritual direction at its best is expressed in such words as *mentoring, modeling,* and *forming.* In fact, not until after the Council of Trent (1545–63) did the image become more that of a director of conscience than a midwife of spiritual consciousness. The Twenty-first Ecumenical Council, known as Vatican II (1962–65), invited a restoration of the earlier tradition, replacing the tendency toward a monolithic, flesh-denying directing with an evocative, world-affirming spiritual diversity. While Catholic spiritual formation has stressed objectivity, sometimes narrowly, Protestantism has stressed subjectivity, sometimes in a "piety" of sentimentality and otherworldliness. Contemporary spiritual direction needs to call upon both traditions in order to fashion souls fit for the twenty-first century.

The present situation, however, is confusing. Twenty-five years ago I sought training from several spiritual directors who worked with Catholic seminarians. Their reply was a confession: "Since Vatican II, we're not clear about what spiritual direction should be or how to do it." They suggested that the Protestant practice of learning counseling skills through chaplaincy programs of Clinical Pastoral Education (CPE) might be more useful than anything Catholics had to offer. Yet recently, CPE personnel are discovering that the secular counseling techniques that have been their models are derelict in regard to spirituality. Today we need spiritual direction that involves a mutuality of director and directee, recognizes a legitimate spiritual diversity, and focuses upon the uniqueness of each individual being formed by the Spirit. So understood, spiritual direction is concerned with faith as a primal trust issuing in commitment, intersected by the church's rich spiritual traditions, and incorporating a diversity of modern approaches to therapy, personality theory, and learning theory.

Currently no agreement exists regarding terminology for spiritual direction. Names currently used include *spiritual friend, soul companion, spiritual companion, shepherd of souls, spiritual guide, mentor, confidant, faith partner,* and *spiritual midwife.* In this book, however, we will use the familiar terminology of *spiritual direction* and *director* as a way of acknowledging continuity with the long tradition spanning not only the church's history, but, as we will see, our Old Testament heritage as well.

My introduction into giving spiritual direction began long ago when a teaching colleague asked for an hour of my time. I assumed that I would be wearing my counseling hat. In such sessions, I usually experience persons as talking around the issue bothering them, hesitant to "drop the first shoe." Only near the end of the session do they dare to drop the second. So I listened patiently to my colleague's scattered conversation as he surfed a number of his activities. Finally, he just stopped, simply asking, "What do you hear me saying?" He had not even dropped the first shoe. Not once had he raised either a hurt or a pressing problem needing resolution. Then I realized that we were involved in something different from anything

I had experienced before. I did not know its name, nor did he, but this was a request for spiritual direction. What he wanted was someone to walk with him in discerning what the Spirit was about in his life. This is what every request for spiritual direction is really—the desire for a companion on the pilgrimage, one willing to participate in a mutual process of discerning, and someone who can hold the person accountable to the discernments. Whatever the method, direction involves support, discernment, and accountability. And the director's role is to be midwife for the Spirit who alone gives birth.

My colleague was intuitively right about how one-with-one spiritual direction operates. The directee provides the material, then asks, "What do you hear?" (or see? or feel? or have a hunch about?) The response has to do with recurring patterns, motifs, avoidances, signs of unease, and momentary excitements. Initially, midwifing means evoking, not controlling, and only later, as birthing is imminent, does the director risk leading, by suggestion. Early entrée, if needed, should be questions as nonleading invitations. Expansion may be invited by repeating phrases, serving as questions, such as, "So you just don't seem to have much energy?" Or just by the phrase, "Tell me more." Careful listening may lead to a point where some coalescence might be useful, beginning, perhaps, as a suggestion posed as a question: "Do I hear you saying . . . ?" The session will probably reach a point where the director might hint of connections seen, venturing such hunches as, "Could it be . . . ?" or "I wonder if . . . ?" Normally, in moving toward tentative closure through insight, the session ends with an assignment. This is because the most important work should happen between sessions. When learning to play the piano as a boy, I never quite got the picture. The lesson was where I thought I was to learn. Instead, the teacher saw the lesson as the time for perceiving what I had learned between sessions through practice. The best assignments in spiritual direction often emerge by asking the person what would be most helpful. After this is decided, the director and directee need to agree on how support can best be given and how accountability can most helpfully be established and maintained.

Some of the greatest theological treatises are actually classics in spiritual direction. Some take the form of confessions (e.g., Augustine); others are journals (e.g., John Wesley); still others are notebooks (e.g., Howard Thurman); and some are collections of letters of spiritual direction (e.g., François Fénelon). In their varied ways, they bear witness to the fact that all theology is autobiography, and all spirituality is pilgrimage. Thus, Paul Tillich's three-volume *Systematic Theology* is not so much a summary of Christian doctrine as it is the explicit distillation of Tillich's own pilgrimage for meaning within a Christian context. Every person is a theologian, with spiritual direction a powerful way of rendering self-conscious that meaning in terms of the spirituality of one's daily autobiography. Theological living and spiritual pilgrimage go hand in hand, with spiritual direction the means of their correlation.

When spiritual direction is understood in this fashion, these are some of the ways I have gleaned to express what is involved:

- Discerning the shape and meaning of the Spirit's workings in one's life

- Envisioning the kind of person God dreams each individual can become

- Paying attention to God's urgings for the sake of spiritual maturity

- Celebrating, struggling, encouraging, reflecting on, and discerning God's workings by sharing one's faith journey with a trusted person

- Establishing and maintaining a growth orientation in one's faith life

- Providing as support a delicate balance of tenderness and toughness whereby one is no longer inclined to hide but is willing to be held accountable so as no longer to postpone becoming who one is

- Opening the road by which one can affirm his or her authentic identity

As for the role of the director, I like to image it as entering the lives of others in such a way that the director is able to sing their song when they forget the words—knowing best which verse to sing and whether to sing it in a major or minor key. The Roman statesman Cicero described such a person as able to speak healing words at the proper season. Directors know the weaknesses of their directees yet continue believing in them, even when they stop believing in themselves.

To be able to do this, the director's own spirituality is crucial. Persons cannot do psychotherapy without undergoing psychotherapy themselves, lest they work out their own demons on others. Likewise, persons should not give spiritual direction who are not themselves receiving it, lest they project their egos onto others. The ideal director is transparent rather than translucent, serving as an instrument of the Spirit's workings and modeling a centered serenity. Put another way, wounded people are best healed by directors who have known themselves as wounded. Consequently, these directors are particularly capable of patient compassion, for they know what it is like to be where others are.

Spiritual direction, the tested method for gaining the courage to stand responsibly before God, is necessary for every Christian. As a lifelong process, it is the search for God within God's search for us. Having said this, it is possible to identify particular needs that make direction especially urgent. Often these are times when God's incognito (mystery) is experienced as a stumbling block:

- Resolving issues from one's past

- Accepting one's limitations and/or those of others

- Internalizing the values by which one wishes to be formed

- Making wise and necessary commitments

- Establishing and nurturing healthy relationships

- Choosing and being held accountable for particular spiritual disciplines that can feed one's soul

- Learning how to be faithful to a community of support and accountability

- Making spiritually mature decisions at major junctures, such as a vocational calling or choosing a life companion

- Dealing with times of burnout or dry-up, as evidenced by the shutting down of one's feelings, imagination, and/or intellect

- Crossing the threshold into one's uncharted landscape

- Encountering faith crises that eat at one's commitment

Now that I have indicated some of the scope of these needs, here are several definitions of spiritual direction, gleaned through conversations with others who have had extensive experience in giving and receiving it. Spiritual direction means:

- Facilitating the total fulfillment of a person through the relationship of that individual with nature, other persons, and God

- Providing companionship on someone's pilgrimage; walking together in the Spirit so as to provide support, discernment, and encounter; integrating spiritually the intersection of the person's intellectual, emotional, social, and cultural contexts

- Receiving help in exploring the paths down which one is being drawn, recognizing the errors that lurk, the moods in which one hides, and the temptations that spread their illusions, so that one may stand firm in the full light of God

- Relating with another mature Christian before whom one is willing to be vulnerable and held accountable, expecting to hear prayerful guidance during the struggle to discern God's active presence in one's life

- Engaging with someone who stands beside and walks with a person; confronting, challenging, proposing, and modeling; doing so in such a manner that the person can sense God's affirmation of his or her worth, and God's confidence in that person's potential

- Discerning God's initiative in terms of where one has been, what one is looking for, what one cares about, what one feels strongly for, what one would like to attain, and who one is being lured to become

- Deepening one's identity by growing in awareness of how death and resurrection function in one's life

- Entering a process of illumination that evokes without compelling, unmasking one's self-deception in order to be totally receptive to the beckoning of God

- Accepting the gift of a presence by which a self may emerge through faith as a whole person

- Forging an ironic self-knowing in which, through kindly support and wise advice, one is able to accept, affirm, and incorporate what one already knows

In light of these varied definitions, you can see the importance of establishing a common image between director and directee as to their respective roles. It makes a difference whether those giving direction see themselves as directors, spiritual companions, guides, gurus, or mentors. Likewise, it matters whether directees see themselves as pilgrims, apprentices, learners, discerners, journeyers, sojourners, disciples, or self-discoverers. Thus, an important part of spiritual direction is attaining a compatibility of image.

TYPES OF DIRECTION

While I will later develop in detail the types of direction, it is helpful here to identify and provide an overview of the eight different types of spiritual direction.

1. PERSONAL DIRECTION

The serious Christian is always involved in self-direction. While favorite disciplines in this regard are prayer and journaling, the most widespread form of personal direction is between author and reader. Spiritual directors for many folks include Henri Nouwen, Thomas Merton, Richard Foster, or Annie Dillard. Most of us have a minilibrary of favorite spiritual books, most apparent by their worn covers and markings in the margins. To these we keep returning for personal direction, for the journeys of these particular authors help us focus our own. A test for identifying the nature of one's personal direction is to observe where one turns for help when encountering an uncertain issue—is it scripture, canon law, a theological classic, journaling, a phone call, or what?

William Paulsell's surmise as to why his friend wanted a period of separation from others says well why most of us get involved in serious personal direction:

> He wanted to be by himself, "not to nurse his wounds, not to count his victories, but rather quietly to take all the mysterious fabric of one's life and there lay it all out and trace the hand of love that somehow ordered all things, the good and the bad, the crooked and the straight, the bitter and the sweet, the whole of it . . . and then to take the whole thing and throw it over one as a garment woven in love."[3]

2. FRIENDSHIP AS DIRECTION

The universal need for at least one close friend is deeply related to direction. The distinctive characteristics of friendship indicate as well what one needs and expects in spiritual direction. Aelred of

Rievaulx (twelfth century) indicates that friends, above all, draw each other out of themselves. Such friendships are classic in the church's history—Teresa of Avila and John of the Cross, Catherine of Siena and Raymond of Capus, Benedict and his sister Scholastica, and Francis and Clare of Assisi.

Not long ago a friend sent me an anonymous "alphabet of characteristics of friendship," a list which, slightly edited, provides the marks of friendship that characterize good direction. A friend:

Accepts you as you are.

Believes in you.

Calls to support you when you most need it.

Doesn't give up on you.

Envisions you as whole and fulfilled.

Forgives, often without being asked.

Gives unconditionally.

Helps in surprising ways.

Invites you to share your life and his or hers.

Just likes to be with you.

Keeps you honest and self-aware.

Loves you for who you truly are.

Makes you feel important.

Never judges, only holds you accountable.

Offers support.

Picks you up when you are down.

Quiets the hurtful memories and present fears.

Remembers you, especially on special days.

Sings the positive things you tend to discount about yourself.

Tells the truth with love.

Understands you, sometimes better than you do.

Values your thoughts and feelings.

Walks beside you.

X-plains the things you do that confuse you.

Yells only when you just won't listen.

Zaps you into excitement for living a life of grace, beauty, joy, peace, and service.

Such honored marks of friendship are, for the Christian, *means* rather than *ends*. The end is the fullness of life lived because of and for God's sake, and thus on behalf of one's neighbor. So oriented and motivated, friendship is a profound kind of spiritual direction. This becomes especially true when friends contract to make explicit this kind of spiritual relationship.[4]

3. MENTORING AS FORMATIONAL DIRECTION

Inevitably, we all have heroes and heroines, serving as role models who draw us toward the outer boundaries. What an incredible difference it makes spiritually whether these models are rock stars, saints, sports heroes, world leaders, TV comedians, or Christian companions. I remember the sorrow I felt several decades ago in discovering that for many women with whom I worked, our sexist society had deprived them of role models to emulate. Yet this condition is now becoming true for all of us. One by one our heroes and heroines are having their clay feet exposed, so that the differential of trust between these heroes and con artists narrows. Direction as mentoring requires models who have "been there" and yet have not fallen, experienced but not succumbed, suffered but gained wisdom through it all, and have so much by wanting so little. Without such models, the horizon becomes painted gray with skepticism.

Learning, at its best, often occurs through apprenticeship. So it is with spiritual growth, under the tutelage of someone through whom one can do and be something of what he or she has done and is. In the Appalachia of my experience, one could become a coal miner only if someone was willing to "take you in" and work by your side until you could dig coal on your own. Recently, I was blessed by learning to pilot a plane at the hands of a person who was in love with soaring. When I made the transition from a Protestant to a Catholic cleric, the bishop wisely assigned me to a priest willing to teach me how to "hear confessions" by trusting me to hear his own. Alcoholics Anonymous assigns a sponsor to each new member, one who as a "recovering alcoholic" models the way to recovery.[5] Likewise, the Catholic Rite of Christian Initiation of Adults (RCIA), a six- to twelve-month program to prepare for confirmation, incorporates this apprenticeship approach of spiritual mentoring. The RCIA weekly sessions are a form of corporate spiritual direction, but, in addition, each participant is gifted with a spiritual mentor who attends all the sessions as a partner, providing ongoing support and friendship, even after confirmation. These expressions of spiritual direction as mentoring recall the relationship of early searchers to the desert fathers and mothers. Daily they would approach the hut of such saints with the request, "A word for my soul."

4. MUTUAL DIRECTION

The mutual spiritual direction in which I was involved for several years involved a monthly dinner at our favorite restaurant. We divided our time, making clear for each segment who would receive and who would give. Direction is not like having a good conversation, in which, analogous to tennis, the ball goes back and forth. In direction, the ball continues to be bounced on one side of the court. In conversation, one person might say, "I had a bad day today," and the other individual might appropriately respond, "Me too." Then each "antes in," ideally without either person dominating the focus. In direction, however, an appropriate response would be, "Tell me about it." When one session of our mutual direction reached closure, we took a dessert break, making clear that the focus of direction was changing to the other person.

5. Communal Direction

The advantage of spiritual direction in a group setting is that a person learns not only how to receive direction but also how to give it. In addition, one has the advantage of additional support and multiple feedback. An important example of communal direction in Protestant circles were the "bands" of two to six members that arose in the 1700s in Herrnhut, the Moravian community of Count Zinzendorf in Germany. Their declared purpose was to "confess your sins to one another and pray for one another, so that you may be healed." Adapted and made mandatory within the early Methodist movement, as we will explore, this process of sharing and being held accountable rested on a positive answer to one question: "Do you desire we should tell you whatsoever we think, whatsoever we fear, whatsoever we hear concerning you?"[6] Sessions began with the director speaking about the state of his or her own soul, then asking searching questions of the other members. The grounding for such communal spiritual direction remains in the General Rules of The United Methodist Church, found in *The Book of Discipline*.

> Such discipline assumes accountability to the community of faith by those who claim that community's support. Support without accountability promotes moral weakness; accountability without support is a form of cruelty.[7]

Such communal direction works best when the group drafts a "rule" to which its members are willing to be held accountable, with each member translating that rule into particulars best suited for the individual's spiritual growth.

6. Personal Discernment through Corporate Direction

In this kind of direction, an individual asks for spiritual guidance from a group in making a major decision, such as discerning his or her vocational direction. This practice, sometimes called a clearness session, is described in Appendix 1.

7. Group Discernment through Corporate Direction

In this type of direction, group decisions are made through a process of discernment, rather than the traditional "majority rules" mentality as set forth in *Robert's Rules of Order*. See Appendix 2 for a more detailed explanation of group discernment through corporate direction. The classic expression of group discernment in scripture occurs at the Jerusalem Conference, where the early church confronted the issue of whether the "Jesus movement" would be a Jewish sect or a new reality in which Gentiles were to be free of Jewish customs. Acts 15:28 describes how the decision was made: "It has seemed good to the Holy Spirit and to us. . . ." Discerning the will of God through the Spirit is what spiritual direction is all about.

8. One-with-One Spiritual Direction

There are a number of options within this type of spiritual direction, ranging from an informal relationship to a contracted service with a trained professional director. To understand what this involves, it is helpful to distinguish therapy, counseling, and spiritual direction.

- *Therapy* is required when debilitating mental or emotional anguish or pain becomes so severe that one is no longer able to cope with daily living. Whatever the particular therapeutic methods used, they tend to be characterized by dialogue. Therapy usually concerns itself with repressed memories, bringing them to the surface so that they and their surrounding emotions can be expressed. The working assumption is that such knowing frees a person sufficiently to cope with daily living.

- *Counseling* is needed to resolve a problem, clarify an issue, or sort out a particular situation, usually for the sake of making a decision. Whatever methods are used, they usually evoke "now" feelings that clarify the implicit issues. The working assumption is that by providing firm support, the pros and cons can be identified, and the person is thus able to make a decision and follow through with it.

- *Spiritual direction* encompasses the totality of one's life—body, mind, and spirit—as these function in one's environment of meaning. While therapy deals with coping, and counseling with deciding, spiritual direction deals with lived meaning. Within this general understanding of spiritual direction, I find it important to distinguish between *situational* and *contextual* directing.[8]

Situational direction is illustrated by the philosopher José Ortega y Gasset in identifying the human need for "a periodical and thorough going over the accounts of the enterprise that is [a person's] life, and for which only [that person] is responsible."[9] Here the directing occurs within the individual's own defining situation.

In contrast, contextual spiritual direction operates intentionally and explicitly from within a particular context, in our case Christian. The particular version that this Christian context takes (which we will develop later as one's "Theological World") is the one in which the directee implicitly and/or explicitly operates as a Christian.

Nonetheless, in contextual direction there are some working assumptions from which the Christian director operates. Here they are, in skeletal form:

- Each person carries baggage from the past (both "original" and "actual" sin).

- Discovering, owning, and unburdening oneself of this dark side are redemptive ("confession").

- The basic need driving each person's life is for unconditional love.

- Because this need can never be fully satisfied through human relationships, attempts to do so lead to frustration, luring us into dead ends of inadequate coping.

- God, as known in the Christ event, can provide the experience of grace by which the person can be healed and made whole.

Put succinctly, Christianity is about healing, and spiritual direction is a primary instrument for enabling it. The process is holistic, in which *spiritual* means the integrative formation of body, mind, and heart. This Christian context helps persons identify the spiritual dimensions of their daily world. When one learns to see ordinary experiences as sacred, such sensations as smelling soup and hearing rain become recognized as spiritual experiences. Yet, in contrast, spiritual direction may bring the discernment that the operating context in which one lives, moves, and has one's being destroys that person's identity. This usually happens when a "world" has been imposed upon the person or expected of him/her. In such situations spiritual direction had best entail a process of conversion to a viable alternative.

While situational direction can be distinguished rather clearly from therapy and from counseling, contextual direction incorporates aspects of both. To illustrate, Alice Miller, one of the finest secular psychotherapists, identifies the primal situation most often requiring therapy as the deprivation of unconditional love as a child. The freedom she identifies as available through secular therapy provides courage sufficient to acknowledge that such love never was and never can be available to anyone. Through grieving this realism, the self is freed from the torment of a doomed game.[10] Contextual direction agrees with this analysis, but only at the human level. The Christian context affirms much more: The unconditional love that by nature every person craves, and without which one's life is restless and thwarted, is available on another level, that of the spiritual.

In providing this context, Christian spiritual direction recognizes that neither therapy nor counseling is really "value free." It is not difficult to recognize the contrasting value contexts underlying the therapies of a Freud, Jung, Maslow, or Frankl. Thus, while a secular counselor may profess to bring no context to a difficult marriage situation, working assumptions are always present. The counselor cannot avoid being influenced by his or her own perspectives on responsibility to and for oneself, spouse, and children; the meaning of making and breaking promises; and the intentionality implied by sexuality. Therefore, contextual direction is not as unusual as one might think. The real difference is that Christian directors make intentional their working context.

Yet the Christian director must not impose his or her own *version* of this context. The initial discernment is of the meaning-context actually operative within the person's own situation, moving it from the implicit to the explicit. Once identified, the task is to appraise the success of this context in nurturing the person's fullness of life, doing so within an awareness of viable options. But operative throughout is the director's own personhood that suggests quietly the availability of Unconditional Love. Thus, even though a Christian director might do situational direction in certain circumstances, this operating context is still implicitly present. That is our reason for being involved. But the director's task is not conversion, in the sense of specific denominational allegiance or particular theological versions of the Christian faith. The Christian context is born of the awareness that since the primordial human craving is for Unconditional Love, authentic healing occurs in a caring context in which such love is implicitly available.

Incorporating certain therapeutic and counseling dimensions into contextual direction is often necessary and desirable. Even though the basic aim of direction is to discern God's healing presence and movement within the person's life, this process entails learning about the self, especially one's motivations. The type and degree of this incorporation depends on the director's skills and training, the depth of blockage encountered, and the time available. Even so, what remains distinctive is the holistic context in which such ingredients and methods are enfolded. Even when a person's pilgrimage requires professional therapy, it is usually advisable for spiritual direction to parallel the therapy, providing a Christian context for the healing. Therapy ends when one can cope. Counseling ends when one can decide. Spiritual direction never ends, for growth is eternal.

SPIRITUAL DIRECTION:
A Short History

The Bible's first story concerns spiritual direction. Adam and Eve had regular appointments to walk with God "at the time of the evening breeze" (Gen. 3:8). When one evening they failed to meet their appointment, God knew that they had failed in their accountability (Gen. 3:9 ff.). In Israel's history, spiritual direction became institutionalized in the prophets. Their function was twofold. They were to be the spiritual directors for the nation as a whole. "The word of the Lord came to me, saying: 'Go and proclaim in the hearing of Jerusalem'" (Jer. 2:1-2). In addition, they were spiritual directors for particular persons, especially the kings. The direction that Nathan provided for King David is classic. Using the method of mirroring through story, he told of a wealthy person with many sheep who stole the solitary lamb of a poor man. In anger, the king shouted, "The man who has done this deserves to die." Nathan replied, "You are the man!" (2 Sam. 12:1-7) David accepted the direction, acknowledging, "I have sinned against the Lord" (2 Sam. 12:13).

Acceptance, however, did not occur with the greatest of Israel's prophets—Jesus. In refusing his direction, the people killed the director. Luke portrays Jesus' direction as unconditional support for the poor and firm accountability for the rich, with special judgment reserved for Israel's religious leaders, who were supposed to provide the people with reliable spiritual direction. While some of Jesus' direction was with words, it was through his presence that he was the director par excellence. Jesus was involved in multiple types of direction. While he called many, his direction took on ever smaller configurations. We have "the multitudes," the five thousand, the five hundred, the seventy sent out two by two, the Twelve, the three disciples closest to Jesus, and finally "the one whom Jesus loved." The contrasting ways in which Jesus directed these different groups is intriguing. For the many, he taught in parables. Afterward, with the Twelve, he often explained such direction in straightforward language (e.g., Matt. 13:10 ff.). The special few he drew apart just to be with him (e.g., Mark 14:33 ff.). While Jesus' key directive is "Follow," his key invitation is "Come and see." For the apostles, spiritual direction meant doing what Jesus did, speaking as Jesus spoke, and healing as Jesus healed.

In so doing, Paul became a spiritual director for the Gentiles. He knew that he was not an eloquent speaker, yet in becoming a conduit for the Spirit, Paul's life became a model of direction: "I am content with weaknesses, insults, hardships, persecutions, and calamities for the sake of Christ; for whenever I am weak, then I am strong" (2 Cor. 12:10). His practical contribution was in perfecting direction through mail to such an extent that his letters became sacred scripture as direction for us all. In some letters, his direction was wrapped with strong praise: "I thank my God every time I remember you, constantly praying with joy in every one of my prayers for all of you, because of your sharing in the gospel from the first day until now" (Phil. 1:3-5). In others, he expressed forthrightly the strong need for accountability, expressing graphically his disappointment in the people's behavior: "I wrote you out of much distress and anguish of heart and with many tears" (2 Cor. 2:4). He trained Timothy and Titus to help him in this ministry of spiritual direction, both through visits and with letters. Likewise, bishops in the early church were chosen from among the people precisely for their abilities in this ministry of support and accountability, especially needed in time of persecution.

When Christianity became widespread after the conversion of Emperor Constantine (A.D. 312), serious Christians substituted for the previous ideal of martyrdom a call to solitary battle in the desert, the citadel of the demons. Here they quickly discovered that such places were quite hazardous without support and accountability. Thus, the desert fathers and mothers became directors for each other. As their fame for holiness grew, people came out from the towns for spiritual direction, asking, "Abba, a word for my soul." Abba ("father") became the title "abbot," and those persons who in their spiritual aloneness (monachus) opted for ongoing direction became known as monks. The monasteries that resulted were communities of corporate direction in which to live seriously a life of disciplined growth. They were also available as "hospitals" for the spiritually sick, whereby persons could stay a while before returning to common life.

In time, monasteries expanded this ministry into "schools," the name coming from schola, meaning leisure. They permitted leisure from labor and regular responsibilities sufficient for a person to discern the meaning of his or her life. Monasteries, and the universities that grew from them, broadened the parameters of spiritual direction, providing increased resources for fulfilling the mind (philosophy), the body (science), and the spirit (theology). Something of this intent is preserved in English universities, where each student is assigned a tutor who functions as a guide for the journey, helping the student appropriate uniquely the diverse opportunities encountered.

Martin Luther was a product of such monastic direction, since he was a member of the Hermits of Saint Augustine. Even at the Diet of Worms, where he refused to recant, he wore his monastic habit. Two features of Luther's reform have particular significance for spiritual direction:

1. He developed the idea of the priesthood of all believers. Reacting to priestly corruption, Luther insisted that confession (and thus spiritual direction) could be done with fellow Christians. During the Nazi period in Germany, Dietrich Bonhoeffer restored this understanding in his underground seminary. "In the presence of a psychiatrist I can only be a sick man; in the presence of a Christian brother I can dare to be a sinner," he said. And who is qualified to give such spiritual direction? "He who himself lives beneath the Cross."[11]

2. Luther's decision to marry was an effort to make the Christian family the Reformation's equivalent of the monastery in providing spiritual direction. Even in my own childhood home, we had a "devotional corner" where my father functioned as the family's "spiritual director," offering prayers, reading the Bible daily, and often giving commentary. The family Bible was our rule and our book of canon law, in which were registered the family's spiritual pilgrimages—births, baptisms, confirmations, marriages, and deaths.

As we shall explore later, the parsonage home of John Wesley's upbringing was explicitly such a place. Susanna, the mother, was the acknowledged spiritual director, even to the point of having one-with-one direction weekly with each child in the family. This practice so influenced Wesley that he considered spiritual direction essential for sanctification ("growth in grace" or "holiness of heart and life"). In fact, he made it an organizing principle, establishing group spiritual direction as a way of renewing the Anglican Church. It is this insistence upon disciplined discipleship under communal direction that is Methodism's central contribution to the ecumenical church.

Unfortunately, throughout the church's history, this tradition of spiritual direction has been largely squandered and almost lost. Mild vestiges of it remain in the idea of godparents, traditionally responsible for supporting and holding the parents accountable for the spiritual direction of their child. The loss is so significant that a case can be made for understanding the modern crisis of the family as a crisis in spiritual direction. Largely lost are family prayers expressing concern for others, Bible reading as the context for growth, bedtime prayers as daily "confessionals," and family meals as "little Eucharists" of thanksgiving in sharing one's flesh and blood with one another. All of these disciplines have become the victims of TV dinners, eating on the run, and overcrowded and conflicting schedules. Likewise, spiritual formation that was once provided by the larger society is in crisis, as witnessed to in the breakdown of such primary institutions as marriage, neighborhoods, religious orders, and congregations. In fact, loyalty to one's employer is no longer a given, nor is it even a factor in professional sports. An offhanded comment I heard recently from a deacon indicates the influence of our culture—he remarked that his grade-school daughter no longer attends church because it conflicts with cheerleader practice every Sunday morning. Ours is a post-Christian era, and to the degree that being authentically Christian is becoming a countercultural calling, spiritual direction is indispensable.

Yet, opportunities and availability of personnel for spiritual direction are lean. Ministers and priests who once imaged themselves as pastors in the spiritual sense are being pressured into limiting even their one-with-one sessions to crisis counseling. And while renewed interest in spirituality is a welcome testimony to the dehumanizing impact of modern society, without provisions for spiritual direction, it will remain only a symptom. Ironically, the real direction often provided in the church is, more often than not, inadvertent. It is happening in the space made available for outside groups, where during the week a host of twelve-step programs occurs for every kind of spiritual struggle, from alcohol and drugs to obesity and gambling.

We may be on the threshold of rediscovering a crucial Christian premise: *Without lifelong support and disciplined accountability within the context of Christian vision, Christianity does little more than justify, make palatable, and provide coping skills for a way of life that is intrinsically sec-*

ular and often un-Christian. Without direction, the current hunger for spirituality is derelict of perspective, and the resources themselves disengaged from the end for which they are intended as means.

THE *WHY* OF SPIRITUAL DIRECTION
As Universal and Christian Necessity

The meaning of being human is sufficient reason to understand why spiritual direction is needed. But that need is exacerbated by the phenomenon of a larger cultural quest for personal authenticity through interiority. Many persons in modern culture exhibit a growing disaffection with their external environment—the vacuity of runaway consumerism, the violence of a politics of power, the injustice of structural inequality, the insecurity of nuclear deterrence, and the suicide of ecological exploitation. In such a "value system" that renders the individual an expendable commodity in a throwaway economy, the only hope for many seems to be in a pursuit of interiority. The phenomenon of spirituality is the quest for a "who" and "why" in reaction to a world of "what" and "how."[12] Thus, in our society of speed, efficiency, and activity, it is not difficult to discern the why of spiritual direction.

1. *Action-reflection.* Life is action, but without intentional reflection upon that action, existence lacks both self-consciousness and intentionality. "Action-reflection" is a basic way we learn, and the test of such learning is its "livability"—the authenticity of life so lived. For the result to become intentional as commitment, accountability is necessary, providing perseverance to resist the human inertia against change. Spiritual direction renders this process self-conscious. Mary is a model. While she "treasured all these words and pondered them in her heart" (Luke 2:19), when the mystery of her pregnancy occurred, she sought out Elizabeth "with haste," no doubt engaging in mutual spiritual direction for three months with one who herself was strangely pregnant (Luke 1:39, 56).

2. *Doing and being.* In a society so charged with the dynamic of "doing" that time for "being" is crowded out, life loses its stabilizing perspective. Thereby, without the discipline of spiritual direction, everything is susceptible to being sacrificed on the altar of having, with living diminished to postponed existence.

3. *Loss of Mystery.* Each of us is a walking miracle. Our hearts beat for decades without any thought on our part, while the mind stands amazed before the phenomenon of a hundred billion light-years. And yet, in a binary age, everything is either on or off, profit or loss, yes or no—with engagement occurring as sound bites rather than poetry, and efficiency declaring that loss of time is a primal sin. Without spiritual direction, the loss of Mystery is lethal.

4. *Wanting/needing.* In our culture of instant gratification, self-discipline gives way to self-pampering. Without the discernment that spiritual direction entails, wanting and needing become hopelessly confused.

5. *Superficiality and depth.* Our culture is increasingly intolerant of persons who refuse to be defined by the narrow parameters of the normal and expected. Blessed are those who crave to know and experience what it means to be thoroughly human. Through spiritual direction, these individuals can become recognizable a mile away, by the way they look at the horizon.

6. *Supportive accountability.* Our society, which views principles as relative and values as flexible, needs to heed this witness from the president of a Christian denomination: "Unless I have a spiritual director with whom humility can be nurtured and perspective preserved, I do not see how I can keep from arrogance over the power that I have, and the breadth of power I might be tempted to seek." Arrogance is the inevitable state of every group and every person when supportive accountability is not operative.

7. *Nurtured growth.* Growth is built into the fabric of existence. Either something grows, or it dies. But without intentional formation, growth gets out of hand. The definition of both cancer and a sick society is uncontrolled growth. In today's society, formation is

largely an aftermath of the competition of special power interests for economic control of things both large and small. Christian spirituality forces a primary question: Is growth of the person totally open, as if we are clay to be formed? Christianity firmly insists that the answer is no. The apt analogy is the relationship of acorn to oak. If an acorn were given "freedom," it could not become a maple. Instead, the options would be to become a healthy oak or a contorted self-contradiction. So with humans, for the "image of God" is so structured within each person that the options are (1) to love God with all our hearts, souls, strength, and minds, or (2) to become twisted, tortured, and frustrated creatures. There is a nonnegotiable structure in the very fact of our existence, so that freedom is the invitation to pilgrimage within the "stages on life's way."[13] Literature abounds with Faustian stories, such as those by Marlowe and Goethe, fascinated by an apparent inevitability—that the temptation to be more than human reduces us to becoming less than human.

Thus, Saint Paul's concern for his "little children" was that they become fully human. His task as their spiritual director was to see that "Christ is formed in you" (Gal. 4:19). Christian spirituality holds that this process of formation involves movement in degrees. In the monastery, we symbolize this movement in the transitions from observer to postulant to novice to temporary professed, and finally to solemn profession for life. Alcoholics Anonymous understands the movement and provides tokens as markers along the pilgrimage of healing. Researchers such as Erik Erikson, Jean Piaget, and Lawrence Kohlberg conclude that there are stages in psychological, educational, and ethical development. The same holds true in spiritual development. And while such a theologian as Sam Keen criticizes James Fowler's research as domesticating the wild Spirit into a tame pigeon, Keen himself discerns stages of spiritual growth: child, rebel, adult, outlaw, and, finally, the foolish lover.[14]

8. *Calling.* Christian spiritual direction involves more than the general stages of spiritual growth. Theologians have long held that there is a divine intentionality for each person. François Fénelon,

one of the classic spiritual directors, understands spiritual direction in terms of God's making us read the residue at the bottom of the heart. This special providence informs Jesus' teachings: "Do not worry about your life, what you will eat or what you will drink. . . . If God so clothes the grass of the field . . ., will he not much more clothe you?" (Matt. 6:25, 30). Fénelon insists that each life is precious in its singularity, offered by God in a path unique to that person.

Spiritual direction operates on this understanding by recognizing levels of intensity. At the most common level, discernment is of the Spirit's working in one's daily living. A second level involves vocational discernment. Each life, taken as a whole, is a calling. Blessed is the person who is able to perceive that intentionality. Third, direction helps one live as a Christian *in* one's calling, fostering qualities of sensitivity, care, and hospitality within the structures and definitions of that calling as provided by society. Here we hear the New Testament admonitions for the Christian to be a good citizen (e.g., Titus 3). But some persons are called to yet a deeper level, where direction is for those called to be a Christian *through* their calling. At this level, one's passion is to transform society's definitions and structures. Thus, the banker defies the practice of redlining, the educator resists testing in favor of a holistic pedagogy, and the parent approaches child rearing as an art form. Finally, perhaps for just a few, are the "hermit souls." Here the beckoning is to relinquish everything, content with nothing less than losing oneself totally in God, whatever and whenever that might turn out to mean. These are the Christians pushing the perimeters, somewhere near the outer edge.

9. *The shadow side.* There is still another universal compulsion requiring spiritual direction. In a sermon to his fellow monks, Matthew Kelty insisted that even they were shrouded in darkness where strange inner forces are at sway.[15] So it is with each of us, tossed by moods and feelings and emotions, tainted by despair and hatred and envy, tempted by pride and ambition and the desire for power. This is our shadow side, in which is rooted the anatomy of all human tragedy. Emerson is right: History is the lengthened shadow

of the person. Spiritual direction is a way to exorcise the dirty basement in all of us. But we are not inclined to do this without God as the "Hound of heaven," biting us with fresh feelings from past wounds, driving us to open the creaky cellar door. While we may wonder how one person can possibly change the broader status quo, wrestling into submission one's resident demons would change significantly the miniworld that one populates. Thomas à Kempis insists that each of us has a final battlefield on which we are called to face down the foe within. It does not take long for a perceptive spiritual director to discern "a word" for each of our souls. We do not hide well the "what" of our shadow world. The hard part, however, is that we are not inclined to hear it—or, if we do, we are incapable of acting upon it without help. Spiritual direction enables us to deal with the "why."

10. *Games.* Each person needs to come to the point where he or she is tired of games. This occurs when one is called upon to put everything on the line. Dag Hammarskjöld, secretary-general of the United Nations from 1953 to 1961, describes such a moment: "I don't know Who—or what—put the question, I don't know when it was put. I don't even remember answering. But at some moment I did answer yes to Someone—or Something—and from that hour I was certain that existence is meaningful and that, therefore, my life, in self-surrender, had a goal."[16] This is the call, known or unknown, to begin the pilgrimage intentionally, which is what spiritual direction is all about.

The *How* of Spiritual Direction:
Diverse Processes, Persons, and Contexts

The *how* of the varied types of spiritual direction is best sensed in the basic method used in giving and receiving one-with-one spiritual direction. Since we will spend an entire chapter developing this idea, here it is sufficient to give a short overview of the steps involved.

Step One: Greeting. It is important for the director initially to set an ethos of "We're in this together, and I'm hopeful." A straightforward beginning should make serious the often meaningless greeting "How are you?" In spiritual direction, the conditioned response of "fine" is inappropriate. Whereas in normal conversation, to give a truthful answer would likely embarrass the greeter, in direction the question is serious: "How are you, Sam? *Really!*" This is a revision of Wesley's primal question: "What is the state of your soul?" For the response to be honest, spiritual direction must exemplify the marks by which Saint Paul characterized the church's presence: where persons speak the truth in love and share one another's joys and sorrows.

Step Two: Acknowledgment. The director needs to clarify the reason for meeting together and guarantee the confidentiality of the session.

Step Three: Invitation. The director invites the directee to share randomly, encouraging him/her to say whatever comes to mind. The directee needs to understand that no advance preparation is expected, such as bringing tentative conclusions to the session. The ambience should be such that the directee is not tempted to wonder, *What am I supposed to say?*

Step Four: Listening. The conversation that follows will be both verbal and nonverbal, intentional and nonintentional. The director listens, intent on the movement of the whole session as event, from unexpected feelings to inclinations to yearnings to blockages to clarity to goals to discipline to accountability. Repetitions, recurrences, motifs, and themes are noted, so as to detect the invisible logic seeming to function as binder. Essential is a sensitivity to the *whys* beneath the *whats* that result in the requests for *hows*.

Just this morning I met with someone entering spiritual direction for the first time. The invisible logic that emerged led from trouble with his present ecclesiastical authority to problems with authority in general, to deep anger over his parochial education as a youth, to a father who always told him he only produced at 80 percent, to intense workaholic tendencies throughout his life. Then it circled back to putting on forty pounds this past year, to other behaviors lacking in self-control, to a final recognition of a long overdue rebellion emerging in flagrant ways of saying no to anything and anybody who "tries to tell me what to do!" With heavy tears, he finally described his mystifying behavior as beginning to make sense. In our next session, we will work on the "therefores."

Step Five: Assimilation. Effective discernment depends on the director's ability to convey a deeply caring attitude, creating an environment in which harsh and distressed feelings are drained through the director's willingness to take them on himself/herself. The method is like skimming off the protective film so as to be able to siphon some residue from the bottom of the pan. Even if there is little need for the director to do more than nod appreciatively and appropriately, it is amazing how often the directee finds this a "helpful" session. The underlying request is more than just wanting problems solved—often the real request is a yearning to be heard, to have one's fragile places held tenderly.

Step Six: Consequence. From illumination, the session moves toward closure by establishing together an assignment to be done between sessions. This might entail focusing on a particular behavior or an appropriate spiritual discipline, followed by determining how accountability might best be established and maintained.

Step Seven: Ending. After scheduling a follow-up session, the director needs to promise ongoing support, convey appreciation for what has happened, and express hope regarding the quality of pilgrimage that is unfolding.

DIVERSITY OF DIRECTOR AND DIRECTEE

Spiritual direction entails appreciation of the Holy Spirit's wildness, defying lines and margins, coming exceptionally, creatively, distinctively, and uniquely to each person. Yet there are general personality patterns within this diversity that can be helpfully identified as aids in direction. While we will explore a number of these later, it is important to illustrate here the contrasting way in which extroverts and introverts tend to function. Extroverts, in order to discover who they are and what they need to be about, naturally share openly, both orally and conceptually. They usually find the conversational method of spiritual direction relatively easy, with communal direction particularly appreciated. Introverts, on the other hand, are not inclined to share with others until they have finished internally the basic work of sorting, weighing, and tentatively concluding. Thus, conversational direction is less natural and may be difficult, making one-with-one direction preferable to communal direction. Consequently, in direction it is important to assure the introvert that random thoughts and feelings, rather than thought-through summaries and conclusions, are worthy of being shared. Invite the directee to let things tumble forth, like playing a game. Likewise, in discerning both assignments and accountability, there needs to be a clear appreciation for the strengths and difficulties of both introverts and extroverts.

Relatedly, directors need to prevent their own Christian version from functioning as normative. This issue was painful in my own life. Raised as an only child by introvert parents, I was forty years old before I sensed that my life was in any way spiritual. Judged by my parental model of introvert spirituality, I was a spiritual failure. It never occurred to me that there might be such a thing as an extrovert spirituality. And so it may be with many persons today when they face the type of spirituality often taught as normative. Listen, for example, to William Law (1686–1761), a classic spiritual writer receiving new appreciation today: "Although God is present everywhere, God is only present to you in the deepest and most central point of your soul. Your natural senses cannot possess or unite with God." While many current writers make such spirituality the ideal, what we really have is an introvert type of spirituality—being heralded by those with introvert propensities as if it should be the primal spirituality available for all. Certainly there is truth in speaking of this depth of soul as "so infinite that nothing can satisfy it or give it any rest, but the infinity of God." And certainly we should be sympathetic if this spiritual dimension is offered as a corrective for our culture's enormous emphasis on the outer dimensions of doing and having. Certainly our starved interiority must be encouraged to reach for something more, something different. The tendency of many writers today, however, is not only to elevate such interior spirituality as being superior but to make it normative.[17] Saint John of the Cross with his "dark night of the soul" and the anonymous writer of *The Cloud of Unknowing* are now standard models for this spirituality of introversion.

As spiritual directors, then, we dare not do violence either to the breadth of spirituality or to the rich diversity of human personality. Extroverts need to explore the interiority of life. Introverts are well advised to discover the vastness of the Spirit's intersection with billions of galaxies and the surgings of oceans. But neither encouragement should neglect or discount the way in which each person is most naturally fed. Thus, denizens of each personality type are called to mature spiritually in terms of their strengths, and at the same time they are invited to take gingerly steps onto the shadowed slopes of their spiritually undeveloped sides. Both are key in spiritual direction, because the God who speaks in a "still small voice" is also the God radiantly incarnate in rendering all things events. The God who emerges as Mystery when one quiets the senses into stillness is the God who ravishes all our senses daily at sunrise and sunset. There are the graced moments of losing oneself in God in amazing foretaste of our "falling asleep with Christ in God." And there are ecstatic participations in the cosmos as Christ's fleshly body, in stunning foretaste of resurrection as the promised kingdom. As in most things, we are right in what we affirm and delinquent in what we dismiss.

The director, then, must understand the diversity of Christian spirituality and recognize the diversity of persons in such a way that direction becomes a matter of discerning the fit toward which the

Spirit beckons. And while life is lived from the inside out, *spiritual direction entails exploration from the outside in.* Augustine speaks of loving and then doing as one will. He says this because inevitably one will do as one loves. Direction focuses on discerning the object of one's love by listening to its manifestations. Throughout the process, exterior and interior are in ongoing dialogue.

In such discernment, it is crucial that the director not become the person's superego. We can sense this if the directee shows an undue need to please the director. As a result, direction becomes an imposition rather than midwifing, the only experience of love possible being some conditional version. In contrast, direction must rest on the assurance that, no matter what, one is a child of God. Only then can one be open to choice as an expression of openness to the Spirit's blowing where it will, involving the person in the discernment process at each step. While most directors today do not intend to impose a particular view, the dynamics involved in directing can be subtle. I learned this painfully one winter evening when one of my grown daughters scheduled a visit. Finally she blurted out, "Dad, you always encouraged us to be our own persons. But all my life I have lived with the burden of never wanting to disappoint you!" It took her thirty years to say this. In the time since, we have grown by retracing the steps of our relationship. This journey has led to a working distinction between needing and appreciating approval.

All that I have said so far can be summarized in this statement: Spiritual direction is an art. Different directors bring various talents to the process, just as directees bring unique conditions and needs. In my own direction, I seem to do best at discernment—sensing underlying dilemmas and drawing hidden connections. Other directors are particularly creative in providing assignments that bring about the precise changes a person needs. Others possess an uncanny ability to draw people out, blessed with an infinite patience. Still others convey a profound sense of support, encouraging the healing of such fears as abandonment. Part of spiritual direction as an art, then, comes in meshing the sensitivities of the director with the contours of the person seeking direction.

FINDING A DIRECTOR

A question I hear often is, "How can I find a director?" Someone once said that when the pupil is ready, the master appears. Maybe, but in my experience, finding a director also involves looking and asking. If what one needs is basically feedback and accountability, situational direction might be sufficient. For this, some persons have even had success with a person who is not spiritually inclined. This happened for one pastor I know by observing a young lawyer who faithfully attended the important meetings in town, exhibiting a caring sensitivity and a keen conscience. An invitation to have lunch together gave birth to an arrangement by which the two could hold each other accountable to their visions.

If more of a spiritual companion is needed, you might begin by listing persons in your church who seem to have it together spiritually. Consider also such issues as gender, age, geographical proximity, and possible availability. In approaching a potential director, it might be best to avoid "spiritual direction" language. Suggest having lunch, meeting for coffee, or spending a little time together after a church meeting. The stated reason might be as simple as, "Let's get to know each other a little better." The person's response often indicates whether that person will be appropriate as your spiritual director.

The second indicator, sensed after spending time together, is the degree to which that person has an ability to listen, rather than needing to draw the conversation to himself/herself. Does the person seem caring and understanding? If the time together doesn't seem right, it only cost you a little time, and maybe the bill for a meal. If it goes well, offer a concrete suggestion, such as: "What would you think about having lunch once a month? I would appreciate your feedback on some of the things my life is about.

Maybe I could do the same for you." A pastor may find it best to seek someone outside his or her parish, for the best sort of spiritual companionship occurs when there is no vested interest in the relationship. Confidentiality could also get sticky.

A mutual arrangement of situational direction served me well for several years, but my initial monastic experience triggered awareness of the need for contextual direction. What I especially needed was one whose spiritual maturity promised for me only what I dared to imagine. That was seventeen years ago, and his mentoring continues through letters and a monthly visit.

For persons needing contextual direction that might involve such intentional matters as the healing of memories, a professional director is advisable. One might inquire at such places as the local Roman Catholic chancery, a monastery or convent, a spiritual retreat center, schools that offer degrees in spiritual direction (they keep current lists of graduates), and places that offer certification, such as The Shalem Institute for Spiritual Formation (Bethesda, Maryland) and the Academy for Spiritual Formation (Nashville, Tennessee). Clinical Pastoral Education is available at many hospitals, but be attentive for chaplain supervisors who are sensitive to spiritual matters. Mainline denominations are beginning to keep lists of available spiritual directors, and the denominational offices sometimes know of professional therapists who practice within a Christian context. The latter are harder to find and are best trusted when recommended by persons whose experience has been positive.

൸

Having explored the *what, why,* and *how* of spiritual direction, we are now ready to investigate how these areas interplay so as to respect the spiritual diversity that makes each person unique.

Chapter 2

✠

SPIRITUAL DIVERSITY: THE TAILOR-MADE NATURE OF SPIRITUAL DIRECTION

LIVED THEOLOGY AND DIVERSE SPIRITUALITY

Spirituality means living one's theology, and theology means articulating one's spirituality. Although the term *spirituality* is only recently finding favor in Protestant circles, the truth is that most denominations and religious orders began as alternative lived theologies, established by their founders for spiritual renewal and reformation. While these groups play an important role in the rich diversity of Christian spirituality, their uniquenesses tend to become diluted over time. Even within Saint Francis's own lifetime, the Franciscans split over compromising his rule. Present-day Lutherans, Presbyterians, and Methodists are barely familiar with more than the names of Luther, Calvin, or Wesley. While groups might still study the theology of their denominational founder, most people would be puzzled by any talk of restoring that originating spirituality. It is no surprise, then, that recent studies show that a person's choice of a local church has little to do anymore with denominational affiliation.

While this has tended toward an unfortunate least-common-denominator ecumenism, the recent resurgence of interest in spirituality may be giving rise to an exciting *internal* ecumenism. Even though the alternative schools of spirituality tend be neglected in time by the denominations and religious orders that follow, they are nonetheless valid. Together they constitute the beautifully colored threads woven by the Spirit into the church's tradition. One importance of Vatican II is its affirmation of this amazing diversity. Religious orders have been mandated to seek renewal through reappropriating the defining charism (uniqueness) of their founding. But instead of returning to a competitive narrowness, the result has been a new appreciation of diversity as the very means for discerning, broadening, and deepening one's own magnetizing focus. Thus, in my own Trappist order, while this renewal has brought welcome clarity about contemplation as our reason for being, it has also brought with it a new appreciation for Eastern spiritual practices, the importance of spiritual friendship, the centrality of scripture, a concern for the poor, and renewed interest in the power of intercession on behalf of the world.

Some of this diversity is happening within local churches and parishes as well, broadening the spectrum of theological-spiritual options offered there. A generation or so ago, one could walk down the main street of most towns on a Sunday morning with the churches resembling a cafeteria of spiritual alternatives. And while today these same churches have become largely indistinguishable, the vibrant alternatives they once represented have moved inside most of these churches as an "internal ecumenism." This situation is not without conflict, for what were once competitive, exclusive, and rival alternatives are becoming uneasy siblings in the same local church family. But whereas this tension is usually generalized as the conflict between liberals and conservatives, it may better be understood as the birth pangs for a new and authentic spiritual diversity.

To illustrate, one church school class on a Sunday morning might feel quite at home having a Luther as teacher, thriving on the theology of being justified by the saving blood of the crucified Christ. Meanwhile, on the floor below, class members with coffee cups in hand are discussing an outreach ministry to the poor that would make a Calvin glad. The first class might well profit from learning that they are illustrating a host of former churches that H. Richard Niebuhr classifies as being of the "Christ and Culture in Paradox" orientation. In contrast, the common passion for social justice characterizing the second group would render them dues-paying members of Niebuhr's "Christ the Transformer of Culture" type of church.[1] Thus, while his typology of five contrasting spiritualities no longer works in differentiating denominations, it is coming to illustrate the lively alternatives within these churches themselves. Thus, in the sanctuary at 9:00 A.M. with the worship geared toward families, the ethos may be identifiably Wesleyan, trusting that grace will grow to fulfillment. At 11:00 A.M., the service may be more liturgical, with a sacramentalism that would be user-friendly for Anglicans and Catholics. The current trend toward multiple services encourages this phenomenon. More than a nod to convenience or church growth, alternative worship experiences speak to the need of persons to find their niche within an authentic diversity. People today hunger for companions who function on a similar spiritual wave-length, who can share needs with a common focus and experience pilgrimages that just might have the same "travel agent." Likewise, in Catholicism, different Masses draw different clientele, each with a contrasting spiritual flavor. Thus, the scattered "contemplatives" at 6:00 A.M. Mass contrast significantly with the gregarious 9:00 A.M. crowd that thrives on "passing the peace." And with the reemergence of the Latin Mass as an option, the breadth of spiritual alternatives within the local parish is increasingly amazing.

This emerging diversity has significance for doing spiritual direction. In fact, it points to the role direction can play as a vehicle for transcending creatively the present liberal/conservative conflicts apparent throughout these churches. The conservative insistence upon a strong personal commitment needs appreciation. The liberal awareness that there is more than one way of being faithful deserves similar praise. Spiritual direction is a crucial way in which both these truths can be brought together for each Christian. And for our times in particular, it entails intersecting the growing need for disciplined spiritual growth with the availability of the rich spiritual options woven into the church's robe of many colors.

In finding our way within this new Christian situation, spiritual direction must avoid two dangers. On one hand, it is crucial that a directee not be guided in a prechosen way, no matter how excited directors may be about their own spiritual paths. The second caution is an opposite one. In spite of the past penchant for training pastors in nondirective counseling, it is important that present-day Christian direction not be so. Spirituality is not an individualism of picking and choosing tidbits in a flea market of spiritual resources. Such individualism operative within our time has bequeathed 20,780 distinguishable Christian denominations in the world. This figure has resulted from an average of 270 new denominations emerging each year, more than five every week. Projecting from these statistics, there are presently more than 25,000 denominations, with the number growing daily.[2] Flooded by such subjectivity, Christian spiritual direction must regain a sense of the objective. The art of direction involves the skillful interplay of God's objective doing and the delightful subjectivity of the Spirit's playfulness with each person as unique. How to do this is a major concern of this book.

The Spirituality of Question and Answer

This objective/subjective interplay in the church's long life has given rise to its primary doctrines. These doctrines are not content to be memorized and acquiesced to as a required part of the church's "faith package." Rather, *doctrines are answers to the fundamental questions thrust upon all of us in becoming self-conscious about living.*[3] Direction helps us understand the Christian faith in this functional way. Thus, the God doctrine needs to be prefaced by a correlative question: "Why is it better to live than to die?" The question is not "*Is* it better to live or die?" To continue to live rests on the implicit assumption that living is better. And whatever the answer that gives meaning to one's life, it functions as one's "God." That God might mean having one's name on the door of the president's office of a corporation, or having the title "bishop" as one's proper manner of address. Or one's God might entail pampering oneself in a suburban town house equipped with a turquoise Jacuzzi.

Each of us has a God, maybe several, that determines the dynamic of our lives. Ironically, it is often not the one affirmed credally on Sunday morning. One's functional God provides the *why* that flavors the *how, where,* and *who* of one's Monday mornings. Who we are depends on whose we are. A key issue of spiritual direction, then, is to discern from among the plethora of today's options competing for our loyalty which one actually functions as our God. Much of life's tragedy results not only from not knowing this identity, but from the deception of trying to hide that foundational orientation, even from ourselves. Wanting to think well of ourselves, we think far more highly of ourselves than we deserve, hiding the literal crudeness of the motivations behind our undertakings. As much as we try to make it otherwise, people who experience us regularly know our "God" better than we do. This is because the identity of our God tends to be not only unrecognized and unknown, but even unconscious. Saint Paul knew this: "I do not understand my own actions." The good that we want to do, we don't; and that which we do not want to do is precisely what we end up doing (Rom. 7:15 ff.). The why is what we mean by God, and the motivations that spring unconsciously are such that our "discipleship" is usually not at all what we would like to believe it to be. One's "God" is not an ideal, nor a belief, but a living dynamic that can breed myopia. It may be bequeathed to us by parents or molded steadily by class, gender, race, or culture until the complex result becomes a polytheism beyond recognition.

An essential task of spiritual direction, then, is to bring one's *functional God* into self-awareness. And in order for the face of that God to peer out through the mist of guilts, hurts, emotions, yearnings, and dreams so as to be seen "in a mirror dimly," one must receive support sufficient to resist running, and accountability ample for perseverance in what must follow. This may entail vomiting out one's tainted life as confession, or it may mean receiving the encouragement to water the fragile plant of Christian longing into blossom.

This functional approach suggests the manner in which one's God answer is to be assessed. The litmus test is the "livability" of one's God, marked by the depth, breadth, and height of its enhancement for those who live as its disciples. The real proof of the Christian God is not philosophical but simply "How those Christians love!" This brings us back to the question, Are we are free to be and do anything our hearts desire, as long as we can get away with it? At this point, direction involves us with the doctrine of the "image of God." The Christian is convinced that a life lived in free abandon will be buffeted into living proof that we do have an essence, form, or core nature that we must realize, or the result is a life not worth living.

The doctrine of the *human condition* stands in stark contrast to the doctrine of *human nature* (being created in God's image), raising the question: What went wrong? Such a contrast can be experienced in diverse ways: as *separation* (feeling alienated), *conflict* (being oppressed), *emptiness* (rendered invisible), *condemnation* (experiencing guilt), or *suffering* (made to be a refugee).[4] "Truth" is the quality of life that faithfulness to one's functional God renders in response to one's particular version of the human condition.

Spiritual direction, then, not only helps identify one's God, but holds up to that person an honest mirroring of what life so lived looks like. "You will know them by their fruits," says Matthew (7:16). This truth can set in motion a powerful dynamic. Almost as if one is implanted with the Golden Rule, the gnawing question occurs: Why am I acting in a way I would never tolerate others acting toward me? *Original sin* is the Christian doctrine that names this state in which we find ourselves, personally, societally, and culturally—a condition that is far from what we might hope. This means that the human race, as it were, precedes our personal existence. We are the residue of the sins of our fathers and mothers for far longer than the third and fourth generations. None of us enters life neutrally but always with what feels like a deficit or a borrowed account. Our motivations render ambivalent even our first cries and movements. Expressed functionally, this is *originating sin,* for it is out of this self-absorbed center that our subsequent living springs, as attempted answers to this ongoing feeling at our center. This dynamic renders every person's life a pilgrimage, grasping for a meaning as elusive as the mechanical rabbit.

Francis Thompson's poem "The Hound of Heaven" captures the feeling of a life so lived. Often it seems that we are being pursued, fleeing the shadowed corridors and darkened days. But there can come a moment of intersection, claims the Christian, when suddenly we realize that what defies God ravages at the same time our own being. Consequently, the only God who can claim the right to *be* God is the one in relationship with whom a disciple is able to be faithful to his or her true self. Whenever a person begins to experience life as fleeing and chasing, among shadows and hints, that person is ripe for spiritual direction. Then it is that the person can best appreciate the value of a second set of eyes and the wisdom of one without vested interest in the outcome.

THE UNIQUE ANATOMY OF BEING HUMAN

While we all share much in common in terms of the emptiness that tempers our waking moments and gnaws at our passions, each person is nonetheless unique. An impulsing invisible logic shapes the raw ingredients of one's life story into the texture of a unique plot, the energy of which renders each person's life a spiritual quest, conscious or otherwise. This logic is rooted in what we may call an *obsessio*—the pain we most crave to alleviate, the question we most ache to answer, the dilemma by which we are most defined. Each of us would express differently how this *obsessio* is experienced—as life's conundrum that boggles one's mind, or as a hemorrhaging of one's soul, or as the wound that bewilders healing, or as a mystification that renders one's living cryptic. The *obsessio* is what gets its teeth into one at soul depth, establishing one's life as the search for healing. The etymology of the word *obsessio* says it well: "to besiege."

In my own life, the pain that identifies my *obsessio* is the fear of rejection and abandonment. Through spiritual direction, I have traced its entrails back into the earliest shadows, where my spiritual anatomy took on the feeling of being unnoticed and unwanted, except for the wrong reasons. In the lonely hours, I can still feel hints of being unwanted, even when I am by myself. When in the past this feeling took on duration, it could be a burden without relief. And although my pilgrimage into Christianity has been an amazing healing of soul, aging has a way of giving resonance to the familiar echo. The favorite guise with which it comes now is that of not wanting to become a burden to anyone. I thought I had thrown away the box, the one tied with the rope of not being worth keeping. But the logic still operates at times after midnight. If one is a burden to oneself, one would certainly be a burden to others. Such awareness can bring tears, for while a person may learn to live creatively with his or her *obsessio*, the eviction notice never gets fully served.

Spiritual direction is a proven means by which individuals can discern the plot of their lives. Even more than this, it can provide clues to the plot of plots. As you might guess from what I have confessed, my fear of abandonment is rooted in never experiencing from my mother the unconditional love by which I would have known that I was worth keeping. Instead, her love was conditional, for over it fell the shadow that if I did not measure up, it would go away. But there came a special moment in my life—one of extraordinary transition in which the smoldering anger opened out into forgiveness. I suddenly knew why my drivenness to earn those special words from my mother could never have worked. It was clear now. Her whole life had been intent on earning these same words from her father, who never said them—nor could, because he himself had never heard . . . on and on, generation after generation. *Such is the power of one's obsession.*[5]

But there is always a second pole that interacts dialogically with one's *obsessio* to create the impulsing logic of one's autobiography. We can call this the *epiphania*—which means "to show forth," as at Epiphany the wise men returned home with the light of the good news. An *epiphania* is the answer one craves, the scratch for one's primal itch, the salve for healing, the embrace for the craving, the hope for one's despondency. It may emerge in a conversion encounter, or it may be the breakthrough of cumulative moments, or little more than hints, or sensed best as a persistent hope. Whatever its form, the interplay of *epiphania* with *obsessio* is what makes life fluid, searching, restless, energized, intriguing. The intensity of our *epiphania* is the determiner that renders existence a quest worth pursuing for a lifetime. Its absence, or even the weary inability to hold on any longer to one's fragile hope for an *epiphania*, means death. If not physical suicide, this death comes as a slower form of oblivion, whether drug related or psychologically induced. Spirituality is the name for this whole enterprise, and spiritual direction is the method most apt for identifying the plot and providing resources for the journey.

Reminiscent of the workings of an oyster, the reality of an *epiphania* is marked by its capacity so to enfold one's *obsessio* that the grating particle is made bearable. But far more can be involved. Although the *obsessio* is never lost, the promise of an *epiphania* is so to embrace the *obsessio* that it becomes a center around which a pearl is formed. I marvel at this pearl formation in my own life. The feeling of being unwanted has birthed in me an ongoing passion for the marginalized, presently directed toward the poor and prisoners on death row. *Epiphanias* do not so much provide new information as a contrasting perspective that affects import and thus redirects focus.

Ironic though it is, the *epiphanias* in our lives remain as unrecognized as our *obsessios* remain unconscious. Often this is rooted in self-deception about the identity of one's *obsessio,* or even having one at all. To illustrate, some persons find it easier to give gifts than to receive them, for to receive entails an implicit admission of need: "I don't want anyone to do anything for me." Part of the unconscious motivation at work may be that those who give can always take away, so it is better never to have received in the first place. And yet, deep down there is in such persons the persistent ache for someone to care, even as they push others away.

There are other persons whose inability to experience *epiphanias* is because of ears that are unbalanced. A supervisor can give them a positive year-end report on how they are doing, complete with nine strong affirmations. However, these accolades get quickly shelved in their minds, and they let themselves fester instead over the one suggestion for improvement, hearing the helpful suggestion as a hurtful criticism. Whatever form this dynamic takes, it bears witness once again that for all of us our fundamental dilemma is spiritual. For these persons, no amount of human compliments, not even a merit badge sash full of them, will ever be effective until the holes in the bottom of one's colander-soul are named and plugged. The only *epiphania* capable of touching their *obsessio* has to do with a homecoming for the prodigal son.

There are still other persons who seem wise enough to seek spiritual direction, knowing that the *epiphania* they need is to "experience God." But in their determined effort to effect an undeniable contemplative encounter with the Divine, they render themselves oblivious to the blessings and hints and promises all around them—*epiphanias* capable of filling the senses to overflowing. Just last month, a person came to me asking for "intense direction," for he knew he would always be restless until he had "a real experience of God." He was theologically informed and knew many of the major resources for spiritual discipline. Still, for him, God remained absent.

As we sat together on the deck of my hermitage, all around us the birds were singing gloriously, the autumn leaves were dancing earthward with colorful pirouettes, and hawks overhead were waving their wings in apparent joy. Yet in the middle of this theater of glory, choreographed by the Master Artist, this pilgrim sat, staring at the ground, mournfully lamenting that he had never experienced God. What could I say, except: "Look!" But he could not see. So his assignment was a "forced feeding." I asked him to spend the morning down at the lake, taking off his shoes and socks, and wiggling his toes in the water. "But what do you really want me to *do?*" he asked, puzzled. I hesitated to suggest skinny-dipping. I settled for, "Skip rocks and wave at the hawks." He had much to learn, and yet by lunchtime he could speak about the gifts of God. The afternoon session was to explore the primal cause(s) of his spiritual blindness and deafness. In time the confession emerged: the tension in the home provided by his "fine Christian parents" was actually such that he had been forced to turn inward for refuge. He admitted, "It will be scary for me to turn around and look out!" As he left my hermitage, my prayer was that maybe he could experience the gift of the wind in his hair as the fingered touch of the God he wants so much to experience.

Finally, there are other persons who deny having *epiphanias* because it seems easier to prove they are alive by rehearsing a bruised past. Therefore, periodically they pull off the scabs of past hurts rather than undergo the healing that begins with confession: that the power of the past exists only in the power we grant it in the present. What they need to hear is, "Pick up your mat and walk" (John 5:8, NIV). As T. S. Eliot insisted, "April is the cruellest month," because it stirs up the rocky soil that defies growing, challenging the roots in their paralysis of dormancy.

Whatever form the myopia takes in blinding us to the *epiphanias*, I have yet to meet anyone who, when the scales are removed, is not able to discern moments of grace. Likewise of our deafness, Jesus insisted: "Let anyone with ears listen!" (Matt. 11:15). Spiritual directors provide the eyeglasses and hearing aids for discerning *epiphanias*.

THEOLOGICAL WORLDS

Each of us is engaged in this spiritual dynamic of *obsessios* with *epiphanias*, but the precise plot resulting from their interaction is what constitutes each person's uniqueness. The result of this engagement determines one's "Theological World." It is how we domesticate the dynamic of our space and time as "home base." While each person's World is unique, my research indicates that the Worlds overlap so as to form identifiable clusters. The result is a working typology of five Theological Worlds that is useful in spiritual direction, identifying the varied ways in which the dynamics of *obsessio* and *epiphania* tend to operate. With such an aid, the spiritual director is better able not only to identify the *obsessio* underlying a person's World, but also to suggest the sort of *epiphania* that is needed and provide the disciplines most likely to open a person to receive.

Elsewhere I developed the "Theological Worlds Inventory" as a tool for helping identify a person's primary, secondary, and tertiary Worlds.[6] In still another book I extensively describe each of the five Worlds, complete with representative expressions from painting, music, literature, mythology, and theology, by which the directee's World can be identified and enriched.[7] In Appendix 5 of this book I have created an abbreviated version of the "Theological Worlds Inventory" that can be used in spiritual direction.

The *obsessios* and *epiphanias* whose opposite interactions provide the rhythm for each of the five Worlds are these:

WORLD 1: Separation and Reunion

WORLD 2: Conflict and Vindication

WORLD 3: Emptiness and Fulfillment

WORLD 4: Condemnation and Forgiveness

WORLD 5: Suffering and Endurance

In spiritual direction, a basic task is to discern the World in which the person is functioning. In **World 1**, the feeling is that of **longing**—for the "more" beyond anything that ordinary living seems able to fulfill. At its edges and wrinkles, life has about it a mystery, an ingredient that seems squeezed out of so much of today's living. Many persons with whom one interacts seem oblivious to this mystery, satisfied with what society provides. Yet if this is all there is, something is wrong, very wrong. This craving for more makes one feel isolated, separated, as if one doesn't belong. The big picture, this huge cosmos, gives one the sense of being an orphan. World 1 residents long to go "home," resonating with Judy Garland as she sings of birds flying over the rainbow: "Why, then, oh why can't I?" Life seems like a quest to understand the Mystery of the Whole, yet sometimes it would seem enough simply to be enfolded by it.

The feeling of the *obsessio* characterizing **World 2** is more that of **anger** at the condition of the world. It is not right that we live in societies comprised of winners and losers, rich and poor, powerful and weak—where everyone is forced to compete and do each other in. Self-interest is the primal dynamic of history, with violence the gaudy red thread woven into the social fabric. Nations war against nations, races against races, gender against gender—this is wrong, and one's life needs to be an effort at change. The foe is any system that dehumanizes the very people it is supposed to serve.

World 3 is inhabited, in turn, by those who feel deeply inside themselves what it means to be self-estranged—to have a low self-image, as this condition is currently expressed. One feels an *ache,* as if needing to cloak one's nakedness from others. But deep inside, unable to hide from one's own weaknesses and shortcomings, one becomes preoccupied at times with the conclusion that one isn't very lovable. This is why so often World 3 residents feel invisible, insignificant, of little regard, and unheard. Life seems like a futile effort not only to keep from being rejected, but just to keep from being disregarded, as a nobody. One feels inclined to act like an outcast, whether in church or community or even in one's own household. The feel is emptiness, void, ache—somewhere near the pit of one's stomach. So one tends to flounder, often aimlessly, for one doesn't know what to do about it.

In *World 4,* the dynamic has to do somehow with immorality. While the residents of this world would like to blame others for the conditions around them, inevitably they cannot avoid confessing the taintedness of their own motivations, no matter what they do. Down deep is a feeling of dirtiness, wrapped in *guilt;* for in all honesty, we, like Adam, are tempted by "forbidden fruit." Again, Saint Paul says it well when he confesses: "I do not understand my own actions. For I do not do what I want, but I do the very thing I hate" (Rom. 7:15). At dark times, one feels morally sick, so that, as the General Confession puts it, "There is no health in us." Of all the Worlds, World 4 acknowledges the pervasiveness of temptation and sin, and with it, the tendency to hide our apparent impotence to become clean. The primal sin, then, is a defensive self-deception without which one is unable to live with oneself. Consequently, life is edged by the fear of getting caught. We know of Christ's command to love, but the only motivation that encourages us into action is the self-contradictory one of "What's in it for me?" Thus, World 4 residents are like Adam and Eve, continually throwing themselves out of Eden as fugitives.

The feeling of *World 5* is heaviness, for it seems that whatever can go wrong will—sooner or later. The dilemma is not one for which we can blame the cosmos, or society, or the self, as in some of the other Worlds. Rather, the feeling is that of being **overwhelmed,** as if a victim simply of the way life is. The Appalachia of my childhood was such an environment of deprivation. But even the rich can experience it, whether downsized from without, or being eaten by cancer from within. One way or another, suffering seems to be the lot of human beings. So, like Job, a World 5 resident feels like a refugee. Unable to exist without being scarred, one is tempted not to feel anymore, worn down to a cynical fatigue.

These five portraits are sketched out with a heavy marking pen, so that one can feel something of the contrasting Worlds that result from these diverse ways in which *obsessio*s are experienced. The spiritual director needs to bring compassion to the task, capable of sufficient empathy to enter into the Worlds of other persons. One must feel with them, encouraging any venting that is needed, willing to be awash with the myriad emotions that may come flooding out. The director must never forget that all of us are bruised reeds, weak and fragile at soul depth. Thus, anyone who treads with muddy boots into the inner chamber of another's soul flirts with spiritual murder. Speaking perhaps of this fragile soul-child within each of us, Jesus is clear that those who cause such a one "to stumble" would be better off drowned (Luke 17:2).

Spiritual direction not only identifies the *obsessio* of one's Theological World, but it also helps open persons to the *epiphania* for which they hunger and thirst. In World 1, the yearning is what mystics through the centuries have discovered. By losing themselves in the Whole, they become unified with the ultimate Mystery. Therefore, the home that such persons crave is not this finite world. Yet they can be blessed with moments of foretaste. Bernard of Clairvaux understands this *epiphania* when he speaks of foretastes of dining at Christ's wedding feast, where there is "fullness without disgust, insatiable curiosity which is not restless, an eternal and endless desire which knows no lack, and lastly, that sober intoxication (Acts

2:15) which does not come from drinking too much, which is no reeling of wine, but a burning for God."[8] Protestant hymnology provides abundant illustrations. In "Breathe on Me, Breath of God," we sing of being "wholly thine, till all this earthly part of me glows with thy fire divine." Or in "Spirit of the Living God," we urge "Melt me, mold me, fill me, use me. Spirit of the living God, fall afresh on me."

Spiritual direction can also help residents of World 1 experience life sacramentally. Through the transparency of things, it seems as if the veil is lifted, and at least for a moment one can see by not seeing, and know by unknowing. The fear of abandonment that often shadows this World is taken up in an experience of total belonging, beyond all separation. "Who will separate us from the love of Christ?" asks Saint Paul triumphantly. "Nothing in all creation will be able to separate us from the love of God in Christ Jesus our Lord" (Rom. 8:39). The craving here is to return from whence we came, losing ourselves forever in God.

Seen from the perspective of this *epiphania*, there is a still point to the circle of life's whirling wheel—an axle, as it were, whereby in the stillness of contemplation one experiences the "eternal now" around which time circles as being less than real. Yet citizens of this World can also be fed by the ongoing cycles of nature, in their liturgical pirouette of birth, death, and rebirth. But whatever form the *epiphania*s of World 1 may take, they are variations on the theme of reunion of all things into God as their Ground.

The *epiphania* for residents of World 2 is quite different. In fact, the previous *epiphania* might sound to these residents like an escapism of "pie in the sky by and by." The craving within World 2 is what we pray in the Lord's Prayer: "Your kingdom come . . . on earth. . . ." The good news is the vision of a new heaven and a new earth where "death will be no more; mourning and crying and pain will be no more, for the first things have passed away" (Rev. 21:4). Theirs is the God who takes sides, deeply committed to the poor, the captive, the blind, and the oppressed. "If God is for us, who is against us?" (Rom. 8:31). We are called to be cocreators in completing creation, living now as if the end is already present. And the strength to do so comes from faith in the God who makes and keeps promises.

Here the discipline needed might aim at establishing a creative balance between being and the drivenness to do, fostering as well a habit of reflection to accompany one's actions. Residents of this World may need help in setting aside images of spirituality as quietism, aware only of an introvert spirituality. Rather, the brand of spirituality they need is one in which "justice and peace will kiss each other" (Ps. 85:10). While persons in World 1 are inclined to speak of Elijah's God of the "still small voice," the God of World 2 will speak, as with Moses, from the plane of history, with a broad brush and a voice marinated in anger against powers and principalities.

The *epiphania* for World 3 is different still. Here, to lose oneself, as in World 1, would feed the *obsessio* more than enable an *epiphania*. Even losing oneself on behalf of social justice, as in World 2, would endanger losing that which truly matters—the sacredness of one's self. In World 3, persons matter, every single one. Therefore what is needed as *epiphania* is a deep sense of acceptance, of being valued, of being wanted, of being indispensable—like each lily and every sparrow. The God who needs to be experienced here is the One who turns the house upside down looking for the lost coin and will not rest until I am found. It is the God who indeed leaves the ninety and nine to seek me out, and God carries me back, the lost lamb, in his arms. I am precious, for I am God's pearl of great price.

Central to this *epiphania*, then, is a love that has no conditions tacked onto it. The love that residents of this World have known threatens to be withdrawn when one doesn't measure up. "Do this, and then maybe." Or "Be this, and then perhaps." Thus, no matter what is done, one can never accumulate enough merits to purchase the belonging one craves. The *epiphania* that matters is unconditional love as a free and gracious gift. And once experienced, one's potentialities are beautifully released. The syntax is no longer "you must" but "you may." The *epiphania* for this World is such freedom.

The director doing direction within this World needs to remember how important ongoing affirmations are for these persons. They may be supersensitive to small matters as signs of rejection, such as how they are greeted. Thus, it is particularly important to find things to celebrate and to encourage in their pilgrimage. While this focus on the self might seem selfish, actually it is this very judgment that often is a blockage for residents of World 3. Likely they have been brought up on the dictum "Those who find their life will lose it" (Matt. 10:39), until the giveaway program of unconcern about the self leaves little to give away.

World 4 persons tend to be turned off by the *epiphania* of World 3. Preoccupation with the self, rather than being an *epiphania*, is a graphic illustration of the *obsessio*. A person's condition is not that of being empty, needing to be filled by God. Rather, the dilemma is that the relationship with God is itself ruptured. Thus, World 2's efforts at transforming history are romanticism, for history's plot displays arrogance. And this plot never changes—only the cast of characters. World 3's stress on individual effort and self-fulfillment, in turn, only encourages persons to compete more vigorously in the competitive struggle for status and power. Thus, the real *epiphania* can appear only on the other side of confession, in vomiting out the duplicity in one's soul— in coming clean. The spiritual direction offered by John Wesley's classes was intent on making this happen, asking of each person seeking membership, "Do you desire to be told your faults, all of them?"

Thus, the *epiphania* needed in World 4 is that of forgiveness, pure and simple. Then it is that one receives the miracle of reprieve, for in no way does one deserve it. I am accepted not because of my acceptability, but in spite of my unacceptability. This is the new birth, in which everything is rerooted, emerging as conversion through gratitude. As the old hymn says, "Amazing grace! How sweet the sound that saved a wretch like me!" The spiritual director might be tempted to help citizens of World 4 not be so hard on themselves, to "quit bad-mouthing themselves." Don't. Residents of this World need the vehicle of "tough love"; they need to hit the bottom in some real sense before the way up becomes possible. Somehow they know, although they may try all kinds of games to avoid it, that what they need is full confession and full forgiveness. Nothing less will touch the *obsessio*. Consequently, the director may need to function as priest, granting absolution—or may need to work with a pastor or priest who can.

In World 5, the *epiphania* is quite different, for, in one sense, it is really no solution at all. If suffering is a fact of life, this cannot be changed. Thus, resolution comes not in removing anything but in changing the way we deal with it. "I'm a survivor" is a phrase often identifying residents of this World. Yet the real *epiphania* entails more than surviving. The goal is enduring—outlasting with integrity. Integrity, in turn, is the determination to persevere, no matter what. The courage for doing this rests in understanding Christ as the Suffering Servant, the One who does not remove anything but promises that "we are in it together." Because this Companion God suffers with us, we can endure to the end, even making defeat a moral victory. As Mark 13:13 says, "The one who endures to the end will be saved." Suffering can be the refining fire whereby "we are afflicted in every way, but not crushed; perplexed, but not driven to despair" (2 Cor. 4:8). In providing spiritual direction for persons in this World, the director must understand what will help them spiritually. Unlike *epiphanias* characterizing some of the other Worlds, which refocus attention elsewhere or provide forgiveness, direction here helps the person drink life to the dregs, one day at a time—and never alone.

The characteristics of these five Theological Worlds can be charted in this fashion:

THEOLOGICAL WORLDS

	FEELING	OBSESSIO	STATE	ATONEMENT	CHRISTOLOGY	EPIPHANIA
TW1	Longing	Separation as being abandoned	Alien	(To mediate) Love as tearing the veil	Revealer	Reunion as homecoming

	FEELING	*OBSESSIO*	STATE	ATONEMENT	CHRISTOLOGY	*EPIPHANIA*
TW2	Anger	Conflict as being oppressed	Warrior	(To combat) Love as taking our part	Messiah	Vindication as the new earth
TW3	Ache	Emptiness as being self-estranged	Outcast	(To model) Love as filling to overflowing	Example	Fulfillment as wholeness
TW4	Guilt	Condemnation as being judged	Fugitive	(To take away) Love as forgiving the unworthy	Savior	Forgiveness as adoption
TW5	Over-whelmed	Suffering as being undone	Refugee	(To write off) Love as outlasting with long-suffering	Companion	Endurance as integrity

The Jesus that any of us claims is a remembered one. Thus, in the New Testament we have diverse theological interpretations, for each writer perceives Jesus as the *epiphania* through eyes shaped by the writer's magnetizing *obsessio*. Put another way, declaring Jesus to be the Christ is to affirm that the Christ event is one's *epiphania*. *In every case, unconditional love is the answer.* But, as evident in the chart under "Atonement," the way in which that love is experienced differs with each World, and thus there are contrasting images of Jesus as the Christ. In spiritual direction, then, we need to be sensitive to remembrances by different persons with different personalities because of different needs experienced in different places—and thus a different Jesus as the Christ.

Consequently, it is important in spiritual direction that theology be understood as the conceptualization of this diverse interaction by which particular Worlds are domesticated. Theology is not an end in itself, as if it were an intellectual exercise for those so inclined. Thus, the value of such conceptualizations as Merton's "general dance," or Bonhoeffer's "secular Christianity," or Bultmann's "radical obedience," or Tillich's "sacramental principle," or Letty Russell's "partnership in ministry" is to describe particular ways of living as a Christian. What the spiritual director needs to understand, then, is that theology is always a conceptual expression of the particular World that the author is thereby declaring to be home. Taken together, the five Theological Worlds usefully illustrate the viable, alternative ways of existing spiritually. In providing theological resources for persons further down the road, the director will do well to know the "neoliberalism" of Paul Tillich and Thomas Merton as powerful portraitures of World 1. Liberation theologians, such as José Miguez Bonino and Gustavo Gutiérrez, express well the anatomy of World 2. Process theology, as developed by John Cobb and Marjorie Suchocki, gives fine intellectual refinements to World 3. Neoorthodoxy, such as incarnated in the early Karl Barth and Donald Bloesch, gives flesh to the contours of World 4. And C. S. Song, Dietrich Bonhoeffer, and Søren Kierkegaard capture in contrasting situations the common hope instilled in World 5.

Relatedly, the spiritual movements and personages dotting the church's history in lively fashion are all ready resources for spiritual direction. Thus, citizens of World 1 will thrive on the contemplative dimensions of monasticism, distilled by such mystics as Saint John of the Cross and Teresa of Avila. World 2 residents will be at home with the broad swath connecting the Augustinian tradition to the Reformed spirituality of John Calvin. World 3 is as Franciscan as it is Wesleyan. World 4 is as Lutheran as it is Pauline. And World 5 has resident saints from the desert mothers and fathers to the sectarians of the radical Reformation.

In chapter 1, I described the vision of Christianity that in claiming me enabled my conversion. It centered in the incredible promise of a "new heaven and a new earth," in which God shall wipe away every tear from our eyes and death shall be no more. While there had been hints of *obsessios* from other Worlds, it was spiritual direction that helped me claim as primary my unrecognized residency in World 2. This made sense, for even as a Protestant I found my spiritual friends at the Catholic Worker House. Even now, direction continues to make changes in the decor of my World. My optimism of the 1960s is fading into a realism making common cause with the "nevertheless" of World 5. And a sobering of the effectiveness that gave hope to the marches of my World 2 activism has meant pulling an altar to the center of my furnishings, bringing new appreciation of the sacramental hope that World 1 knows. Yes, in a sense, we are all eclectic. Yet there must be a home base to which we keep returning for centering. Mine will always have a World 2 motto etched on the lintel: "Thy Kingdom Come."

It is helpful, then, to understand Christian spiritual direction as functioning within contexts of structured diversity, such as offered by the contrasting Worlds. The process follows:

- *Discernment* of a person's *obsessio*, with its accompanying feelings and memory images.

- *Invitation* for healing within the context of an appropriate *epiphania* that identifies with hope the World in which one exists.

- *Enticement* into furnishing that World faithfully as one's home.

By so operating within the context of diverse Worlds, spiritual direction may well be a foretaste of the ecumenism of the future. Let us end this chapter, then, by witnessing to the power of a particular Theological World to transcend the divisions and past conflicts that are supposed to render us foes. World 4 will serve well as a dramatic example. While it is home for most Protestant evangelicals, what follows is an abridged Roman Catholic testimonial that any evangelical could enthusiastically embrace as his or her own. It was written by Father André Louf, world-renowned abbot of the Cistercian monastery of Mont-des-Cats in Katzberg, France. It is his description of the spiritual restoration he sees as characterizing those who are Trappist monks. I cannot imagine a more classic description of World 4.

> The joy of a redeemed life rests in the knowledge that all our sins are drowned in God's mercy, as our guilt is devoured in Christ's love. Each day from our neediness a new person arises, whereby through forgiveness we can embody peace and attain deep serenity. Little difference remains between repentance and thanksgiving, for we have been broken down and rebuilt from top to bottom, by pure grace. We have learned how to forfeit our weapons, defenseless before God. Naked and shattered, with only empty hands, we are joyous, for God has given us permission to be weak. Our wounds have blossomed into wonder, and so to live is to give thanks and praise to God. And so it flows forth, that our relationship to all others shall be as a kind and gentle friend. How could it be otherwise, for in acknowledging who we really are, the defects of others no longer irritate us, and their weaknesses evoke only our sympathy? In the tender compassion of our God, we can relate to all sinners in the world as brothers and sisters. Daily, our favorite prayer is that of the publican. Like breathing itself come the words: "Lord Jesus, be merciful to me a poor sinner!"[9]

In being grasped by the exquisite beauty of contrasting Worlds, each of which is an authentic version of the Christian faith, one can better sense how spiritual direction needs to function within the World of the directee, not that of the director. Such direction may result in a person's declaration of spiritual bankruptcy, boarding up the World which one has been bequeathed—scraping away the clutter in search of the base *obsessio* on which to pour a new foundation. Or it might take extensive remodeling, reclaiming as one's own the World into which one was born. Or, still again, the invitation involved might have to do with better housekeeping, walking through the rooms with loving tears of new appreciation. In all this, the company that a director will need to provide may keep changing locations. At times, it may mean rummaging together in the basement. It may mean holding hands while opening creaky doors leading to an attic. It may mean having coffee together by firelight in the family room. Or still again, it may mean looking quietly together through an upstairs window toward the horizon, beyond today's flapping laundry. Wherever direction occurs, the joy of the spiritual director comes in helping a precious human being find a home.[10]

CHAPTER 3

✛

COMMUNAL SPIRITUAL DIRECTION:
THE WESLEYAN MOVEMENT
AS MODEL

DIVERSITY AND A GENERIC LOOK AT REDEMPTION

We have been concerned with giving manageable order to the diversity of Christian spirituality. One's faith creates a World in which one lives, moves, and has one's being. But undergirding these Worlds, is there a fundamental rhythm that makes these types variations on a common theme? Understood generically, yes—much like a skeleton relates to a living person. As we have seen, councils and theologians throughout the centuries have distilled the diverse Christian answers into doctrines that serve as repositories for these lived meanings. These doctrines have little meaning if isolated from the fundamental questions of human existence to which they are attempted answers. Spiritual direction, in turn, is the process for helping these generic issues to arise in the context of one's living, bringing an awareness of how they shape the context of one's World. One cannot refrain from living implicit responses to that for which Christian doctrines are explicit expressions.

The overarching Christian doctrine is *salvation,* meaning "to render healthy and whole." "Salve" is an ointment for healing, in the sense that "there is a balm [salve] in Gilead to heal the sin-sick soul." To understand how this works, the Christian is forced to distinguish the human condition (the way we are) from human nature (the way God intended us to be). Spiritual direction always involves such a distinction, for persons seek it because they are not like they believe they want to be or should be. *Original sin* or *originating sin* is the doctrine we have identified as indicating that our dilemma is deeper than not always being able to do the right thing. What gnaws at us is the state of our being, characterized by the proclivity to draw everything into the orbit of one's self. Whatever concrete expression this state takes as one's *obsessio*, it always involves a social continuity. No child is born into or reared within a neutral environment. The *obsessios* of the parents are bequeathed to the children in an "endless line of dis-splendor." I have never done spiritual direction with anyone who was not seeking healing from the universal dilemma Paul identifies in himself: "I do not understand my own actions" (Rom. 7:15). He expressed the need for spiritual direction as a cry: "Wretched man that I am! Who will rescue me from this body of death?" (Rom. 7:24).

Here we have expressed the christological question that life pressures each person to ask, one way or another: Who, or what, can function as the Christ (i.e., Messiah or answer) in my struggle for wholeness? There are many names for the orientations competing to be one's christological *what,* providing impetus for one's redemptive process. Christians are persons who claim that for them Jesus is the Christ. From this perspective, all other christological options tend to be variations on three primal temptations: the three *p*'s of possessions, power, and prestige. These temptations are such powerful rivals that even Jesus confronted them, not only during his forty days in the desert, but, like us, for a lifetime. After Jesus' first successful encounter, the tempter merely retired "until an opportune time" (Luke 4:13). Thus, the powerful enemy which Christians must face head-on in their redemptive struggle is modern society itself. Here these three primal temptations, functioning as today's principalities and powers, are no longer regarded as temptations, but as the very promises that function as the heartbeat of contemporary life. The anatomy of modern society, without which it would collapse, is the daily lure to make self-interest the orienting motivation of each person. This societal formation is such that it makes little difference what form the promised *epiphania* takes, as long as it is an expression of the lures that play upon selfishness as one's basic motivation. For the Christian, Paul's cry in Romans 7:24 expresses for all of us the feeling of suffocating under society's barrage: "Who will rescue me from this body of death?" Advertising screams constantly in almost every arena, hustling christological promises. Against all this, Paul's confession in verse 25 is the triumphant alternative: "Thanks be to God through Jesus Christ our Lord!" *Jesus is* the Christ.

Redemption is the doctrinal name for the process affected by one's christological orientation. Justification, in turn, raises the doctrinal question: When does this redemptive change take place? All of us ache to justify ourselves, to feel that our lives are not in vain, or wasted, or unclean, or useless. This explains why what we say is so often defensive. But whatever our response, the Christian insists that every attempt at self-justification only traps us more, for self-interest can never motivate us not to be self-interested. Therefore the Christian answer is the doctrine of grace, as opposed to works. Any answer that cannot be earned must be a gift, given by the gracious God who loves us *in spite of* ourselves. Our justification is in spite of our unjustifiability.

Sanctification (the process of growth in grace) is the doctrinal name for the living that results from one's justification. The secular name for this is lifestyle. The ongoing internal change always has an external expression. Just as every institution in corporate America is expected to establish a mission statement, so the Christian needs to have a mission statement—a creed or rule.

The goal of this inevitable process of sanctification is one's answer to the church's doctrine of glorification. Here we return to the point from which we began in the previous chapter. That which one's life attempts to "glory"—to worship or praise—functions as one's "God." That which brings life glory, into which one loses oneself in its meaning, might be the triumphant finale of a Super Bowl victory. But for the Christian, the glory is touched in the triumphant finale of Handel's "Hallelujah Chorus": "And He shall reign for ever and ever . . . Hallelujah." In Christian tradition, the two themes, around which all other candidates are variations, are the choice of self or God. As one writer put it, persons who love themselves seek their own glory, but those who love God love the glory of their Creator.[1] This completes the circle for the Christian— in response to the human condition, our human nature is restored through the redemptive process in which Jesus is the Christ. Our regeneration and sanctification mark a life that glorifies God as Father of our Lord Jesus Christ.

Life for each person, then, is a pilgrimage, structured by implicit answers to unavoidable questions. Spiritual direction, in turn, is a fundamental method for making explicit these working assumptions—examining in their light one's conscious commitments, testing in the face of alternatives the quality of life so lived, and structuring a supportive accountability through which ongoing growth becomes intentional. This renders life an action-reflection process whereby one's fruits become the way in which a person can be introduced to oneself. At times the process is gentle, but there are times in which the director may invoke the Spirit, in Kierkegaard's words, to "pour salt on open sores and wound from behind." Christian spiritual direction is built upon the certainty that the Holy Spirit will not let persons rest in their inauthenticity. An anonymous hymn of the sixth century expresses this well, singing of "Christ the Craftsman, Christ the Builder, Christ the Master Architect, who, blow after blow, shapes each living stone." God's own promise puts it more gently: "I shall live in them, and I shall walk the corridors of their hearts."[2]

This general anatomy of the salvation process has been well preserved for Protestants in hymnology:[3]

1. Our sinful condition as an open invitation—"Only Trust Him"

2. The miracle of God's action—"Amazing Grace"

3. Living in joy at the promise—"Standing on the Promises"

4. The will to mission—"Take the Name of Jesus"

5. Hope as glorification—"When the Roll Is Called Up Yonder"

Expressed doctrinally, the anatomy looks this way:

• *Prevenient grace:* God's going before us and working in us, rendering life a quest.

• *Justification:* God's action for us, empowering our acceptance.

• *Sanctification:* God's ongoing action and our life of response, making our pilgrimage a growing in grace. As Wesley put it, in our lives and our conversations, in our eating and our drinking and whatever we do, we must learn to do all to the glory of God—for to God we owe every thought, word, feeling, and action. An Anglican collect serves well as our daily prayer: "Cleanse the thoughts of our hearts by the inspiration of the Holy Spirit that we may perfectly love thee, and worthily magnify thy holy name."

• *Eschatology:* Evangelization for the sake of the kingdom.

- *Glorification:* God's promise as a correlation to such living.

From the church's dialogue of human questions with doctrinal answers, then, emerges the skeleton around which each Theological World becomes an enfleshment, made distinctive by the diverse *obsessios* and *epiphanias* that render us who we are. Such enfleshing entails a process that passes through stages of formation, or what Wesley calls "degrees of faith." Using the monastic analogy, such growth, which is supported by spiritual direction, begins as retreatant (the curious one) and moves to the observer (the sampler), then postulant (the inquirer), novice (the learner), temporary professed (the trial run), and finally, solemn professed (life commitment).

TOWARD AN ECUMENICAL SPIRITUAL DIRECTION BASED ON COMMUNAL FORMATION

One of the church's most remarkable ecumenical efforts in putting together the intricacies of spiritual direction as a "both/and" rather than an "either/or" has been the Wesleyan movement. Part of its genius is its intriguing blend of Protestant and Catholic wisdom. It insists on original sin yet human transformation, sanctification as well as justification, an emphasis on the uniqueness of each person but within the context of an organic community, human effort interplaying with divine choice, human appropriation as well as divine grace, sacraments effecting social holiness and personal piety within a High Church liturgy. All of these function within the creative rhythms of fast and feast, emptiness and fullness, knowledge and discipline. This movement understands Christian living as vigorously ascetic yet world affirming, as a "vital piety" that is intellectually rigorous, and as a centering upon scripture rooted in a passion for cultural expression. Wesley himself was a disciplined solitary who insisted on group life, a churchman who saw the church's renewal through an *ecclesiola* in *ecclesia* (a little church within the Church), a person of mystical propensity who operated within a finely honed conscience, and a pilgrim whose penchant for personal salvation entailed a passionate commitment for the poor and marginalized.

Expressed another way, the Wesleyan movement combined sectarian discipline with the universality of grace. This impressive blending was in part the product of the highly ecumenical nature of John Wesley's family upbringing. There he experienced a convergence of Anglo-Catholic and Puritan ideals and their accompanying resources, which James Nelson characterizes this way: "The colorful and creative contemplative piety of the Catholic Reformation and a sacerdotal-sacramental devotion in the elder Wesleys' adopted high-church commitment was grafted onto the grimly serious, ascetic-flavored, highly literate, legalistic, moralistic, biblical piety of their Puritan ancestry and early education."[4] Actually, at least four sources interplayed in Wesley and the movement that flowed forth from him: Anglo-Catholic sacramentalism, Puritan discipline, Moravian experience, and Reformed passion for social justice. This accounts for why scholars have found in Wesley's preaching characteristics drawn from Lutheranism, pietism, English puritanism, and Anglican Reformed.

Ironically, while these elements express well the apparent antinomies characterizing the church through the ages, the Wesleyan movement did not attempt to resolve the conflicts. Instead, it embraced them in such a way that the resulting tension became a rich ecumenical spirituality. The clue for how this was possible is this: *The very rationale for the Wesleyan movement is spiritual direction.* The result is a remarkable intermingling of personal discipline within a framework of supportive corporate accountability, sacramental means of grace laced with secular means of appropriation gleaned from practical wisdom, and ecclesiastic faithfulness applied as a total lifestyle within the secular world. The fundamental understanding at work is that Christianity rests on givens that evoke obedience in the form of a "rule," necessitating spiritual direction done with a warm heart so that persons become enabled to live by the

Spirit more than the letter. This view rendered spiritual direction an art form more than a regimented program, through which the Spirit carves each person as an original work of art. Expressed another way, spiritual direction rests on two premises: (1) Being a Christian mandates spiritual companionship on the journey, and (2) Salvation is the Spirit's unique dance with each person.

The United Methodist Church, through its mergers, has endeavored to respect its basic tradition by retaining, on the one hand, "the various landmarks of our several heritages," while, on the other hand, remaining aware that "the transcendent mystery of divine truth allows us in good conscience to acknowledge the positive virtues of doctrinal pluralism even within the same community of believers."[5] Such was the spirit of Wesley, who asked "in essentials, unity; in nonessentials, liberty; and, in all things, charity." This achievement is such that there is good reason to hope that the present-day interest in spiritual direction may bring with it a rediscovery of the deeply ecumenical spirituality and communal spiritual direction model that once characterized the Wesleyan movement.

THE ANATOMY OF WESLEYAN SPIRITUAL FORMATION

The home of John Wesley's upbringing was, in effect, a mini-monastery. Susanna as mother functioned almost as novice master, being quite self-conscious about spiritual direction being the defining purpose of a family. She was explicit in her pedagogy, articulating the state of every child in terms of the human condition, insisting on discipline as necessary for opening each child to confession, followed by an experience of grace. The results were "a rich and yeasty mélange of spiritual activities adapted to the child's age and capacity, and woven into the variegated content of the historic Christian tradition. It was biblical, liturgical, devotional, and at significant points mystical."[6] Every Thursday evening was set aside for John's spiritual direction session with his mother.

The continuity between this early training and the founding of the Holy Club at Oxford (1729) is clear. John and Charles Wesley attempted to restore within the university setting a structure of spiritual formation, using a method analogous to the ascetic practices by which a novice is formed in a monastery, including journaling and supervised discipline. This experiment was not simply a supplementary activity for John Wesley while attending Oxford but was his creation of a fundamental way of doing spiritual formation, one that he wanted continued after his graduation. He became convinced that this model of spiritual formation should be made available not only for clergy but for laity as well. His ministry in Georgia was essentially an experiment in such lay formation. "Wesley married his experience with the Holy Club to the Moravian adaptation of the German Pietist conventicle and re-established his university experiments with clergy cultivation as an institution for spiritual formation of the laity."[7]

Wesley's own spiritual pilgrimage evidences a continuous and consistent line. He learned from Peter Boehler and the Moravians what he identified as a piety of the servant, whereby his total life was to be a search for holiness. His Aldersgate Street experience of May 24, 1738, showed him that servanthood should no longer spring from a sense of duty. It resulted from the free gift of adoption in which the intimate relationship that resulted was one of being a child of God. God has "taken away *my* sins, even *mine*, and saved *me*." A dim analogy to what this meant for Wesley was something one of my five daughters expressed: "I know you love us all, but somehow you make each of us feel special." Paul states this key experience theologically: "It is that very Spirit bearing witness with our spirit that we are children of God" (Rom. 8:16). Yet, for Wesley to preach this spirituality was an invitation without content unless opportunity was provided for corporate spiritual direction that could provide disciplined growth in living this new relationship. The various strands of his personal pilgrimage came together in the conviction that while discipline is not a requirement for receiving

God's gracious acceptance, it is a joyous consequence rooted in a passion for pleasing the divine Lover.

From Wesley's pilgrimage came four primary questions that continue to be asked today of United Methodist candidates for ordination. These questions echo implicitly the spirituality expected of the laity for whom these candidates would be spiritual leaders:

1. Have you faith in Christ?

2. Are you going on to perfection?

3. Do you expect to be made perfect in love in this life?

4. Are you earnestly striving after it (perfection in love)?

This theme of "going on to perfection" is easily misunderstood. The preferred term is *holiness,* meaning an ongoing inner transformation ("regeneration" or "new birth"), marked by a change of heart. The term *perfection* can mean either an attainment or a process, such as "being holy" versus "becoming holy." Wesley meant the latter. Perfection does not mean that mistakes will not be made, or that temptations will disappear, or that one will never again hurt others. Forgiveness remains a lifetime necessity. Rather, perfection involves a new disposition toward God and therefore neighbor, characterized by a purification of one's *intention*. One is purged of any intent to maliciously and intentionally harm or cause misfortune to any person or group. This goal requires an ongoing process, for deeply at work is a diabolical deceit in each of us—not only in deceiving others but even more in dealing with ourselves.

The human dilemma is a misdirected will issuing from a diseased heart. The distinction involved is between "Sin" as our self-centered state of being and "sins" as the willed offenses that result. Thus, ignorance is not a cause of our misdoings as much as it is a self-imposed symptom. Consequently, most persons spend their lives on the surface, dealing with symptoms as if they are weeds to be mowed rather than having roots to be pulled out.

The disposition that results from experiencing God's gracious love is a forgiving, gentle, and generous heart. Yet Wesley was realistic about the gap between our human condition and this transformed state, remaining suspicious of what Dietrich Bonhoeffer later called "cheap grace." This is why the *discipline* of spiritual direction was mandatory, guaranteeing that there would not go unchallenged any hint that our perfection renders us worthy of that grace. Likewise, his suspicion of subjective experience becoming a primary guide of action without scripture being the norm required spiritual direction as a process of *discernment*. Christians need to be empowered by the ongoing support that spiritual direction gives, making the relationship of forgiveness and unconditional love an ongoing reality. Thus, we have spiritual direction as discernment, support, and discipline.

Christian life is to be as rigorous and disciplined as the regimen characterizing an accomplished musician or athlete. And just as the impetus for the musician is a love of music and the athlete a love of the game, so Wesley insisted that happiness follows from holiness. His recurring theme is that the Christian is "happy and holy." This resembles the monastic idea of joy as the inner tranquillity and persistent peace serving as one's bedrock, no matter what the outer circumstances or the inner emotions. Wesley's words on his deathbed testify to that centering: "The best of all is, God is with us!"

THE WESLEYAN MOVEMENT AS CORPORATE SPIRITUAL DIRECTION

Wesley's approach gave birth to one of the church's most fruitful movements in spiritual direction. Its importance for us today is twofold. First, the spirituality and methods of spiritual direction institutionalized by the Wesleyan movement are ecumenically rooted, drawing from the rich heritages of both Protestant and Catholic traditions. Second, it discloses spiritual direction as a central reason for the church's existence. Our concern in this section is to make available this artistry of communal spiritual direction as it unfolded within the Wesleyan movement.

The Wesleyan approach to direction has three foci: *growth in grace* as the goal of Christian existence; *corporate spiritual direction* as a central means for such growth; and the church's *means of grace* as primary resources for this pilgrimage. Conceiving this movement as an evangelical order within a Catholic ecclesiology (that is, High Church Anglican) is a helpful way of illuminating the ecumenical nature involved. Ernst Troeltsch interprets the history of Christianity in terms of two communal expressions: the church-type and the sect-type.[8] The church-type accepts the secular order of society, attempting to influence it by universal principles drawn from Christianity as intended for all of humanity. The sect-type, in contrast to the values of society, aspires after an alternative inward perfection through direct, disciplined personal fellowship among group members. The value of the first is its appeal to large segments of the population, made possible by watering down the demands of faith. The value of the second is its faithfulness to the radicalness of Christianity, so stringent that it restricts Christian living to a smaller group. The genius of the Wesleyan movement is that it forged a way by which the sect-type can function creatively within a church-type context. The renewal of Christianity today is likely to depend on our ability to do precisely this.

The way in which the Wesleyan movement was able to accomplish this was by becoming an evangelical order within a Catholic (Anglican) context. Some Catholic scholars today lament that the dynamic that forced this movement to become a separate denomination could have occurred creatively within the Catholic Church. Here there would have been available a long history of rigorous discipline and spiritual diversity made possible through the encouragement and support of religious orders. Be that as it may, an example of a religious order comparable to the Wesleyan movement is the Franciscans. Here there is a "first order" (monks), a "second order" (nuns), and a "third order" (laypersons living a spiritually disciplined way within ordinary societal life). This Franciscan "third order," presently with over one and a half million members, functions in a manner comparable to how Methodism desired to function within Anglicanism.

One can actually argue that the Wesleyan "third order" was a creative conduit for monastic spirituality, for Wesley drew widely from the sweep of Christian monasticism. He appreciated the desert monastic fathers and mothers, of whom Macarius the Egyptian was his favorite. Other favorites included Bernard of Clairvaux (Cistercian Order), John of the Cross and Teresa of Avila (Carmelites), and Ignatius of Loyola (Jesuit). That the Wesleyan movement functioned as an order is witnessed to in England where Methodist society meetings were never permitted to conflict with Church of England services. Wesley's strong doctrine of the church centered in his insistence on Holy Communion as an essential means for spiritual growth, thereby requiring vital participation in the sacramental life of the Anglican Church. No Methodist structures, then, whether societies, classes, or bands, were to be a rival to or a substitute for the church. As an order, then, the Wesleyan movement was in actuality a sect-type functioning as a vital ingredient within a church-type.[9]

Unfortunately, in this country the American Revolution was deeply disruptive for this structuring. When most Anglican priests returned to England, the order was largely left without its priestly and sacramental base. A contrasting but related phenomenon occurred in England when the Anglican Church became reluctant to give the sacrament to members of the societies. This necessitated introducing the "love feast" from the early church into the class structure. Even today in corporate spiritual direction the love feast can be useful, especially since it can be an entirely lay event. Nonetheless, Wesley was clear that there could be no substitute for the sacramental means of grace, and thus opposed any separation from the Church of England. When the societies became separated from the Anglican Church, however, the result was that they no longer functioned as an order within the church but as an independent sect forced increasingly to function as a church-type. The loss was twofold. In becoming a church, the sectarian characteristics of an order were increasingly sacrificed, namely the disciplined personal faith birthed by communal spiritual direction. This meant the dilution of what Wesley called the "prudential means of grace." And separated from their sacramental base, in turn, the Methodists were never able to recapture the fullness of what Wesley insisted upon as the "instituted means of grace." It was only a matter of time until, as a mainline, broadly based denomination, Methodism became only marginally disciplined and minimally sacramental.

This twofold diminution characterizes much of Christianity today. On the one hand, the more sacramentally inclined churches are depleted of groups resembling a "third order" that can offer a serious and disciplined spirituality to the laity. On the other hand, the more sectarian-like churches that stress deep personal spirituality tend to lack a firm sacramental base for such growth in grace. There is reason to identify the present resurgence of interest in spiritual direction as a hungering for the creative blend of church and sect that characterized the Wesleyan movement at its inception. In fact, the conflict straining every major denomination today is, in effect, a struggle between a liberal inclusivity based on diversity, and a conservative insistence on radical commitment. This is the tension that the Wesleyan movement rendered creative.

THE WESLEYAN MOVEMENT AS A RELIGIOUS ORDER

Religious orders are characterized by three kinds of discipline.

1. *Spiritual direction.* Spiritual direction is the key method for providing supportive accountability for growth in grace. Susanna Wesley was John Wesley's spiritual director. He, in turn, was the spiritual director for the early class meeting leaders, who then became the spiritual directors of the persons placed under their care. And the most capable members of each group, in turn, became

the directors of their own groups. And "that he might have more time for this great work, he appointed a day when they might all come together, which from thenceforward they did every week." And from there, "their number increased daily."[10] Interestingly, the day of the week John chose for this first class meeting was Thursday evening, the night of the week which his mother had set aside for his childhood spiritual direction.

The essence of the Wesleyan movement was disciplined care of souls. And, characteristic of an order, every member was supposed to be under spiritual direction. So essential was this that Wesley forbade his preachers to preach anywhere that communal spiritual direction would not be available when they left. His passion was to promote spirituality as practice, which he called "practical religion."

2. *Rules.* The second feature of any order is having a rule *(regula).* This functions as the group's reason for being, to which spiritual direction is to hold each person accountable. Wesley had a rule for his societies, classes, and bands. The necessity of having different rules for communal direction groups emerged from the different intensities that characterized persons along the spiritual journey. This structuring, again, resembled monastic orders with their ascending movement from postulancy to lifelong vows. In the Wesleyan movement, persons could move from one group into a more stringent one—from classes, to bands, to select societies. This movement toward "perfection" as the goal of one's striving was intent upon the lifelong commitment to live the monastic equivalent of a "solemn professed."

Monastic rules generally have three dimensions: to empty, to refill, and to feed. This is precisely the way in which Methodism's General Rules are divided—to refrain from, to be fed by, and to do for. In addition, the preaching houses of early Methodism were much like priories (religious houses headed by a prior or prioress) and were sometimes called that. In fact, Wesley's declaration of what his groups were about would make a fine rule for any monastery:

A company of [persons] having the *form* and seeking the *power* of godliness, united in order to pray together, to receive the word of exhortation, and to watch over one another in love, that they may help each other to work out their salvation.[11]

For this to happen, spiritual direction was central, with a prescribed monastic-like rule for leaders to use in each group of twelve at their weekly corporate sessions.

- "To inquire how their souls prosper." That is, to help discern the state of each person's spiritual pilgrimage.

- "To advise, reprove, comfort or exhort, as occasion may require." Each person at each stage is to be recognized as unique, and thus in need of differing degrees and types of support and accountability.

- "To receive what they are willing to give toward the relief of the preacher, church, and poor." *Social holiness* was the term coined for this dimension. Authenticity of one's spiritual growth is to be measured by the degree to which one's life is lived for others, especially the marginalized.

Now we are led back to find equivalence with Saint Francis's three orders. The "first order" in the Wesleyan movement would involve the ordained clergy. The "second order" would be composed of the lay preachers, or what Francis called the "brothers." The "third order" would consist of the laity. Also intriguing is the way in which the United Methodist Women, throughout their history, have functioned much like an order within the church, significantly autonomous in structure, mission statement, and budget.

Just as several documents often serve compositely as the rule of an order, the same is true of the Wesleyan movement. For instance, in my own Trappist order, there is the Rule of Saint Benedict, the Charter of Charity (inaugurating the founding), the Constitutions and Statutes of the order, and the House Rules of the particular monastery. Similarly, Wesley identified his initial rule as "the scriptural doctrines of the Church of England as contained in the Articles of Religion, the Homilies, and the Book of Common Prayer." Faithfulness to these documents was expected of early Methodists. In time, five basic sources began to function as a rule: (1) The General Rules (1743); (2) the Articles of Religion; (3) *Wesley's Explanatory Notes upon the New Testament* (1754); (4) *A Collection of Hymns for the Use of the People Called Methodist* (1780); and (5) the Large Minutes (1789). Together they functioned as the *regula* by which the spiritual discipline of each Methodist was to be formed.

3. *Canon law.* The third type of discipline characteristic of an order is its functioning under canon law. In church history there have been twenty-one ecumenical councils, whose purpose was to create "widely applicable norms to protect and foster church unity." These norms were called canons.[12] The codification of these canons, done in 1500, remained in place for the Roman Catholic Church until revisions in 1917 and again in 1983. The Methodist equivalent is appropriately called *The Book of Discipline.* It is possible to map the movement of Methodism from being an order within a church to functioning as a church by observing the degree to which the *regula* became of "historic interest" and *The Book of Discipline* became almost totally a book of canon law. This shift has entailed a loss of Methodism's originating genius as rooted in a firm systemic base for spiritual formation through corporate and personal spiritual direction. Taking its place is Methodism's present genius for polity, the primary rule tending to be legal regulations for institutional ordering. This identifies the dilemma of most modern churches as well—what has been lost is a basic discipline for daily, personal spiritual life, nurtured by spiritual direction within a structure that provides supportive accountability.

Spiritual Direction within an Ecumenical Spirituality

The early Wesleyan movement borrowed richly from many traditions, which accounts for its widespread appeal. It likewise seized upon anything practical that could be used as an instrument for spiritual growth. Wesley's genius was in knowing where to look. Not even his idea of corporate spiritual direction was original. He took over the idea from the religious societies already present in the Church of England. The idea of more intense bands he borrowed from the Moravians. As a result of such eclecticism, what we have is a wonderfully balanced ecumenical approach to Christian spirituality. This approach can be summarized with Wesley's own admonitions:

- *Preach our doctrine.* This centers in grace of three kinds: prevenient, justifying, and sanctifying.

- *Inculcate experience.* The point here is that only beliefs that are experienced produce transformation.

- *Urge practice.* The result of transformation is discipleship.

- *Enforce discipline.* Spiritual direction is the method by which one moves through discipline to discipleship, from general principles to specific actions.

In order to temper the quietism of the Moravians on the one hand and the predestinarian tendencies of the Calvinists on the other, Wesley made ongoing use of the term *seek*. Relatedly, Saint Benedict's classic rationale for being a monk is "to seek God." And if one is to seek, the question that follows is, "How shall I seek?" In answer, Wesley insists that there are identifiable practices for our searching, called the "means of grace." These are rooted in the conviction that God will not leave us without resources through which God promises to act. These means of grace are of two types, the "instituted" and the "prudential," both having positive and negative dimensions intended to be balanced through spiritual direction.

THE INSTITUTED MEANS OF GRACE

Wesley identifies the instituted means of grace as being "outward signs, words, or actions, ordained of God, and appointed for this end, to be the ordinary channels whereby [God] might convey to [all], preventing, justifying, or sanctifying grace."[13] As means, they are never to be mistaken for ends. There are five in number, regarded as "invariable"—that is, they do not change, nor are they optional. Thus, in spiritual direction, we are to be wary of a Christian who says, "I do two of these, but the third I do not find useful." God institutes these as the Christian's nutritious meal, not options from which to select, as in a cafeteria line.

1. *Prayer.* A Christian must be a person of prayer. This includes personal, family, and public prayer, and in each case prayer is to be exercised in both a silent and spoken manner. Here, as throughout Wesleyan spirituality, the word used over and over is *regular*—regular prayer, scheduled prayer, methodical prayer. Thus, one is not simply to pray when one feels like it. Prayer must be practiced regularly, daily.

2. *Scripture.* Wesley expressed this means as "daily meditation on scripture." Again the emphasis is on regular practice, whether one feels like doing it or not. How does one meditate upon scripture? Again Wesley's words: "Hear it read in the context of prayer." This is precisely the monastic practice of *lectio divina* (sacred reading).[14] His instruction for this practice is to pray before, during, and after reading, and then practice what you hear. This is simply a way of saying that one must read scripture with the expectation that God will speak. Such reading is not done for the purpose of religious instruction or for practical functions such as sermon preparation. It is the practice of bringing oneself expectantly before the Word to be addressed personally. It makes sense, then, that as preparation one

asks to be purified by God. And only in the attitude of prayer might one anticipate revelation of the Word through the word. The centrality of this means for Wesley is clear: "Let me be *homo unius libri* [a person of one book]. The scripture is my rule of doctrine, of practice, and of experience."

3. *Sacraments.* While "the sacraments" explicitly meant two for Wesley, with the additional "ordinances" practiced by the Anglican Church, Wesley had available an equivalent of the seven sacraments of the Catholic tradition. Yet for both Protestants and Catholics, baptism and Eucharist are primary. Through baptism, the Holy Spirit enters one's life, sowing the spiritual seeds that formation will nurture into growth. Here the Spirit marks us, engrafts us, and enjoins us. Thus, baptism functions so as to provide for "regeneration or the new birth."[15] Regarding the Eucharist, two points in particular mark Wesley's understanding. The Eucharist is so essential that he encouraged daily Communion. Second, the Eucharist can be a converting event. That is, Communion is objective, and as an empowering event, it is essential for one's journey.

For Wesley, the sacraments are not simply signs or even symbols, functioning only as reminders of what is already known or experienced. This would make them sacramentals. In contrast, sacraments are vehicles of the Spirit's workings—to transform and to strengthen. As objective means, they do for us what cannot be done in any other way. This understanding is explicitly stated in Article XVII of the Articles of Religion. The sacraments "are not only badges or tokens of the Christian [person's] profession, but rather they are certain signs of grace, and God's good will toward us, by which he doth work invisibly in us, and doth not only quicken, but also strengthen and confirm, our faith in him."[16]

4. *Fasting.* This practice was regarded as so important that even today at the time of ordination the United Methodist candidate is asked, "Will you recommend fasting or abstinence, both by precept and example?"[17] When Wesley quizzed his preachers, he did not ask, "Are you fasting?" The question was in the form of a concrete

directive: "*How* do you fast every Friday?" This weekly act was designed for reasons both physical and spiritual. It was done to strengthen the will, as a liturgical act, for ascetic reenactment of our contingency before God, as identification with the poor, and for the sake of good health.

5. *Christian conferencing.* The first four instituted means of grace are familiar to most Christians. The fifth one, however, being less familiar, invites extended description. It is called *Christian conference* [*con* = to be able; *confer* = to consult, honor, advise]. This was Wesley's way of declaring spiritual direction to be a mandatory means of grace. One cannot be a Christian alone. Further, one is forever becoming a Christian, thereby requiring mutual sharing for the sake of supportive accountability. Spiritual direction is the event whereby our sorrows are divided and our joys multiplied. Largely for practical reasons, Wesley favored corporate spiritual direction. The only requirement for entering a group is a desire to make use of the means of grace, and a willingness to be held accountable for their use. Each session normally contains these elements: hymns, prayer, study, mutual sharing, specific guidance, and service. In a real sense, the goal of direction is service, for the process is so to transform one's daily living that one will inevitably be found where people are in need—such as jails and the homes of orphans and widows. In addition, class leaders are to collect contributions from members so that after class expenses are paid, aid is provided for poor members.

In the Wesleyan movement, groups for Christian conferencing are arranged progressively according to spiritual maturity. Two groupings are basic. *Societies,* the most inclusive, are for every member. In addition, each person is to participate in a *class,* usually with twelve members, and normally arranged geographically. At the beginning of the movement, the members of a class did not meet together. The class leader visited each member separately in his or her home, providing individual spiritual direction. In time, however, Wesley came to recognize the value of the multiple direction that a group can provide. This arrangement also provided training whereby members could themselves learn how to be spiritual directors. Class leaders met weekly with Wesley or with the clergyperson in charge to inform this person "of any that are sick, or of any that walk disorderly and will not be reproved." In effect, this gathering functioned as an ongoing training consultation in how to master the skills of doing spiritual direction.

Each class had four distinguishing marks:

a. *Voluntary*—Membership was intended for those who were serious about their faith.

b. *Inclusive*—Members covered the social gamut of rich, poor, servants, and masters. These groups were so open that before long there was a flood of poor, underprivileged, unlearned, and societally unwanted persons. In class sessions these individuals finally experienced the transforming acceptance of which society systemically deprived them. As one interpreter put it, these classes gave to people who were faceless and worthless on the streets outside the chapel a new respect, dignity, and vision.

c. *Intimate*—Total confidentiality was a standing rule.

d. *Permanent*—Perseverance was expected.

The heart of the spiritual direction provided in these class sessions was an honest sharing of individual needs and problems, covering every arena of daily living, with all the members expected to respond with support, insights, and accountability. On the assumption that sin is a wholesale addiction that no one should have to bear alone, ample opportunity was provided for members to verbalize all kinds of feelings within the context of shared faith, including their doubts about the Christian faith itself.

Interestingly, the forceful questions that Wesley provided for use in these class sessions are quite similar to the monastic "chapter of faults." For spiritual growth, there are orders in which monks meet together weekly for corporate spiritual direction. Each monk is given an opportunity for "self-accusation," followed by feedback from others as to how well he lives the rule. Wesley took such direction so seriously that he inquired of people seeking membership, "Do you desire to be told of your faults?"

At the beginning of the Wesleyan movement, preaching was the entry point for the redemptive process. Converts then became members of a society and subsequently became part of the class system. In time, however, the class became the probationary entrance into the societies. With this change, the movement functioned self-consciously as a sect, with perseverance in spiritual direction considered essential for membership. This process became so systemic that a ticket system was developed, with class cards, renewed quarterly, required for admission to society meetings. The abundant stories we have of these early class meetings sound much like a contemporary Alcoholic Anonymous meeting. The conversion of lives effected by these sessions, however, represented a broader spectrum, from alcoholics and derelicts to prostitutes and criminals, with all sorts of variations of those that society might call "normal."

Wesley was amazed by what he saw happening through the spiritual direction operating in these classes. He was able to describe this quite simply. When persons begin to "bear one another's burdens," they come quite naturally to "care for each other." To make this dynamic self-conscious, he declared that class members are to "watch over each other's souls, bearing one another's burdens." As in most things with Wesley, this had a scriptural base: "Confess your sins to one another, and pray for one another, so that you may be healed" (James 5:16).

One advantage of such corporate spiritual direction is its inevitable expansiveness. Receiving direction for one's spiritual growth develops the abilities one needs for giving it. (That brings to mind Frank Laubach's motto for those taught to read: "Each one teach one.") With this insight, Wesley gave deep significance to Luther's idea of "the priesthood of all believers." Although each communal direction group had a facilitator, each member was to assume responsibility for every other member and for the group as a whole. Here we reach the heart of direction: *Receiving and giving spiritual direction are intended to form a dynamic whole.* We can see this by recognizing the basic triads that came to characterize corporate spiritual direction as it developed through the classes:

- Encouragement/examination/service

- Fellowship/training/mentoring

- Connecting/listening/bearing

- Supporting/loving/caring

- Sharing/discerning/growing

- Evangelizing/nurturing/educating

In time, the Wesleyan movement found the need for more intense groupings, moving to spiritual depths that could not be expected of all members. Here the "societies," comprised of "classes" functioning collectively as a church-type, once again discovered the need for groups more characteristic of the sect-type. The result was the emergence of *bands,* usually comprised of four to five members, organized on the basis of such factors as age, gender, and marital status. Twenty percent of the Methodist membership entered such bands. And out of these, in turn, were drawn persons for *select societies,* chosen for their spiritual maturity. These persons were so advanced in spiritual formation that no leadership was required, permitting the Holy Spirit to be the unhampered Spiritual Director. But whatever the type of group, the method was the same: mutual encouragement, examination, and service within the context of the "Christian conference" as a means of grace. This whole arrangement has been called the Wesleyan Pyramid, and it is based on the intensity of one's growth in grace. A better graphic today is that of a circle, with a centripetal dynamic drawing toward the center a dedicated nucleus called to serve as the heartbeat of a renewed church.

While United Methodism has lost much of this amazing heritage of Christian conferencing, there still remains one vestige of the original structure. Annual conferences, geographically arranged, converge in a yearly gathering of several days. Originally these conferences were the vehicle for corporate clergy spiritual direction. In contrast to their present versions, the original concern was far more spiritual than organizational. They had as their context a powerful collage of proclamations and exhortations, love feasts and Eucharists, in the midst of which preachers were expected to open their souls and their ministries to one another. The primal focus was the spiritual condition of both preachers and their societies. The working assumption was that in conferencing with one's peers, pastors would receive the spiritual direction of supportive accountability without which they could not, in turn, be spiritual directors for their congregations. The whole reason for the church's being, then, centered on spiritual direction. And where it occurred, it exemplified the marks Paul used for characterizing the church—a place where the truth is spoken in love and where joys and sorrows are deeply shared.

Charles Wesley captured in his hymns the essence of corporate spiritual direction at its best. None says it better than this one:

> Help us to help each other, Lord,
> each other's cross to bear;
> let all their friendly aid afford,
> and feel each other's care.[18]

THE PRUDENTIAL MEANS OF GRACE

In our description of corporate spiritual direction within the Wesleyan movement, we have alluded to the prudential means of grace, but we give them particular attention at this point. The prudential means of grace, also known as the "works of mercy" and chosen specifically for pragmatic reasons, are optional in the manner in which they can be done. Indicatively, Wesley's deep concern for the uniqueness of each person made him aware of the diversity of individuals and their circumstances. Therefore he insisted that spiritual formation and direction be tailor-made, using whatever optional disciplines and resources might best help each person grow in the Christian faith.

The instituted means of grace, as we saw, are vehicles through which the Holy Spirit promises to work for our enablement. The concern is to empower inner holiness. Equally important, however, is outer or social holiness. Here the weight falls on discipleship, but in such a way that grace and works form a dynamic whole.

The General Rules structure the prudential means of grace according to three types. The first rule contains a negative dictum: Do "*no harm,* by avoiding evil of every kind"(italics mine). Using the monastic analogy, the specific injunctions enumerated under this first rule are for the sake of cleansing by emptying, without which one cannot be filled. The representative acts from which one is to refrain are far-ranging: swearing, drunkenness, fighting, uncharitable conversation, acquiring costly apparel, singing questionable songs, useless diversion, and self-indulgence. The measure deciding such matters is the negative Golden Rule: Do not do to others what we would not want others to do to us.[19]

The second rule contains a positive dictum: of "*doing good* of every possible sort, and . . . to all" (italics mine). On the one hand, these actions of social holiness are inclusive, such as feeding the hungry, clothing the naked, and visiting the sick and imprisoned. On the other, one is to provide service to "the household of faith," especially the poor. The first rule was concerned with emptying; this second one focuses upon feeding.

The third rule, in turn, deals with how each Christian is to be fed in order to be capable of such social holiness. Although God's enablement is freely given, one must avail oneself particularly of the channels through which God has promised to feed us. These include, as we have seen, public worship and church meetings, the Word proclaimed, the Lord's Supper, family and private prayer, Bible study, and fasting. Wesley includes them here so as to assure that outer holiness overlaps with inner holiness in the ongoing process of spiritual direction.

These prudential means of grace are a way of insisting that sanctification involves more than personal cleansing. Sanctification embraces the whole social order, for it is there in particular that the sins of selfishness and injustice are rampant. In giving spiritual direction, then, it is imperative that no Christian be permitted to become preoccupied with the self. The gospel calls for personal cleansing so that one is enabled to work for the sanctification of the world. Wesley held firmly that Christianity is a social religion, so much so that it is destroyed if rendered solitary.[20] Social holiness begins by taking full responsibility for the lives of one another within the context of class membership, a test for which is how deeply the material needs of each member are the concern of all.

But social holiness dare not become exclusive by remaining internal to the group. It moves out inclusively, making of religious concern the political, economic, and social arenas, with particular emphasis on the poor, prisoners, slaves, addicts, and illiterate. This requires a holy dissatisfaction with the state of society. A mark of the ecumenical nature of this approach is the degree to which the current *Handbook for Today's Catholic* list of required "works of mercy" summarizes the Wesleyan social holiness agenda: (1) Feed the hungry; (2) give drink to the thirsty; (3) clothe the naked; (4) visit the imprisoned; (5) shelter the homeless; (6) visit the sick; (7) bury the dead.[21]

In strong contrast to today's church, a powerful symbol of the social holiness expected in corporate spiritual direction was the insistence that finances were regarded as not to be private in any way. In fact, corporate spiritual direction means nothing less than the practice of mutual economic vulnerability. Wesley himself was the model for how possessions were to be at the disposal of those in need, when at the age of eighty he still walked the winter streets of London collecting money for the poor. Early societies created schools for the poor, medical clinics, drug dispensaries, and provided room and board for the destitute. A question by which class members were forced to exercise such concern was this one, posed as God's question: "How didst thou employ the worldly goods which I lodged in thy hands?"

Wesley's shorthand rule sounded simple: Gain all you can, save all you can, and give all you can. Yet it is crucial that we do not understand this dictum in crass fashion. What Wesley meant stands in dramatic contrast to the drivenness of persons today for personal gain. He is clear that the only gain permitted is one that treats all persons as sacred. And as for "saving all you can," this was in no way an advocacy for stock portfolios. Believing that God alone is creation's rightful owner, we can only be stewards. Thus, luxuries of any kind are to be regarded as signs of faithless stewardship. What Wesley had in mind was frugality, as only a true bargain hunter can understand. But in contrast to today's shopper, frugality of lifestyle is for the purpose of having more money to give to those who have less than you. Anticipating today's liberation theologians, Wesley was convinced that God exercises a "preferential option for the poor." Spiritual direction is the way in which Christians become disciplined so as to function in the same manner. The litmus test was a trilogy: the destitute, the widow, and the orphan.

Inner holiness and social holiness formed a sacred marriage, with spiritual direction functioning as the minister in charge. Yet impressive as Wesley's own disciplined life is in this regard, those of us involved in spiritual direction today must be critical of his restricted application of the prudential means of grace. Lovett Weems is correct in charging Wesley with "being unduly supportive of the existing social order."[22] Consequently, he was unsupportive of citizen participation in government and public decision making, even becoming angry over any efforts against, or disrespect of, the structures of society or church. The unfortunate consequence of this conservative bent for "law and order" is that his concern was to treat the symptoms of social disharmony, rather than to identify and rectify the causes. Two classic statements help clarify the difference. Wesley would applaud this statement by Basil the Great (A.D. 330–379): "The bread in your cupboard belongs to the hungry [person], the coat hanging unused in your closet belongs to the [person] who needs it; the shoes rotting in your closet belong to the [person] who has no shoes; the money which you put in the bank belongs to the poor. You do wrong to everyone you could help but fail to help."[23] In contrast, however, he would be upset, or at least baffled by, the implications of Brazilian Archbishop Helder Camara's statement: "When I give food to the poor, they call me a saint. When I ask why the poor have no food, they call me a communist." Wesley was a saint. Camara was a martyr.

Here we touch perhaps the most controversial aspect of spiritual direction. Since Christianity is intensely social, aiding persons on their spiritual journey dares not leave untouched the implications of living the faith for approaching the dilemmas of society. Jesus taught far more than charity, for he was harsh in his judgment of the way things are. His insistence is upon a way of life in which the first will be last, the rich will be sent away empty, the mighty are to be pulled from their thrones, and the meek shall be given the earth as their inheritance. Jesus's prayer is that this kingdom "come on earth."

Persons will certainly discern social issues differently, and thus their responses will be diverse, as we saw in discussing the Theological Worlds. However, social holiness is such an indispensable ingredient in spiritual direction that Christians dare not be permitted to neglect present-day indicators of the systemic causes of the societal conditions about which Christians must be concerned. Where is the justice in the following facts?

- The world's population is approximately 6.2 billion persons,[24] and the population of the United States is 281 million.[25]

- Almost 800 million people are malnourished.[26] Of these people, 200 million are children.[27]

- One billion people are at the starvation level, approximately the same number of overweight persons in the first world (industrialized nations).

- The wealthiest 20 percent of the world's people consumes an astonishing 86 percent of all goods and services. The poorest fifth consumes only 1.3 percent.[28]

- In 1999 an estimated 61 percent of Americans was overweight or obese.[29]

- Every minute, more than 10 children under age 5 die of hunger.[30]

- In the United States, 1 percent of Americans holds about 90 percent of the nation's wealth.[31]

- Since the mid-1970s, the income of the richest fifth of Americans has grown by 38 percent, while that of the poorest fifth has fallen by 12 percent. Thus, the gap between rich and poor is greater than ever before.[32]

- In March 2002 Bill Gates had an estimated net worth of $52.8 billion.[33] This is more than the total net worth of the bottom 40 percent of all American households put together.

- In 1982 there were 13 billionaires in the United States.[34] In 2002 there were 227.[35]

- In 2000 more than 31 million Americans were living below the poverty level. Of this number, 11,633,000 were children.

- In the United States at the end of June 2001, over 1.9 million people were in prison. The overwhelming majority of prisoners was from ethnic minorities and the lower socioeconomic class.[36]

A helpful way to draw the important distinction between symptoms and causes so as to be useful in spiritual direction is to distinguish between *acts of mercy* and *acts of justice*. Two verses from Isaiah are illustrative. Acts of mercy can be expressed this way: "Is it not to share your bread with the hungry, and bring the homeless poor into your house; when you see the naked, to cover them?" (Isa. 58:7) Acts of justice, on the other hand, are those that "loose the bonds of injustice, to undo the thongs of the yoke, to let the oppressed go free, and to break every yoke" (Isa. 58:6). In doing spiritual direction, it is useful to see how this distinction works itself out in practical actions.

	ACTS OF MERCY	ACTS OF JUSTICE
FOCUS	Individuals	Systems
COMPLIANCE	Voluntary	Punitive consequence
MEANS	Supplemental opportunities Complementary resources	Legislation, boycott, strike, nonviolent resistance
ISSUES (Examples):		
HUNGER	Emergency assistance	Food Stamp program
ENVIRONMENT	Neighborhood cleanup	Legislate clean air and water regulations
HEALTH	Free health clinic	Universal health insurance
VIOLENCE	Monitor one's TV watching	Organize a boycott of violent films
EDUCATION	Tutoring	Head Start
RACE	Dinners for Ten	Affirmative Action

Throughout the Wesleyan movement, then, spiritual direction is the necessary instrument of support, discernment, and accountability through which the redemptive process is enabled. While corporate spiritual direction was used more frequently than one-with-one direction for practical reasons, both were important. In addition, the third major type of spiritual direction—personal spiritual direction—played an important role as well. The individual journals kept by traveling preachers as a spiritual discipline reveal how deep was the personal direction in which each one was involved. After researching these journals, James Nelson concludes that they disclose "an unbelievably rigorous regimen of private prayer, devotional and scholarly reading, Bible study and meditation, fasting, and confessional dialogue with one another and with lay folk."[37] Here we have evidence of the vigorous interplay of all three types of spiritual direction. Each clergyperson, serving as a model for the laity, not only gave and received corporate and one-with-one spiritual direction but also was involved in intensive personal spiritual direction.

Essential to the genius of Wesley's contribution to the ecumenical church is a spiritual direction that was wrapped in an ecumenical spirituality resulting from the creative fusion of sectarian discipleship with the universality of grace. The Reformation insistence on justification by grace through faith was broadened to include the Roman Catholic insistence upon nurturing grace. And while at every point God's initiative is made prior with the concept of prevenient grace ("coming before"), the Catholic emphasis on human action became an organic part. Thus, we have an ecumenical spirituality of grace and response, justification and sanctification, justice and love, personhood and community, church and sect, Protestant and Catholic.

Chapter 4

✛

THE ART OF ONE-WITH-ONE
SPIRITUAL DIRECTION

ISSUES THAT CALL FOR SPIRITUAL DIRECTION

Perhaps the best way to learn is through apprenticeship. So it is with spiritual direction. Thus, it may be helpful to step inside the workshop of a spiritual director, as it were. In observing how I do spiritual direction, it is important to understand that there is no single right way to do it. In fact, each director must draw from a variety of approaches, depending on the person and the focus of concern. By reviewing the kinds of cases with which I have been involved, we can sense the spectrum of needs that trigger requests for spiritual direction.

> *Accountability:* where a person knows what needs to be done but
>   is not able to do it faithfully without being held accountable
>   by some individual or group.
> *Addiction:* food and drugs are the most frequent issues.

Burnout: a frequent spiritual condition, especially of clergy.

Coping: needing resources for managing excessive anxiety, etc.

Crisis: may be personal, vocational, relational, or calling.

Curiosity: for example, about the spiritual life.

Damaging personality characteristics: for example, resentment, jealousy, drivenness.

Deeper life: wanting more than than just a "normal life."

Discernment: needing help in figuring out what is going on in one's life and what direction the future needs to take.

Emotions: not being in touch with one's feelings, or having feelings that threaten to get out of control.

Family dysfunctionality: for example, unhealthy interaction with one's spouse or children.

Guilt: where someone or something in the past needs to be forgiven.

Healing: with 60 to 70 percent of physical ailments classified as psychosomatic, much sickness has spiritual causes.

Immobilization: feeling paralyzed or "stuck."

Impasse: incapable of resolving circumstances that serve as blockage.

Incarceration: the special spiritual needs of prisoners—dealing with loneliness, fear, innocence, and an uncertain future.

Intervention: on occasion, one may need to offer direction in situations or for persons where a request has not been made.

Issues: for example, facing a possible abortion, or marriage tensions.

Junctures: when an important decision needs to be made.

Negative happenings: dealing with such events as the suicide of a friend, being fired, or helping a friend or spouse to die gracefully.

Ongoing failure: the inability to "do anything right."

Self-image: for example, a sense of insecurity or inferiority, usually rooted in the past.

Physical handicaps or sickness: for example, facing deterioration through disease such as Parkinson's disease, or the possibility of death from cancer.

Practice: needing help in choosing and maturing in the use of particular spiritual disciplines, such as contemplation or *lectio divina.*

Prioritizing: bringing balance to an overextended life.

Quandary: for example, struggling with issues of faith, as in serious doubts, or inclination to change denominations or faiths.

Referrals: for example, being asked by a bishop to "work with" dysfunctional pastors.

Sexual identity: as in dealing with homosexuality.

Situations: for example, being drained by one's work environment, pastoral charge, or the winter blahs.

Soul companion: for persons whose spiritual journey is at a depth where they need to be understood and be assured that all is well, finding perspective for assimilating the "surprises" of the Spirit.

Transitions: for example, a new job, vocation, or retirement.

TYPES OF DIRECTION NEEDED

From this spectrum of focused *issues* that might confront the spiritual director, we can identify various *types* of direction that may be needed. Sensing this scope can help those interested in serving as directors to become clear about their strengths, limits, and needs in regard to knowledge, abilities, and experience. The director is then better able to determine the types of direction he or she is prepared to undertake. Further, knowing the needs that may trigger a request for spiritual direction helps a director anticipate when in actual sessions the director might be outside his or her "comfort level" and need to make referrals. Usually, however, it is possible to control the level to which a direction session is encouraged or permitted to go. For example, a person may ask for help in developing a prayer life. The director can deal precisely with that request, or can invite movement into a deeper level, probing, for example, why the directee wants a deeper prayer life and/or is presently having trouble developing one. Whereas spiritual direction in its fullest and deepest sense entails taking soundings in all directions, some directors may need to draw narrower ground rules. Additionally, the director must be attentive to how deep a particular directee may be willing or able to go, sensitive to when the person may be reaching that boundary, and be prepared to pull back as soon as such signs appear.

1. *Spiritual discipline.* Of all the types of direction in which a person might be involved, most direction will be variations on the theme of helping the directee "become more spiritual." Requests can take the form of "Help me with my prayer life," or "I am not spiritually fulfilled by just going to church and serving on committees." In response, the director may simply need to provide options in spiritual disciplines and faith styles, such as those found in Chapter 5 and the Appendixes. The director should not take responsibility for providing *the* answer. In fact, the director is not to be a problem solver but must have enough discernment to suggest concrete ways in which the directee can be challenged to work with the leadings of the Spirit. One way of doing this might be to suggest visiting a place where a deeper variety of spirituality and practices is available for the experiencing. A weekend at a monastery, for instance, might be helpful, providing a concentrated dosage that invites persons to take their spirituality to a deeper level. In my experience, nothing so deepens spirituality for ministerial students and clergy as a one-week immersion as monks. But whatever approach is decided upon, it is important to establish some form of accountability structure, as each of us has difficulty persevering in new ways of living when confronted daily by the old habitual ways.

2. *Spiritual inquiry.* A director might be surprised to discover that someone is drawn to him or her because of who he/she is. Sensing what it looked like for Jesus to be a man of prayer, the disciples were drawn to ask him, "Teach us to pray." As I have shared previously, a new phase in my own spiritual direction began when I was drawn to approach a hermit monk and state quite bluntly, "You are what I need to be about." I didn't know what I was look-

ing for, but I wanted it nonetheless. As I look back on it now, I was attracted by his internal joy, a quiet happiness, and an absence of my own drivenness always to be doing. It was clear almost from the start that I could never be who he is (an introvert) or live as he does (a mystic)—nor would I want to. But "he knew," and so somehow he could help me find my own path. The image I had during our sessions was of the childhood game "Find the Thimble," where his task was to tell me when I was getting hot or cold.

3. *Spiritual discernment.* Some individuals may not really know what to ask. All they know is that "things are not the way I would like." The data comes by encouraging the person to talk at random about anything that comes to mind. Open-ended questions invite arenas to be examined, such as, "Does your work give you satisfaction?" Or, "How are things with your spouse?" Or, "What do you do in your spare time?" These are all concrete but indirect ways of asking, "How's your soul?" In such cases, the person needs a spiritual friend who can walk alongside, sharing together what is seen. Other situations may entail hidden blockage so deep that therapy is required. In cases where the blockage is more apparent, it may give rise to crisis direction, such as dealing with a dysfunctional marriage. There are other situations where the discernment needed is a *spiritual futuring.* The most challenging of this type of discernment I have done is with a prisoner locked in solitary confinement for the rest of his life. As a result, he is now a hermit monk, for whom a change of heart has transformed his cell into a hermitage where he prays daily for the world and its needs.

4. *Spiritual crisis direction.* Sometimes a particular circumstance weighing heavily upon a person can initiate direction. This resembles the counseling with which most clergy are familiar—dealing with marriage crises, grief, wayward children, sexual affairs, and unethical practices. In spiritual crisis direction, however, as in all spiritual direction, we must remember that our work is *spiritual.* Unlike secular counselors, spiritual directors are responsible for surrounding the person with the gracious presence of God, whether the person

experiences God as Unconditional Love, Merciful Questioner, Forgiving Friend, or Gracious Confidant. Just as a conclusion often flows from the way a question is phrased, the result depends in part upon the spiritual context in which the process is placed.

5. *Spiritual counseling.* The director cannot always know the type of spiritual direction needed just on the basis of a person's request. There are few cases of spiritual direction in which the past is not a factor, but for some persons the shadow of the past is heavy. The director must discern whether the directee is someone with problems or has a problem personality in which the person *is* the problem. Therapy may be required, either because of the depth of blockage involved or the duration of work needed. The director must surmise whether this person has the inner strength to tackle the pilgrimage at a therapeutic depth, and then whether he or she might be open to the suggestion of referral. There are times when spiritual coping is all that can be expected. It is helpful to develop a list of therapists, identified by their type and approach to therapy. Avoid therapists whose professionalism you have no reason to trust, who are unsympathetic to spirituality, who are dogmatic about using only one method, and who use medication without accompanying verbal therapy. While mood-altering drugs can be useful in some cases, only rarely should pharmacological coping be considered as a long-term solution. Since the person's soul is at stake, spiritual direction, done simultaneously with therapy, can be beneficial.

The longer-range spiritual counseling I do is usually a variation on the theme of low self-image, rooted in situations of childhood lack of affirmation by parents and/or siblings. The director should not try to be a therapist in the usual sense but a *spiritual* counselor. The heart of all spiritual healing consists of varied ways of discovering, experiencing, and trusting the unconditional love of God. How this is enabled depends on the personality involved, which in turn suggests the disciplines most likely to evoke this new context for living. Since this love that is needed is in significant contrast to what the person has experienced before, it will usually occur transparently, through the director's patient and caring acceptance. The rejection such persons usually feel is that no one has ever really cared enough to listen to them. Thus, the mere fact of spiritual direction is in itself healing, for intense listening is at its heart. In being listened to, one can begin to sense that one is worth being listened to. In finally feeling heard, one can begin to risk self-disclosure, making possible the process of discerning the patterns at work. Healing is underway when the person is enabled to see the connection between past and present, between latent resident feelings and an experience of the present itself.

Such perception, however, is only the beginning. In many ways, direction has to do with repetition. Even after connectional insights seem clear, the director will need to keep asking what seems so obvious: "Does what is happening with you at work this week feel like what you used to experience from your father?" Direction involves breaking the false connections with which a lifetime of rehearsal has branded the person. Yet there is a fine line between the necessary repetition of one's *epiphania* and the counterproductive rehearsal of one's *obsessio*. Unless carefully directed, reiteration can be like picking at a scab, bringing the hurt of the past into a present hurting, instead of moving into a new remembrance that returns the memory finally to the past, and from which a new future can emerge.

Henri Nouwen suggests ingredients that spiritual counseling might encounter: fears and anxieties, guilt and shame, sexual fantasies, greed and anger, joys and successes, aspirations and hopes, reflections and doubts, dreams and mental wanderings. But most of all, he insists, the focus will be people—family, friends, and enemies—those who make us who we are. While spiritual counseling involves discovering and confessing and sorting and prioritizing, the essential context through which the whole process must move and have its being is the mysterious Presence of the One we call God.

6. *Spiritual resourcing.* Directors, by definition, are spiritual resources. This may entail hearing what amounts to confession and

providing acceptance on the far side of forgiveness. Or the person may need help in "naming the name," learning to perceive daily occurrences as spiritual events. In a society whose theme song is "What's in It for Me?" the quest in spiritual direction to live spiritually and think theologically necessitates some degree of conversion. Helpful, then, are liturgical acts and sacramental objects as aids in symbolizing support and accountability. Oil, for example, can render a promise sacred, while a special rock or a broken reed for one's desk or nightstand can serve as a sacramental parable.

THE ART OF SPIRITUAL DIRECTION

Having identified the sorts of issues that often precipitate spiritual direction, and having named the types of direction likely to be involved, we are ready now to explore more concretely what one-with-one spiritual direction is like. In entering the process, the director should avoid making two contrary mistakes: (1) On the one hand, avoid rushing into the mode of problem solving, as if responsible for making everything right; (2) On the other hand, the director's listening should not be based on the premise that the problem belongs only to the directee. Spiritual direction is hard work for both persons. It involves a listening beyond hearing, intent on discerning a clarity that transcends the person's emotional maze and convoluted intricacies of behavior. The director must be aware that multiple levels will be operative. For example, persons may have a fear of consequences, fear of discovery, fear of implications, fear of guilt, or fear of actions to which direction may push them. Furthermore, persons typically come to spiritual direction with an urge for a particular outcome, a penchant for easy solutions, a desire to come out feeling innocent, an inclination to blame others or circumstances, and a tendency to be defensive.

Thus, it is important for the director to come to the session prepared in specific ways.

- Through prayer, anticipate receiving the person as one for whom Christ died.

- Become aware of any personal bias or partiality that might operate in this particular situation, such as gender, ethnicity, or appearance. Be aware of how the directee's issues or situation might parallel your own, triggering your own unresolved tensions. Be sensitive in advance to any conflict of interest, such as issues of friendship or confidentiality. Be attentive to anything that might lead you to favor a particular outcome to the direction.

- Be in touch with your own temptations, foibles, and sins of the past, so that nothing shared is likely to surprise, offend, tempt, shock, or undo you.

- Come to each session having dealt sufficiently with your own ego needs so that you feel no need to be a "savior" or even to feel appreciated. Be content rather to be a conduit, a transparency, a means, a secondary participant, even an observer, in what will happen. Be eager to be unnecessary.

- Concern yourself more with long-range outcomes than short-term coping. Be willing to provide ongoing support in which accountability is clear, concrete, and manageable.

- Believe profoundly in the power of the Holy Spirit to bring discernment, strengthen possibilities, change lives, and provide significant direction—and ask for it.

STEPS OF THE PROCESS

In general, the process of spiritual direction will be one of support, listening, discerning, guiding, suggesting, assigning, creating a rule, and establishing means of accountability. In more detail, the following are suggested guidelines.

1. When someone asks you to be his or her spiritual director, it is wise to *inquire why the person is interested in participating in direction, and why with you.* This not only helps you decide if this spiritual direction is an assignment with which you can be comfortable, but it also enables you to prepare with possible resources.

2. *Having a verbal contract* before the first meeting is helpful, but be sure to reach an agreement by the end of the first session. The invitation to direction often begins informally, with such a comment as "I'd like to bounce some things off you when you have time." A helpful response is, "When?" A more formal inquiry is likely to take the form of, "If possible, I'd like to contract for some of your time to work on. . . ."

3. I use *two different configurations* in doing spiritual direction. The more usual one is a one-hour session, prearranged as to place, time, and length. Scheduling closure at the end of an hour encourages persons not to prolong broaching the difficult issues. The other type of direction is a daylong event, sometimes overnight, intended to be more intense and open-ended. Such direction is for persons whose seriousness calls for deeper conversation and possibly the use of assessment tools. While the process follows the general approach characterizing regular one-with-one direction, there might be miniassignments with time allotted to do them, feedback times, silent time, as well as time for experimenting with particular spiritual disciplines, creating a longer-range rule, and determining effective accountability. Since such intense sessions are often with persons who have traveled a long distance, they may not be ongoing. In such cases, the focus is diagnostic, followed by establishing a direction program to be continued through a referral to the directee's home location.

4. *Pay attention to where a session is held,* with an eye to creating a relaxed environment, a spiritual ambiance, and a guarantee of confidentiality. At the same time, be sensitive to possibilities of harassment charges and other forms of litigation. If possible, another person should be nearby. Such matters make it advantageous to

inquire if spiritual direction can be included within a local church's ministry, thereby having insurance coverage. To the degree that direction is the less formal type of being a "spiritual friend," there is less reason to be legally concerned. I was distressed recently when a district superintendent indicated that he was discouraging his clergy from doing even crisis counseling for fear of litigation. When such fear undercuts a central ministry of the church, it is time to create a "theology of risk."

5. Before each session, *empty yourself of all distractions* in order to be totally available. The event of direction demands your full attention, focused clearly on the directee and aware of the varied nuances at play. Contemplation is a traditional name for what is involved, meaning total participation in what is immediately in front of the director. This is a stance common to composers with their compositions, scientists with their data, mechanics with a car, and doctors with their patients. If you find your attention distracted by a phone call needing to be made or a situation at home needing attention, you will be duty-bound to make the call or check out the situation, even if the directee has to wait. A better approach, prior to the session, is to make a note of any personal concerns cluttering your mind, indicating when you will take care of them. Then let go. The covenant that direction requires is the pledge of undivided attention, free of preoccupations, intent on listening with an intensity whereby one participates in the life of the person in front of you.

6. *Confidentiality* is indispensable in spiritual direction. The directee must be able to trust that everything disclosed in sessions will be held in sacred trust.[1]

7. *Collect resources and make them available* as appropriate in direction sessions. These might include short bibliographies and handouts that introduce spiritual disciplines such as *lectio divina*, journaling, and centering prayer. It is well to have in mind, or even available for borrowing, your own favorite "great books." Having said this, however, resist the temptation to overwhelm a person

with material, for the focus needs to be upon emotions and will rather than on information and concepts.

8. *The initial task is to enable the person to share,* preferably in a spontaneous fashion. Random conversation is best, for if persons have prepackaged what they wish to share, direction tends to be superficial. Beginning the session should be simple. After a warm greeting and a short prayer for trust and illumination, the opening need be little more than "Tell me why you are here," or "How can I help you?" Because such questions can be heard as inviting a conclusion more than as an invitation to provide data, my preference is to be less direct: "Tell me a bit about yourself." Since most people do not usually know how they really are, such an invitation to share can give the person pause to get in touch with what spontaneously surfaces. Listen. Refrain from interrupting. If a question suggests itself, remember it so that you might ask it later. At this point, be content to nod, give affirming signs, or make comments restricted to "I hear you," or "That makes sense," or "That's interesting." Any questions, initially, should be for the purpose of encouraging additional sharing—either in general, or at places where the directee's "passing over" might seem "too quick." Usually the director needs only say, "Tell me more."

9. *Some who come for spiritual direction will exhibit what I call "misplaced energy,"* while others will come with blockages that have drained them of emotion and thus energy. The first type of person populates Dostoyevsky's novels—people of passion and vitality, floundering, perhaps misdirected, but energetically seeking. This type is usually amenable to direction. The second type inhabits T. S. Eliot's writings. He characterizes them as products of modern life—sleepwalkers, unfeeling, measuring out their lives with coffee spoons, without the energy to risk—"paralysed force, gesture without motion."[2] This type of person has a hunch that something is wrong, or he/she would not come for direction. Yet to almost every question, the answer is a tired variation on the theme of "I don't know." The person does not seem to feel anything, leaving the director to do most of the work of the session.

Successful spiritual direction is almost impossible with someone who cannot feel or refuses to feel. The problem is usually blockage, often deep enough to require therapy. Help is available only through painful and persistent plumbing of *why* such persons are unable to get in touch with their feelings. The "inability" to feel deeply is usually a threatened unwillingness to risk becoming alive. It is a defense mechanism set up to cope with the fear of reexperiencing what was unbearable in earlier life. To evoke feelings, then, is to risk the emergence of repressed memories as a frightening threat in the present. Thus, this latter type of person is more likely to need therapy and is destined for more hurt before there can be real healing and new life. This person's hope rests in the assurance that "the Lord is near to the brokenhearted, and saves the crushed in spirit" (Ps. 34:18).

10. *In some cases, directors will find themselves on a "fishing expedition,"* casting bait in order to hook a clue about the true situation. Discovery and diagnosis are at least half the task of spiritual direction. In these situations, a "Sentence Completion Inventory" can be helpful.[3] An inventory can easily be constructed by listing some of the persons and dimensions tending to appear in all our lives, and writing sentence-starters with a subject and possibly a verb. For example, "Mothers should . . ." or "My one wish is . . ." or "At home, I. . . ." It is fascinating how quickly themes emerge, giving the director clues worth exploring.

11. *The primary task of the director,* especially at the beginning, *is to listen.* Do this not only with ears but with eyes as well, reading the silent clues. Detect body language, translate tone and hesitancy of speech, along with implicit feelings, moods, and habits. Be attentive to your own hunches about what is going on. I find it useful to have a paper and pencil for making notes, informing the person in advance that note taking is an aid to help me listen, remember more clearly, and discern patterns. To allay uneasiness, I give assurance that the person can have the notes at the end of the session. No one has ever requested them, but in some cases I have given a

directee copies for remembering particular insights mutually discerned. If the person takes my notes as offered, I ask him or her to bring them back to the next session. Otherwise, I keep these notes in a locked file, available for reviewing before the next session.

I usually begin taking notes by placing at the top of the page "vital statistics" as they emerge, such as: divorced, two children, bookkeeper, Lutheran, born on an Iowa farm, only child. Each of these notations may be laden with implications, but I resist exploring them at this point. Under any of these statistics I might add additional data as it emerges. Then I begin to record issues or images as they occur through the random sharing. The basic task is to look for recurring persons and themes—such as "mother," "need to be important," or "anger." These I circle. I draw a line down the right side of the paper, providing a wide margin where I can make running written comments. These might include questions worth exploring later, disciplines or resources that come to mind as potentially useful, and hunches about resolution. Be very slow to offer any of these when they first emerge. Best left until later, they will filter themselves through the sharing process. Paper and pencil help me to be "in dialogue" without interrupting the flow of the monologue.

As the sharing continues, I begin to connect certain circles with lines, suggesting to myself possible patterns of connection between persons, situations, themes, issues, or behaviors. For example, worth connecting with lines might be "cold father," "older brother," "problems with men," "fearful of. . . ." Persons seeking spiritual direction are often unaware of their behaviors actually being unconscious reactions with real consequences. As a result, they are unaware of causes, feeling mystified by what they do or fail to do and by their built-in difficulty in changing this. For spiritual direction to have lasting effect, it needs to go beyond the level of coping, providing countervailing disciplines. Healing has to do with identifying and coming to terms with the internalized causes.

12. While the above description best characterizes the "spiritual counseling" type of direction, it is helpful in other kinds of

direction as well. *When asked to do more ordinary discernment, or simply to provide resources for spiritual growth, or to deal with a crisis, the director should always be attentive to the causes*—to the "whys" beneath the inquiries and the needs. How deeply the person needs or wants or is able to go is another matter. Minimally, however, it is important to establish an accountability structure that will help counter avoidance patterns. Rarely are the parameters suggested by the initial request sufficient for the spiritual direction that is actually needed.

13. *There are various psychological and spiritual tools available for use in direction,* as described in the Appendixes. Some require professional certification, while others do not. It is helpful if directors have used some of them in their own pilgrimage. Then, with some experience, the director can sense, for example, where a person might be according to the Enneagram, the Myers-Briggs Type Indicator, or the twelve-step process of healing. While useful to the director, these guides can also be helpful to directees who resist emerging insights, or are out of touch with their feelings, or lack self-awareness. They will likely find one or more of these inventories intriguing. Such tools are also helpful for persons who are eager to discover more about themselves for the sake of spiritual growth. Be sensitive as to when such tools might be intrusive, for keeping things simple is usually the most effective way of encouraging change.[4]

14. *The first part of each spiritual direction session* we have described as a *conversational sharing* for the sake of clarifying the person's situation, using simple open-ended invitations such as: "Tell me a bit more about. . . ." The director usually senses when it is time to ease into the next stage, which might take on the ambiance of "Could it be that . . . ?" Or "Have you ever wondered . . . ?" Or "Do you think there might be a connection . . . ?" It is best to inquire if the person sees a connection rather than first telling the connection you see. Self-discovery and self-recognition are most effective.

15. *Illumination is the goal of this stage,* out of which a person is able hopefully to affirm that "things are clearer now." Both director and directee usually know when the session has accomplished what

is realistic to expect. In moving toward closure, the director might simply ask, "Where do you think we are in all this?" And perhaps later, "Where do you think we need to go from here?" The desired goal is a conclusion sufficient to establish an assignment, one that will help the directee move into new ways of being. That reminds me of what someone once said to John Wesley when Wesley wanted to stop preaching: "Preach faith till you have it; and then, because you have it, you will preach faith." This is what discipline accomplishes. Relatedly, Fénelon insists that just as faith is believing without seeing, so the Christian loves without feeling. In other words, our actions must be rooted in the will rather than our emotions; otherwise we could never love our enemies. It is impossible to have warm feelings toward those who abuse us, but it is possible for us to will what is best for them instead of to will them evil. The intent of accountability in spiritual direction, then, is a disciplined re-formation of the will.

16. Throughout the session, *the director needs to be attentive to what might be the most helpful assignment,* sometimes as an experiment. The simplest is assigning a spiritual discipline. For example, if centering prayer might be helpful, describe the practice briefly, perhaps providing a handout or suggesting a book for the person to read. Inquire how this could best work into the directee's day and for what length of time. It is important that the assignment be clear, concrete, and "doable." Even in more complex situations, closure should result in something that the person is to do. It might be an assignment to draft a week's schedule that would make it possible for the person to give priority time to what was agreed upon. Or it might be an inventory of how the directee uses his or her time during a typical week. Or the person might promise to refrain from some activity, or to try fasting for a set period.

17. *When the assignment is mutually established, an accountability structure should be agreed upon.* Without this, nothing is likely to result. A question is generally helpful: "How can I help you be faithful to this agreement?" I marvel at the value of electronics for accounta-

bility. The directee might promise to e-mail the assignment by a particular day, with the understanding that the director will rattle his/her cage if he or she doesn't. Another accountability option is to call in assignments by phone or to send the director a copy of his/her record of daily faithfulness. Memory aids, such as posted notes, are helpful. However accountability is done, its goal is to practice ways of being open to the Spirit as actor. For this, encourage the use of the church's means of grace. A director's tokens of support can include remembrances of important events in the person's pilgrimage, such as birthdays, anniversaries, death dates of relatives and friends, and the beginning date of direction. The supreme compliment, I have learned, is the frequent use of the person's first name. When a telemarketer asks if "Mr. Jones" is there, I hang up. When the voice asks, "Is this Paul?" I am a soft touch.

18. Before concluding the session, several things are helpful. First, *summarize in appreciative fashion what has happened,* emphasizing the positive and happily anticipating the follow-up contact. Second, *decide about future sessions.* In some cases, all that may be needed is the initial session, followed by ongoing accountability. In other cases, regularly scheduled sessions are best. The "fit" of the two of you may not be right, or the person may not be responsive or responsible, so provide an opportunity to decide that this should be the last session. If the person does wish to continue, suggest a trial time period, such as weekly sessions for a month, then "let's see how things are going." Another possibility is, after several sessions of fairly intense direction so that things are basically in place, the person might be helped to find someone else to be director over the long haul. Unless one does directing professionally, there is a limit to how many directees a person can take on at any given time, and for how long.

19. Ideally, *assignments should be part of an eventual larger assignment, that of creating a "rule" to which one is willing to be held* accountable. Scripture provides examples of rules, as in the Ten Commandments, the Beatitudes, and Paul's characteristics of the Spirit. In addition, all religious orders, such as the Benedictines,

Augustinians, and Franciscans, have rules. A sample rule appears in Appendix 3. Since spirituality is related to one's full personhood, a rule should oversee one's time and space, one's doing and being, one's significant relationships, one's environment, and the use of one's resources. The rule is an intentional spiritual plan, undergirded by sufficient disciplines, support, and accountability for "growth in grace" to be ongoing. This is the goal toward which all spiritual direction ideally moves, whatever the nature of its inception. The rule is more effective if it is written and signed. The "Rule and the Wesleyan Covenant" in Appendix 4 provides a liturgy for marking the occasion as a promise to God. Spiritual direction is serious business.

In creating a rule, begin by helping the person identify the invisible rule already operating in his or her life. All of us have one, for we are creatures of habit. After bringing the invisible rule to the directee's awareness, help the person rework it so that it enables the directee to live his or her faith commitment more intentionally. Be attentive to scope (for example, diet, possessions, sexuality, work, leisure, exercise) and authenticity (living a version of the gospel that best touches at the person's deepest roots).

Disciplined accountability is essential not only to becoming a Christian, but also in one's ongoing living as a Christian. New Year's resolutions inevitably fail, because the very person who lacks self-discipline is the one who is supposed to hold himself or herself accountable. Spiritual growth requires three things: (1) a rule to which one promises to be held responsible; (2) one or more persons who will lend support in this pilgrimage; and (3) a clear method by which one is regularly held accountable. A rule is the straightedge by which one's life is measured and rendered straight.

20. *After such a rule is in place, direction from that point on might cautiously be called "maintenance."* The Wesleyan question "What is the state of your soul?" becomes no longer a general diagnostic question but a concrete one concerned with faithfulness to one's rule. The person's response might take the form of a verbal inventory. "In regard to the quality time I promised for my children . . ."

or "I did *lectio divina* five out of seven mornings last week." "Fine" is not an acceptable response to questions about the state of one's soul or how one is doing with one's rule. The director might need to take some initiative, reviewing the tenets of the rule by asking: "How are you doing in regard to . . . ?" "And how about . . . ?" Sometimes a numerical rating question is evocative: "On a scale from 1 to 10 with 10 being high, how do you think you are doing with . . . ?" Finally, "Give me a number to indicate how you are doing overall." If a particular rating seems low (or high), invite the person to elaborate. Be supportive by encouraging what has been done, and "kindly pushy" in providing creative tension for what needs to be done. Remember that the director's task is not to be liked or even appreciated. It entails knowing when persons need to have their song hummed quietly to them, and when it may be time to lance festering wounds. It may even mean going back to the drawing board if the directee says, "I don't think this rule is working well for me."

21. It is useful to *keep a file on each directee,* the main ingredients being any notes taken during sessions and an ongoing record of accountability. Do not trust your memory on anything. Record the assignment for which the next session will be an accounting. Files must be totally confidential. In addition to locking them, you might use a number rather than a person's name on each file, keeping the code in another place. Do not share with anyone the names of persons with whom you are doing spiritual direction. This is the directee's prerogative to share if he or she wishes.

22. The issue of *payment* is a difficult one. Trained professional directors may choose to take their lead from professional health-care personnel in their area, whose rates normally range from $75 to $150 per hour, preferably on a sliding scale. My preference is for professional direction to be done under the auspices of a local church, and thereby dealt with much as that church deals with such ministries as baptisms, marriages, and funerals. I do not charge for spiritual direction, but my directees often choose to express their appreciation by making a donation to one of the ministries in which

I am involved. For most nonprofessionals, giving spiritual direction will simply be a part of their life as Christians. Hopefully group spiritual direction will become a normal activity in each church, both in receiving and in being trained to give direction. And from such groups those who show particular ability in listening and discernment can be recruited for training in one-with-one direction.

SPIRITUAL DIRECTION AS MEANS TO A HERE-AND-NOW SPIRITUALITY

Primary in Jesus's teaching is his emphasis upon living in the *present*. "Do not worry about tomorrow" is a key dictum (Matt. 6:34), and he likens those who are anxious about tomorrow to a fool whose huge building plans are adjourned by an appointment that night with death. Both the gospel and therapeutic research identify the inauthentic life as resulting from living an almost nonexistent "now."[5] This is because many persons are overpowered by negative memories of the past, with the only perceived hope being a nonexistent future. Squeezed between past and future, the present becomes a stunted arena for survival at best. As a result, one of the first tasks—perhaps the primary task—of spiritual direction is to discover the extent to which the directee is held hostage by the past, or preoccupied by the future, needing to be freed for living fully in the present. In fact, I have found this phenomenon to be so pervasive that examining it in depth here seems important, as well as exploring how it might be resolved through spiritual direction.

The unconscious is populated by images of hurts we have received and inflicted, which haunt us through remembering and re-remembering. Usually these wounds date back to childhood when we were particularly vulnerable, repressing "for later" those issues too painful to resolve. But later translates into an unresolved past that continues to chew on one's fragile now. The "once was," in aggressively invading the present, becomes experienced as an "it is so" *now*.

Abundant examples from spiritual direction cases emerge as

variations on such themes as these: "My mother never once said she loved me," or "My sister always said I was ugly," or "I never could seem to please my father." What is remembered is usually from far in the past, most likely forgotten by all *except the recipient*. For him or her, it is anything but "long gone." It is remembered and thus felt as if today—in fact, remembered in such a way that it *is* one's today. And lurking in the present, it can be retriggered at any time—either as inappropriate projection or as a negative "eye shadow," coloring with supersensitivity what one sees.

This process that undoes us involves more than just a *remembrance* of things past. A metamorphosis occurs. It is no long mother or sister or father speaking in his or her own voice through our memory. Their words have become indistinguishable from our own. "Nobody could love me if they really knew me" (implied: because my mother didn't). "I really am ugly" (implied: my sister ought to know). "I never seem able to do anything right" (implied: my dad did everything right).

This transition from "they" to "me" is what swallows up the now, for the past has *become* the present. I am *now* what I was once told I was and treated as if I were. When we are so possessed, our filters become firmly fastened, and what *was* becomes our propensity for seeing things *now*. To illustrate, even if you receive many comments about how good you look in that purple dress, what gnaws at you all week is a single offhanded comment: "I don't know if purple is your color." Inside the rumbling begins: *I wonder what she really meant by that?*

And what of the positive comments received? "They only said that to be nice." Or, "They didn't really mean it." The negative is what is remembered, for it is "proof" of what you have known all along. "Like my sister always said, I really am unattractive."

This process is ironic, for even *if* these hurts from the past were intentional at the time, rehearsing them *gives* others the power to hurt us continually. Rehearsed hurts become disembodied from their source, becoming a state of being. And in losing their source, a person forfeits any perspective for sorting out the present. The feelings simply *are*, apparently uncaused, and so they become a *given* that a person seems powerless to deny. It must be so. As children we were taught, "Sticks and stones may break my bones, but words will never hurt me." Maybe so, but remembering those words can hurt for a lifetime.

Anxiety is the result. It is the name for what one feels when the cause of negative feelings is unknown. For example, I may awaken feeling anxious, until I recall that this is the day of final examinations. Then anxiety is replaced with a natural nervousness. Or when I remember that I haven't studied, anxiety is rightly replaced by fear. But if I cannot find a cause for the anxiety, my present becomes haunted. The only way to dissipate it is by returning through the feeling to its cause, and, once identified, dealing with it for what it is.

Freeing oneself from the control of one's past, then, depends first on identifying concretely the origins of one's negative self-image. This is where one-with-one spiritual direction often needs to start. Second, it depends on learning how to control one's thoughts. Jesus said, "Take no *thought* for tomorrow" (Matt. 6:34, KJV, italics mine). We all know what it means for a thought to "prey upon" our mind. We allow it to settle in until we can't shake it—much in the same way that a melody heard first thing in the morning continues to haunt us all day. Only by intentionally rehearsing a substitute thought or melody can we dislodge it.

A Native American chief once said, "Every white person I meet wants something. Why are they so troubled?" I would answer, "Because they regret something." And those regrets from the past crowd out the present. In an effort to subdue them, one reaches out frantically to stuff full with *quantity* the small portion of the now struggling for its life. The heart of spiritual direction at this point entails relinquishing the *obsessio* from the past for the sake of a *qualitative* present. This is done by reversing the process—moving from feelings to the voices that once confronted one as a child, and then putting the voices in their place *as past* by hearing them from the present as an adult.

But the question remains: How can these voices be silenced? Sister Mary Margaret Funk is helpful here in reappropriating an important insight from the desert fathers, especially John Cassian.[6] A central discipline practiced by the desert fathers was to renounce "mindless thoughts" for the sake of a life of contemplation. In attempting to empty the mind, the desert fathers discovered the following thought process generally at work. A particular thought enters the mind, and if not displaced, it begins a train of thought. The mind moves, almost inevitably, from entertaining the thought to desires, from desires to passions, and from passions to consent, followed by passive and then active engagement. Cassian said these recurring thoughts cluster around the themes of food, sex, possessions, anger, dejection, apathy, vainglory, and pride. The spiritual direction technique that the desert fathers used begins with recognizing such thoughts the moment they appear and letting them go. Otherwise the mental process sets in, escalating until the thoughts have the power to emerge as action.

I remember my first lessons in contemplative prayer. As I tried to empty my mind, a picture show of images kept floating by. My novice master was helpful: "It is quite all right to see mountains; just don't climb them." So I began learning the process of letting thoughts come and go. But certain thoughts in particular must not be permitted to adhere; they must be halted by instantaneous identification. Jesus put such matters graphically: "Everyone who looks at a woman with lust has already committed adultery with her in his heart" (Matt. 5:28). When a man sees an attractive woman, he is likely to have the thought *I wonder what . . .* pass through his mind. At that point he should let go of the thought. If he permits it to linger and begins to entertain the idea, the thought can take hold. The imagination then comes into play, working on the thought, until he sees things actually taking place. This hooks his feelings, and from arousal comes desire. "Before he knows it," he is canvassing his mind for opportunities to be with that woman, maybe even trying a few innuendoes. By then, the only thing standing between wanting and doing is the availability of opportunity. Thus, once the process gets started, whether one does the act or doesn't is hardly any reason for moral pride.

If we do learn how to control random thoughts, either from the past or about a phantom future, what will the state of redeemed living be like? *The feel of the now as the primary place of one's residence is one of joy in living, glorying in the sheer gift of being.* It is the feel of being wholeheartedly in the present moment—*here and now.* It means participating deeply and fully in whatever is immediately before one—whether that is a friend who smiles, a sunset over glistening water, a bird call at sunrise, or even the tingle of life in an arthritic hand. This makes one a contemplative, for when Being becomes conscious of itself through us, that is Presence. In the Presence of the present, there are no problems and no worries. Problems are baggage belonging to the past, and worries belong to a future that rarely happens as expected. Certainly there are past events needing forgiveness, present situations needing to be faced, and future plans that may need to be made. Yet by living in the now, one deals with them from the inside out, rather than being squeezed from the outside in. An example that most people can identify with is the feeling of the moment when forgiveness lifts the weight from one's shoulders, and all is new. Redemption into Christian existence means experiencing the fullness of each new moment, lived so that others also are invited into such fullness.

The cook at my monastery comes to mind. From him I am learning that humor is a test of such wholeness. Secure each moment by being grounded in God, he is able to enjoy ribbing about his cooking. On Ash Wednesday I told him this was his best meal yet (bread and water). If the realm of his living had been a narrow present boxed in by a haunting past, my teasing would have evoked not delightful laughter but either hurt or anger. Whether someone reacts positively or negatively to what is said need have little to do with the words themselves, and much to do with the orientation of the ears that hear them.

The cook's manner of responding helps us understand what one-with-one spiritual direction can accomplish. Spiritual freedom begins when the directee is able to discern from the mind's chatter the identity of strident voices comprising his or her endless memory tape. Identifying the theme of such voices usually is not difficult, for the script is fairly well memorized. Discerning the source of the negative message is more difficult, and sometimes the directee's Christian faith hinders the process. The belief that Christians shouldn't get angry may obscure the identity of the person or persons behind the negativity. Or the directee may use the commandment "Honor your parents" to hide the past, concluding, "They *must* have loved me." As particular faces emerge with clarity, incidents begin flooding back: "Once I spent a month's allowance on my mom's Christmas gift, and all she said was that she didn't need what I gave her." Or "I wanted to hug her, but she pushed me away, saying, 'Go wash; you're dirty.'" The more often these specific incidents "arise from the dead," the more clearly the directee sees the power this accumulated baggage has on his or her present.

Hopefully there will also come a moment of clarity about the "why." For instance, reconciliation with my mother finally came when I realized that the reason for her inability to love me as I needed was that her father had never given her the hugs she craved. Standing by her grave, years after her death, liberation came in embracing our common hurt. I said to her, "Mom, all that either of us ever wanted was to be loved!" Jesus understood this deeply. Discerning that the soldiers were nameless simple folk just doing their job, he was able to pray, even as they were driving in the nails: "Father, forgive them; for they do not know what they are doing" (Luke 23:34).

Even if such reconciliation never comes, a transforming discernment usually can. Healing, for example, is the final realization that the statement "I am ugly" is not a fact at all. Instead, it is the particular voice of a particular person at a particular time with particular feelings—probably of jealousy. Its only truth is the degree to which I permit that memory to rent space in my *now*. From that moment of realization, my past hurts become my present responsibilities, and I am free to cancel their unwarranted authority to define who I am. Yet the voice may persist. "What if my sister was right—what if I really *am* ugly?" The response that spiritual direction can give is this: "Whether true or not, even the most physically unattractive person can glow from within, with the incredible beauty of a free self, embraced by the unconditional love of God." The only ugly person is the one who feels ugly inside, which can happen even to persons who are ravishingly attractive on the outside.

With such illumination, the next step which spiritual direction provides is that of *practice*. When the person is on the verge of feeling depressed, or feels the surge upon hearing something that rubs a sore spot, he or she practices identifying immediately the voice behind the screen. Slapping on it the sticker marked "Past," the person denies that voice entry into the now. Neither *regret* (past) nor *desire* (future) is permitted to lodge in the present, for nothing exists except what the present makes so. What I often hear in initial spiritual direction sessions is the mark of a person who has not yet learned how to be free: "When someone sounds critical of me, it takes days for me to get over it." The support of the spiritual director gives assurance that through practice the directee can identify the echo of the past and thus shake it, freed from its relentless power to take over and "make it so."

Rudolf Bultmann expresses this redemptive process theologically. Salvation is the healing that occurs as a crucifixion of the past in the now, with resurrection being the forgiveness by which one is freed to walk into the ongoing joy of each reborn present. "For everyone who believes, his past life is dead and done with. He is a new creature, and as such he faces each new moment. In short, he has become a free [person]."[7]

For such redemption to occur, two important advantages of spiritual direction need underscoring. First, one gains a trusted, more objective perspective capable of challenging the coping mechanism that is failing. If the person refuses the connection between the "state" and the "voices," or continues to deny their equivalency, therapy is probably needed. Second, since the odds are heavy against self-correction, the ability to change rests upon operating from a new context—the unconditional love of God. Redemption is a battle of perspectives: between knowing oneself from within as unlovable, versus knowing oneself from God's perspective as beloved. Once freed in this redemptive sense, one is ready to move forward on one's spiritual pilgrimage. And the means of grace are what make the *epiphania* lively, over and over again.

CASE STUDY 1

THE CONTEXT

We will now consider two actual cases, illustrating how spiritual direction can work in practice. The first case is an intense several-day event. The second is a typical hour-long session. The directees are described anonymously, with the approval of the persons involved. The first person I will call Tim. He made a reservation about a year in advance to spend a week in spiritual direction with me at the monastery. His first request was a simple one: "Help me become more spiritual." His added request was more difficult: "I want to have a direct experience of God."

Not long into our first session, two things became clear: (1) He wanted to impress me, and (2) the last thing he needed was what he asked for. Tim told me all he had done to become "spiritually alive." He had attended academies and workshops, watched spirituality tapes, memorized countless hymns, and even taught Celtic spirituality workshops for his denomination. He had participated in spiritual direction for a number of years, practiced journaling, and knew all about centering prayer. Clearly, he had no need to know anything more *about* spirituality. Instead, the question to be faced was why he had such a need to know everything, while inclined to flit from practice to practice, immersed in none for the long haul. As the week continued, it became increasingly clear that his knowing was a way of controlling the situations he faced, for the sake of feeling important. Part of his obsession with doing was a way of covering a deep insecurity. He wanted to appear an expert on the very thing he needed, but in so doing, he made knowledge a mental substitute that blocked the experience he supposedly wanted.

As Tim came to realize that I was not impressed, he sensed that he would be wasting his time if he did not stop talking about everything he knew and had done. Through my patient listening he began to trust that I was in this process for the long haul with him. He began to risk being vulnerable, sharing the past. His discussion settled in around his parents and then fastened upon his father, in whose eyes, Tim finally confessed, he had never been able to do anything right. The process was long and painful, but illumination began to come as he realized how much the past had claimed him. His more than ample abilities and achievements in church leadership never seemed to be enough. This was the clue for why he was so driven with constant doing. His past was driving him out of the present for the sake of a hypothetical future when "everything would be all right"—*if* only he knew what more to do. His secret imaginings were that "getting to the top," whatever that might mean, would bring him peace. Peace from what? That was the hard question—but it would be that unrealizable future when, somehow, he would do enough to earn acceptance—*by his father*. It never worked, and now, at midweek, he was beginning to fear it never could. Even at best, he would only be appreciated for what he did, not loved for who he was. His anxiety was that if he ever stopped doing, he would be overwhelmed by insignificance. His life was doomed to the ongoing burden of "never enough."

Ironically, Tim's Christian faith hindered his pilgrimage, at two points. For him, Jesus functioned as the one who promised resolution in the *future*. Do this, and do that, and great shall be your reward . . . someday. In strong contrast, the Jesus he needed to take to his heart was the one who would tell him to take no thought of the morrow, for living fully each moment of each day is sufficient.

Second, Tim knew how to preach the gospel, in fact so well that it cloaked him from realizing that he was a functional atheist. He had made grace a doctrine to be preached, and believing a duty to be performed. He did both so well that they were what he only knew *about*. There it was, at base level. Not only was the graciousness of God's unconditional love for him something he had never really experienced, but he was not even aware that he hadn't. He lived so much in his mind that he shared with me the thought that maybe earning another degree would be the answer.

The hymns he loved to sing and sang to me provided an emotional pleasure that hid the absence of having intimacy with God. Then came a point on Wednesday when he seemed to sense that if only once he could sing from the heart, he would be free.

But how? Not by ascending, as he craved. If at all, it would be by descending—until he could confess an emptiness that only God could fill. Gradually, through our conversations, the anatomy of Tim's situation became exposed. Yet how could he reverse a lifetime of coping, when his persistent temptation would be to make even this "knowing" another achievement, insulating him further from the conversion he needed? When he came to the monastery, he had been convinced that all he needed was a weeklong spiritual companion who could tell him what to *do* in order to have an experience of "feeling God." That was his way of putting it. He wanted me to provide him with information about some "doing" that would make him feel at peace with himself. Instead, for much of the week, my task as spiritual director was to lead him to a crisis of "being."

THE REPORT

Tim returned home after his week of spiritual direction. Our agreement was that he would work with his regular spiritual director in incorporating and reinforcing in Tim's daily life what had happened to him at the monastery. What follows is his written report to his spiritual director back home, describing what happened to him during the week's direction.

⌒

I am several days away from a seven-day spiritual direction retreat with a Trappist monk at an Ozark monastery. He met with me daily for about an hour. I had written to him for help in discerning what the Spirit apparently is doing with me now. Nothing substantially new emerged from this time, as I had hoped, but instead what happened was a surfacing again of the issues that have been present in my struggles for many years. What was most encouraging was the clarity with which they came this time.

A primary focus on which we worked was the need for me to learn how to be in the "being" mode—as a way of compensating for my usual pattern of going immediately to a "doing" mode. What became clear was that even when I seek to be prayerful, I undermine this by attacking it as something to be done. Paul encouraged me "to be" by focusing on what was immediately in front of me—especially with reference to nature. He gave me periods of time and places to be, where my task was to experience—through sight, sound, touch, smell and taste— birds, stream, berries, pines, the crunch of gravel, the sound of the wind. His insistence was that I stay away from both the past and the future, immersing myself in the present.

During worship after our first session, he slipped me this poem that he wrote for me:

> May the stars wink at you,
> the puppies tug at your pant legs,
> the wine smell of fall,
> and the river sing like angels—
> for if you stop DOING
> just long enough to

> BE,
> you might just find yourself
> lost in the divine presence.
> YES.

This invitation felt appropriate, and sounded manageable. Instead, I found it quite difficult to stay in a purely "being" mode. Even as I enjoyed playing with the puppies, and the wonder of the flowing river about a mile from the monastery, I would find myself remembering something or thinking about what I wanted to do next or in the near future. I felt almost driven to DO something, to be useful, to pay my dues, as it were—as a substitute for getting lost in what Paul kept calling the gifts of God. What an extraordinary spiritual practice all this became, especially as I kept recalling Paul's prayer that I "fall in love with life."

The first thing now in my morning daily time apart is to pause before the mystery and beauty of God's creation, seeking to stay in the present moment with all my awareness. It's embarrassing to acknowledge my deficiency in this matter, since I have been teaching and emphasizing Celtic Christian spirituality for the past few years! The Christian Celts seemed to be able to move so naturally back and forth between the being and doing modes. Indeed, they enjoyed God for God's own sake. They approached God not only to be more holy, but simply for the delight of loving and praising the Divine! I have wanted to be open to such, and Paul pressed me in this matter just about every time we got together.

Likewise, I think I have regained "the inward smile" when recognizing that one of my earliest memories as a child was being entranced by the beauty of an autumn leaf, the smell and enchantment of the woods, etc. Further, I remember how meaningful and special were the quiet times we had at church youth camps before breakfast when we found a place alone in the outdoors to be quiet, read scripture, reflect on a hymn, read some devotional material, and pray.

I want now to continue to enter into natural and spontaneous opportunities for being—when eating, walking, bathing, sitting with my wife, etc., and most especially, when I'm with our grandchildren, playing, holding, reading, listening, and being with them!

I know now that a relevant and important way for me to connect with God is through just being present to the gifts of God! I believe the Spirit is praying within me to have less *doing* and more *being*—with all that this involves, which I'm just beginning to face up to, to discover and to learn to practice!

Another ongoing issue that Paul pressed was that if ever I am able to experience genuine "being," I must move beyond my family of origin script—especially in regard to my father. I see now that the issue is how I can allow the Spirit to help me move away from that operative dynamic in which my worthiness is based upon what I accomplish, with the persistent pattern of needing to be the leader, the big "number 1" in whatever situation I find myself. To please Dad. To recognize this is to confess what is obviously spiritually and morally bankrupt. This is to be so vain, and not at all what I want to be, at least in my deepest self before God.

In this regard Paul assigned me to reflect upon and to pray the words of a hymn we had sung in worship the particular day this issue first arose:

> Heaven and earth, and sea and air,
> All their maker's praise declare;
> Wake, my soul, awake and sing;
> Now thy grateful praises bring.
>
> See the glorious orb of day
> Breaking through the clouds his way
> Moon and stars with silvery light
> Praise him through the silent night.
>
> See how he hath everywhere
> Made this earth so rich and fair;

Hill and vale and fruitful land,
All things living, show his hand.

Lord, great wonders workest thou!
To thy sway all creatures bow;
Write thou deeply in my heart
What I am, and what thou art.[8]

I was especially taken by the last two lines! The unpacking in this matter is yielding such rich blessing. I found myself going back to the parable of the prodigal [son] and sensing anew that God is like the father who rushes to meet me with an embrace and kiss, that I am valued not for what I have done, or can ever do, but who I am as a child of God. God does love me unconditionally! I preach that to others. It is time for me to hear it myself!

I've had few moments when I was certain of this love, directly from God. Mostly where I come to suspect God's goodness and love is through the unconditional love I have experienced from my wife. It is such a mystery to me still why she enjoys my presence, has been so supportive over the years, done so many things to beautify our lives, as well as countless so-called little things to express her commitment and love to me! Can it be that God is in the waves of love I experience for her and the awareness that I will love her, even if she should become unable to meet my needs!?! I think that is what Paul wants me to see. Also, there are those special moments with my grandchildren—when they have looked at me with delight and have run and hugged me. It has felt so wonderful, and I wonder now if God was not involved in all of that.

A key seems to be emerging: how can I overcome this addictive behavior of needing to be "significant," that is, this false self of finding satisfaction from what others think of me? I must escape the obsession with what I am able to accomplish, rendered absurd by my inferiority complex since a child, about not being as smart and as competent as others. The key to living more into my true self in Christ is remembering my unconditional acceptance by my wife. Here I live daily the portrait of what justification is all about—the unreserved acceptance and wondrous love by God in Christ. I think I may be getting close to this. But I know now that it is not something I can program or determine.

If I understood Paul correctly, he believes that my healing is centered in the degree to which I can begin truly to believe in the God who is given unconditionally in the Cross and Resurrection of Jesus Christ. What draws me and feels "right on" is the invitation "to stop doing just long enough to be," and to allow and to foster a delight in the gifts of God (that might even lead to my becoming "lost in the divine Presence"!). Paul has helped me to see the possibilities of a sacramental/incarnational approach to life—of experiencing God in and through everything. Yet, as impatient as I am, I recognize it's not going to happen overnight, but at least I have more clarity now than ever before.

A second ongoing struggle that emerged is related—this whole matter of actually grounding myself in God's unconditional love. I think this too is linked with the persistent longing I have for a direct experience of God. In this regard, Paul came on strong with me—that few persons are mystics, and that most of those who have had dramatic engagements with God, such as Teresa of Avila, have had them only after years of spiritual discipline. And even then, Teresa emphasized the danger of focusing on the experience instead of the practical living out of God's love. My wanting a direct experience is like wanting proof, rather than taking a risk by living lovingly. He helped me see again that Jesus' "preoccupation" was not with experiences of God, but with Kingdom living. What Elijah was given was not thunder and lightning, but the still small voice, or "the sound of silence," as one translation puts it.

As in the past, when I confront this matter more directly, I can see the vanity of it all on one level, and how unsound it is theologically and biblically. I guess at my deepest and truest self, what I really want is not so much an experience of God, as simply to be grounded and rooted in God's love! This seems so hard, so elusive for me. Sometimes I wonder about the depth of my belief in God. At one point, I think Paul said I was a functional atheist. I've never felt I was an unbeliever, at least in any ongoing or fundamental sense. But I have often felt on the edge of unbelief, and that my faith is usually one of winter instead of spring and summer, to use the imagery of Martin Marty's *A Cry of Absence*.

I think I'm coming to recognize that my desire, almost my demand, to have a direct experience of God is not getting me anywhere! Perhaps the Spirit's invitation is simply for me to enjoy the gifts of God and lose myself in Kingdom living. At one point Paul said something like, "Tim, you are so focused on experiencing the Pearl of Great Value that you are trampling the jewels of God all around you!"

One morning the abbot gave a homily on being the love of Christ for others. I felt led again to become part of the feeding program for the poor at the church near my home, and I felt returning a concern for the prison ministry that touched me earlier.

Finally, and perhaps related to everything I have discussed, is the whole matter of lightening up, the splendid habit of laughing inwardly at yourself! I suspect this has to do with what Gerald May means by fostering "spaciousness." Paul's symbol of this childlikeness is Mickey Mouse. I believe the capacity for laughter and the experience of joy will become a by-product of losing myself in God, and the ministry of Christ that follows. That's what I want! In any event, I am beginning to open my hands and arms to life and, I hope, to God.

Your incredible patience and support through all of this as well as your prayers, insight, and counsel are deeply appreciated. I look forward to the serious work that is ahead for us.

With love and thanksgiving,
Tim

A CONCLUSION

I have had enough experience to know that this report would not
bring closure. Tim clearly understands now, but only for as long as he
wants to remember. The connections between cause and effect have
been drawn with the red pen of pain. The *obsessio* to be fought now
has a face. But numerous are the times when such an awareness happens in spiritual direction, only to have the next session be one of
reversion. Then we have to rehearse all over again a new episode of
frustrations and repetitive behavior, at the end of which I ask, "Why
do you think you did that?" With a dose of futility, I hear the same
reply as before: "I don't know." Of course he knows, but he "forgot,"
consumed by habit and the heaviness of the *obsessio.*

In Tim's case, we are dealing with a lifelong way of coping.
Deep is the drivenness to impress others with his doing, as a way of
warding off the feeling of being no one. If ever he stopped, he
could live the beauty of the now; but even deeper is the anxiety
over what would happen if he ever stopped doing. As a substitute
for changing, he keeps assembling information and technique *about*
change. The condition that needs to be reversed is a lifetime of coping with an absence of unconditional love. What is indispensable is
for Tim's "new" awareness to be lived and relived, remembered and
re-remembered, over and over, in a disciplined accountability that
blocks any easy reversion. Otherwise, even spiritual direction will
only exacerbate the problem, reinforcing the negativities through
rehearsing the pain.

Anamnesis is a central term for understanding the Eucharist. It
means "a remembrance," with liturgy being a way to recall Christ
powerfully to mind, especially his sacrificial death. This type of
remembrance is what spiritual direction is about. Tim's song that
his director will need to keep singing to him has such words as
obsessio, dad, insignificant, doing, and *dead-end.* And the second verse
needs to crescendo on the words *epiphania, grace, unconditional love,
now, gift, special, joy,* and *being.* They are best sung to him with the

melody of "Love Divine, All Loves Excelling." One helpful disci-pline for Tim would be to read his report weekly. Another would be to do *lectio divina* with chosen scripture passages. The first selec-tion might be Saint Paul's puzzlement: "I do not understand my own actions" (Rom. 7:15). The second might be Paul's own answer, the one that begins "For I am convinced that neither . . . height, nor depth, [nor father, nor mother], nor anything else in all cre-ation, will be able to separate us from the love of God in Christ Jesus our Lord" (Rom. 8:38, 39). I hope that Tim's director provides him with symbols of reminder for his desk, dashboard, nightstand, bathroom mirror, refrigerator door, and his pocket. All of this is a "forced feeding," intent on drowning out the memory tapes through an accountability that boxes him gently into the present. Then maybe, just maybe, someday, Tim will remember on his own.

I wrote the above almost a year ago. Yesterday I received a let-ter from Tim, sharing with me his reply to a pastor who had just asked him to be his spiritual director. Tim wrote,

> If I became your spiritual director, my objective would be to become a companion on your journey—with the Spirit being your guide. I would not want to impose my particular under-standing of the Christian faith on you, for what matters is dis-covering what God is seeking and doing in your unique journey. For this to happen, it would be important for you to share feel-ings, events, and experiences in your present and past that the Spirit invites you to process before God. And while this is a life-long process, God seeks to bless and redeem every room in your dwelling. What I would need from you is a commitment that in whatever way you connect with the Spirit and Christ, it involves time in loving, praising, and enjoying God for God's own sake in the present. Together we can share where God's grace has been apparent and the times when you have resisted that love.

I believe Tim is remembering.

CASE STUDY 2

THE CONTEXT

This woman is a nun, living in community, with whom I have worked on a regular basis for two years. We have explored her past sufficiently to understand rather well the childhood causes of her insecurity, evidenced mostly in her difficulty with group functioning. At the beginning of direction, she was not certain that remaining with her community was where she needed to be or that she was doing what she needed to be about. To give her stability, we developed a rule, giving special attention to being healed of past scars by being fed through disciplines particularly suited to her temperament. We no longer have regularly scheduled visits. She calls when she feels ready, usually every one to two months.

THE SESSION

Coffee around the hermitage fireplace on a cold winter morning was well advised, purveying an ambiance of comfort and trust. The beginning was easy, needing little more than a prayer of thanksgiving and a simple invitation: "Tell me what's been going on." Her response was a review of the major segments of her life: work, the monastic community, and relationships with family and friends. I was pleased that she was able to speak more favorably of her work situation than previously, indicating dimensions of improvement in light of changes she had promised in her previous session to try. Concrete feedback regarding other realms was likewise positive— except for times with the community.

So I invited her to review a typical daily schedule, focusing on a balance of being and doing during the time before and after work. The times and circumstances of difficulty became clear. Probing them for the causes of tension, it turned out that the "they" who "made" her feel insignificant were not the entire community, but only two persons. With this clarification, we were able to understand the personality conflict that two aggressive extroverts would almost inevitably create for this gentle introvert. With her laugh at admitting the obvious, I was careful to suggest as a factor her possible oversensitivity, rooted in scars from her childhood circumstances. "Oh yes, I do need reminding, don't I!" she replied. The nondefensive mood of her re-remembering made it possible for us then to put several recent happenings of being hurt in helpful perspective.

We reached the point in our conversation where she reaffirmed that the ongoing healing she needed against the tendency to feel bruised by others resided in being even more faithful to the spiritual disciplines we had established. This recontexting usually occurred in each of our sessions. Once again she saw the correlation between being less than faithful in her disciplines and being caught by the symptoms of insignificance. We reviewed her daily disciplines to discern which functioned best as conduits for the Spirit's feeding. These turned out to be the quiet times of "being" in her cell, walking though nature in the park, playing and listening to music, and driving out of town with her favorite tapes playing. When she indicated that the quiet times were most important, we considered ways of making her cell more conducive to sensing God's presence. She decided to change some of the pictures on her walls, simplify the clutter, and sort through her clothes to share them with the poor. We agreed about when and for how long she would be fed daily by this sacred quietness. We then reviewed how she would deal with several potentially difficult situations in the coming week. The conclusion she drew was the important one: Awareness of God's unconditional love is what frees her to relate to others without needing their affirmation as the condition for feeling loved.

It seemed time for me to remind her that occasionally she would raise the issue of whether she was where she needed to be or whether she needed to move on. I led her through an inventory of the particular aspects comprising her present situation. At each juncture, we considered options that might give her hope of being better. When we finished, she smiled quietly and said, "I know now that I am where God wants me to be."

We were moving toward closure, so the next question was inevitable: "How can I best hold you accountable to your written rule and the concrete promises you made today?" Agreeing upon an e-mail report within two weeks, we both marked our calendars. I expressed my appreciation for how well she was doing, applauding particular areas of positive contrast between today and a year ago. After a prayer of thanksgiving, my payment was an invitation for lunch at the local restaurant.

A CONCLUSION

Let's call her Sister Jean. She is gentle, quiet, sensitive, and caring, with a fine social conscience. The present focus of her spiritual pilgrimage is the ongoing healing of a fragility forged by a silent and unfeeling home life. She knows that her answer depends on her ability to affirm deeply this truth: "I am unconditionally loved by God." After the first session, I assigned her scripture passages on that theme for *lectio divina*. Since then, the one discipline that has been increasingly valuable has been contemplation or "centering prayer." It is her means of losing herself in God, imaging this healing Presence as falling asleep in the arms of Christ. The spiritual direction Sister Jean needs, contrary to the most appropriate kind for Tim, is that of providing a caring support and only secondarily accountability, very gently done. In our sessions and through short notes and e-mail greetings, I remind her that she is worth listening to. Throughout her spiritual direction, the theological-spiritual environment that is needed is the *epiphania* appropriate for a resident of World 3—a belonging, sufficient to counter her tendency to slide into a sense of emptiness and isolation.

One last observation. I continue to be amazed in spiritual direction by the power of two things: the use of the person's first name, and the reassurance "We're in this together."

Chapter 5

✣

DIMENSIONS, EXERCISES, AND RESOURCES FOR SPIRITUAL DIRECTION

THE TRINITY AND THE DIVERSITY OF CHRISTIAN SPIRITUALITY

Spiritual directors need to know a variety of spiritual disciplines, both for their own maturation and as a repertoire from which to offer directees options for addressing different needs in different situations. These disciplines are rooted in the ways God gives us in which to be understood. For the Christian, these dimensions of God rest in the disclosure that *God is triune*. In fact, the word *God* is not really a proper name but a generic one, functioning as an umbrella for a host of references. Trinity, on the other hand, is a concrete name for God, unique to the Christian understanding. Yet few doctrines have been as misunderstood as this one.

One of the best scripture passages for showing how the good news and the Trinity are one is this affirmation by Saint Paul: "For it is the God who said, 'Let light shine out of darkness,' [God the Father as Creator] who has shone in our hearts [God the Holy Spirit as Sanctifier] to give the light of the knowledge of the glory of God in the face of Jesus Christ [God the Son as Redeemer]" (2 Cor. 4:6). If God were only the Creator, we would be left in our sins, and the problem of evil would be overwhelming. If God were only the Redeemer, then our redemption would pull us out of the world, concerned only for others who are Christians. If God were only the Sanctifier, then faith would be reduced to little more than an isolated inner experience. Thus, for the Christian, God is all of these manifestations in interaction—for God is the Creator who *redeems the creation for sanctified living*. Even more is involved. Our relationship with God is so rich that it is insufficient to equate God the Father with being Creator, and the Son being Redeemer, and the Holy Spirit being Sanctifier. God is all three persons manifested in all three ways.

Christian existence in all its fullness, then, means experiencing the triune God as working with us in these multifarious ways. Failure to do this means that our God is too small, our spiritual life too superficial, our disciplines too sparse, and our living hardly Christian. The following chart is a shorthand way of identifying how this affirmation of God as triune opens a rich array of dimensions for our spiritual life, around which we are able to cluster exercises and disciplines as aids in spiritual direction.

The names on the left side of the chart refer to the *nature* of God (traditionally called the Trinity of Essence), expanded to avoid

	CREATOR	REDEEMER	SANCTIFIER
FATHER/MOTHER	Mystery/ **Ground of Being**	Contingency/ **Sustainer**	Delight/ **Promiser**
SON/DAUGHTER	Order/ **Logos**	Companionship/ **Incarnation**	Sacramentality/ **Presence**
HOLY SPIRIT	Dynamism/ **Becoming**	Homesickness/ **Pursuer**	Call/ **Creativity**

sexist connotation. The names across the top refer to the way in which this triune God *acts* with us (traditionally called the Trinity of Manifestation).

We experience *mystery* because the Father/Mother God as Creator is the *ground of our being*. All that exists is *ordered* because God is the *Logos* of creation. The *becoming* of everything is because of the *dynamism* of the Holy Spirit as *Creator*. In regard to redemption, *contingency* is our way of experiencing God as *Sustainer*. The divine *companionship* is disclosed as God's *Incarnation* in Jesus as the Christ. We experience *pursuit* as the silent, redemptive wooing of the divine Lover for whom we are *homesick*. And for our sanctification, our *delight* is rooted in God as the *Promiser* of a fulfilled future for all things. *Sacramentality* blesses us with the sanctifying assurance of God's loving *presence* in and through the liturgy of things. And, finally, all of God's workings with us converge as *creativity* within an incomplete cosmos for which we are *called* to be the gardeners.

The chart from page 138 can be expanded to suggest what it means to experience each of these manifestations of God in our lives.

1. **Mystery:** losing oneself in the abyss of God in which all things are grounded	4. **Contingency:** encountering the fragility of life in each moment as sustained by God	7. **Delight:** ecstasy in the promise of experiencing all things as the lyric gifts of God
2. **Order:** perceiving God as the Logos of creation holding all things together	5. **Companionship:** knowing God as the Incarnate One who participates with us everywhere in everything	8. **Sacramentality:** grasped by special things as graced channels of God's presence
3. **Dynamism:** experiencing the cosmic dance as the rhythmic heartbeat of God's becoming	6. **Homesickness:** feeling God as the Hound of heaven whose seeking is a pursuit	9. **Call:** acknowledging God's call to be cocreators in completing creation

Exercises

Spiritual direction needs to be concrete. Suggesting that persons work on their prayer life, become more centered, or make more time available for God is not that helpful. True guidance is a dialogue intent on discerning the *whats* rooted in the *whys* in order to seek resolution and healing through the *hows*. Persons seek direction not only because they lack clarity about what is going on and why, but also because they lack resources for changing their condition. Then all nine modes of God's rich manifestation shown on the previous chart are important in providing various spiritual practices for the giving and receiving of spiritual direction.[1]

I. Mystery and the Ground of Being:
Getting Lost in the Silence

Contemplation and the Prayer of Centering

The intent of this discipline is to lose oneself in the fact of being, by quieting the mind, or focusing on one's center. All thoughts are turned off, stopping one in the immediacy of the now. Contemplation means refraining from doing for the sake of being. It means becoming absorbed in what is immediately before one, whether in hearing music, clinically observing an amoeba, nursing a patient, or giving birth to a poem. Such a state has been variously described as resting in the Lord, losing oneself in order to find oneself, dying in Christ, transcending the subject-object split, or falling asleep with Christ in God. While contemplation in its purest sense is a gift (infused), one may prepare for it through a process of emptying (acquired). Whatever the method used, the goal is to turn off the mind. Here is a suggested procedure for centering prayer:

1. Find a place where you will not be disturbed.

2. Assume a relaxed posture; breathe deeply with increasing slowness.

3. Permit a request, phrase, or word to surface from within. Repeat it over and over again, giving the mind an undemanding activity to keep it out of the way, so that the self can lose itself. Any word or phrase, often called a mantra, will do, but many persons find the names of God most helpful, or words such as *peace, love,* or *grace.*

4. Keep repeating your word or phrase at the slowest speed needed to occupy the mind. If the mind wanders, increase the tempo. Then let the speed decrease until a moment comes when all is still. At this point you can experience a peace where all separation is overcome.

5. End the experience gently, with a thankfulness that prepares you to taste the Mystery of Presence in other dimensions of your living.

In the monastery we have two-handled cups, for contemplative reasons. Most people drink coffee mindlessly from a cup held in one hand while doing some activity with the other. The monk grasps the fine shape of his cup with both hands and is thereby rendered unavailable to do anything except to be totally absorbed in the act of drinking, lost in the experience. So done, insurmountable is the aroma and taste of the first steaming cup of coffee on a cold winter morning.

A physical object (mandala) such as a cross or candle can also be helpful in contemplation. This absorbs the mind by centering it through a particular sense. Extroverts in particular find such physical mantras useful. Another aid is a koan, which is a short question that confounds the mind sufficiently to keep it out of the way. For example, "What is the sound of one hand clapping?" or "What did you look like before you were born?"

Mysticism

When acquired contemplation becomes the gift of infused union with God, we have the experience of the mystic. This union is often experienced as ecstasy, in a passionate and intense communion with deeper levels of life and thus God. The mystic Evelyn Underhill identifies four steps or stages in this state:

1. *Recollection:* focusing attention by discipline and simplification.

2. *Purgation:* becoming detached from everything.

3. *Seeking:* a loving unity with all of creation and every living thing.

4. *Awakening:* into a new and rich consciousness, where to be grasped by God is to transfuse life with feeling and depth.

Om

Widely practiced in Eastern spirituality, the om involves a sound made by breathing out in a special way. This sound has been described by various persons as the coo of a dove, the purr of a cat, the hum of a motor, the tone of the sea, the music of a wind chime, and the reverberation of a gong. Each of these sounds contains the inner vibration of atoms and living cells, moving outward into the silent sounds of the spinning galaxies. In the om these sounds echo in one's heart as the heartbeat of the universe itself, as everything is being drawn into Christ. It is healing to lose the limits and margins that separate things into competitive individuality. The value of om, then, is that persons can experience a oneness with everything, melting into God, the primal source.

To do the om, take a deep breath and then make a long "O" sound. As your breath begins to reach its limit, allow the sound to mellow into an "mmm." Take a deep breath, and continue for several minutes, finally mellowing it out into silence. The om can be done with other persons, alternating points of beginning so that the sound is continuous. Our modern penchant for singing in the resonance of a shower may be a vestige of this practice.

IMAGE CONTEMPLATION

In image contemplation, analogies are used to intensify the fact that each of us lives, moves, and has our being in the Creator God. For example, imagine your breathing as God's infusing and departing from your body, God's own dwelling. Or picture the air as an ocean of divine Presence. Or visualize yourself as a favorite thought in the mind of God.

SILENCE AND SOLITUDE

In our society's culture of noise, individuals need to be ravished by silence. Nothing seems more able to remove life's clutter than silence. Yet everywhere we turn, we experience sensory overload that invades every sense until there is no space left in which to *be*. We need silence not only as an experience but also as an inseparable part of who we are. Such silence entails resisting the arrogance of communicating every thought that comes into one's head, as if the world needs our ongoing commentary.

Silence quiets our aggressive and ambitious drives, issuing as they do from our fallen condition. Clamor, on the other hand, applauds the ego's urge to manage, control, and organize all of life for its own glory. This is why we thrive on noise, for it is the sound of seeking positions of power, competing to surpass others in the self-defeating effort to justify our existence. The more hullabaloo one causes, the more important one feels.

In contrast, Jesus was silent for thirty years, preparing for one non-silent year marinated by nights spent in the silent Galilean hills. Mary sat at the feet of Jesus in silence, while Martha made noise in the kitchen. From inward silence comes the urge to avoid idle chatter and gossip; words that inflict pain; cynicism or sarcasm; off-color words and stories; faultfinding; and exploitative curiosity. Out of silence flow words of respect, affirmation, encouragement, compassion, cheer, and hospitality. Honoring silence, our desert fathers and mothers wisely advised, "Go, sit in your cell, and your cell will teach you everything."

While silence is hard to find in modern society, it still resides in woods, monasteries, at lakesides, in recreational facilities at opening and closing time, and one's car as a traveling hermitage. Not even large cities are deprived of silent cemeteries. But people also need silent space in their homes, if only minimally acquired through a mutual agreement to honor a "Do not disturb" sign on someone's bedroom door. Sad is the home where one must fake a need for the bathroom just to be able to take a "breather."

Not only do we need silent spaces, but we also need silent times. These might take the form of a day apart or several days of retreat. In one wing of our monastery, always available for guests, a sign reads, "Silence is spoken here." This is the place where I first felt comfortable being silent in the presence of others, needing only a smile or nod to acknowledge their sacredness. Unlike society, in the monastery silence is the norm with speaking the exception, for one is surrounded by an inexpressible Mystery.

SACRED SPACES

While Catholics have their shrines, every one of us had sacred spaces as children. Our space may have been a tree house, an attic corner, behind the sofa, or under the porch—wherever we went to imagine and to cry. As adults, we need to rediscover such places as creative respite for our spirits: winding roads, sitting rocks, open vistas, tenting spots, nature trails, library nooks, fire towers—whatever we claim as sacred ground.

NATURE

For many of us, immersion in nature is the easiest way to lose one's self. Nothing compares with lying on your back at night, invaded by the incredible panorama of the starry heavens, painted with a brush whose swath is a hundred billion light-years wide. Or you can participate in two daily shows, one at sunrise, the other at sunset. Even a noonday siesta in the grass works to help you taste the peace of resting in the everlasting arms of God. Another option is to take time to look deeply into the eyes of one you love.

CHANTING

We all know the phenomenon of being awakened by a song on the radio and having the tune persist in our mind all day. So it is that monks chant the psalms, providing a simple melody that gives the words staying power. To sing a psalm is to pray it twice. This is easily done by singing the first line of a psalm on the same note and ending the last word on the next higher note. Chant the second line on that same note, ending the last word on the original note on which you began. Continue until the psalm or your extemporaneous prayer is finished.

MEDITATION

In all nine of these modes of spirituality we are exploring, it is helpful to have words capable of evoking the experience. Make your own list, perhaps consulting a thesaurus. As a start in evoking the sense of mystery, consider such words as *fog, secret, puzzle, conundrum, enigma, mystification, puzzlement, riddle, maze, cryptogram, question, perplexity, arcane, labyrinth, web, meander, intricacy,* and *why.*

THE ARTS

George Aichele once defined art as "cultural expressions of those meanings, values, and fundamental structures in terms of which human life is lived." Art helps us pry beneath the conceptual into the mysterious heart of reality. T. S. Eliot speaks of "music heard so deeply" that "you are the music."[2] Music is formed silence. The artist, then, is an unknowing spiritual director, midwifing creation's yearnings in general, and mining the *imago dei* (image of God) within each of us in particular. Research has shown how different types of music affect significantly the mood and behavior of the listener, even a fetus. Therefore, an intentional choice of music is a powerful way to enter a particular spiritual mode. For the mode of mystery, you might try Albinoni's *Adagio in G Minor*, Debussy's *La Mer*, Wagner's Prelude to Act 3 of *Lohengrin*, or Gregorian chant. Paintings are helpful too, such as Monet's many paintings of water lilies, where the shimmering formlessness and endless overflow is like a timeless event. Poetry thrives on metaphor, where everything is more than it seems, with hints of the impossible. It preserves a mysterious ambiguity with an "almost," teasing with a "not quite." It functions, as the poet Wallace Stevens perceives, as "nothing that is not there and the nothing that is." Here poetry, spirituality, and mystery enter into collusion, for as Stevens confided, "The poet is the priest of the invisible."

II. ORDER AND THE LOGOS:
Serenity in the Abiding

THE JESUS PRAYER

The Jesus Prayer is the ongoing repetition of a two-part phrase, best done in rhythm with one's breathing or heartbeat: "Lord Jesus Christ" (as one breathes in), "have mercy on me" (as one breathes out). The desert hermits rehearsed this correlation of the verbal and the physical over and over again as they "mindlessly" wove baskets for their livelihood. This repetitive discipline not only turned a monotonous task into a spiritual experience, but also it imprinted the words so that they repeated themselves on their own all day and night.

HABITS

We are all creatures of habit, having a favorite chair, food, restaurant, pew, song, shirt, and color. For this particular exercise, identify the primary habits in your life, keeping a log. Evaluate them, adding and subtracting, so as to order them in a manner that reflects a Christian way of living. Include such habits as your time and manner of rising and retiring, blessings for the beginning and ending of meals, and the color and shape of clothing as a way of living "liturgically."[3] Worship is the church's favorite way of establishing such spiritual habits.

ROSARY

Protestants have a hard time understanding the power of the Rosary, confused as to its purpose. Whatever else it may be, the Rosary is a calming ordering of the spirit, feeding the strange hunger deep within us for the tranquility of repetition. Fifty times, at the touch of each bead, the person praying repeats: "Hail Mary, full of grace: the Lord is with you. Blessed are you among women, and blessed is the fruit of your womb, Jesus. Holy Mary, Mother of God, pray for us sinners, now and at the hour of our death. Amen." Part of the appeal of rock music to youth is the repetitive, mesmerizing beat, so loud that it gives a demanding order to everything. Repeating the Rosary accomplishes a similar function.

FOCUSED MEDITATION

Digital order is one of the most attractive features of the computer. Once mastered, it offers almost complete predictability—few mistakes; minimal misspellings; all numbered, margined, and ordered. Imaging one's computer this way, one can experience it as a model expressing one's primal task of being spiritually ordered in all things. Likewise, one can be mesmerized by nature. I stand in awe of the glorious order of a dandelion face, the star of an apple cut in cross section, or bales of hay placed at intervals until they fade into the horizon. Let those who have eyes to see do so.

SIMPLICITY AND POSSESSIONS

In a culture where meaning is often measured by the accumulation of possessions, most of us have far more than we need or can even store. Before long, what we own, owns us. Spiritual transformation occurs when a *possessor* becomes a *steward*, keeping with open hands, having as if not possessing, holding all things lightly. Clutter is a mark of negative spirituality, a deterrent to serenity, bringing distraction wherever one turns. In the Old Testament, every seventh day was a Sabbath restoration, and every seventh year entailed a restoration of the fields, with seven times seven years being the Year of Jubilee, in which everything was restored to its just and equal originality. Spring housecleaning is such a "simplicity review." By sorting through last year's accumulation, giving to the poor all that was unused, one brings a new order to the whole, reestablishing sane priorities. Such an exercise is a shaking of materialism, inviting persons to share and co-own equipment, rethinking the wasteful possessions and habits of the nuclear family. The goal is a balanced order of simplicity, harmony, and gracefulness, defying the competitive complexities of modern disarray. Undeniable is the power of exterior ordering to bring interior orderliness.

NATURAL ORDER

Living on a farm wraps one in the profound order of the seasons. Nothing rivals the greenness of a spring day, followed by the quiet laziness of a summer afternoon, the mesmerizing color of autumn, and the breathlessness of the first snow. Seasons forge our sensitivity for the abiding. In contrast, modern society trains us to cool the hot, heat the cold, light the dark, and shut out the sunlight. Living according to the church year, in contrast, brings to life an ordered wholeness. The Middle Ages had a practice called the Angelus. Church bells rang at sunrise, noontime, and sunset, calling the peasants to pray in the field at the same time that the monks were praying in the monastery. Today the hourly toning of the digital watch aches to be so used. Suburban decks are perfect for savoring the ordering of fresh mornings and gentle evenings. As the psalmist wrote, "You make the gateways of the morning and the evening shout for joy" (Ps. 65:8). "I will awake the dawn" (Ps. 57:8).

Form As Beauty

Most of the mass-produced decorations we use to trim our daily environment are gaudy. In contrast, it is a spiritual act to find dishes whose pure form needs no decoration, and furniture whose lines embody a gentle order. Relatedly, the purpose of the camera is to bring order to the transient—stopping motion, capturing moments that deserve to last, and choosing vistas and gestures not to be discarded. The focus of a camera suggests the responsibility God must feel. Likewise, traditions give meaning to events. A remembered, repetitive order weaves a web of sacredness over Christmases, Easters, birthdays, and anniversary celebrations. A useful discipline is to consult with family members or close friends in identifying what rituals actually operate in these relationships, often unconsciously. Determine which rituals are worth preserving, which ones should be remembered but are on the edge of being lost, which ones need to be forgotten, and which ones you hope to establish. The human disposition for meaningful order is evidenced in our fascination with stories of "the way it used to be."[4]

Meditation

Just as we suggested words for meditation on the spiritual mode of mystery, the same is true here in evoking the theme of order. Possibilities are *essence, form, dependability, intentionality, faithfulness, predictability, constancy, structure, shape, pattern, changelessness, solidarity,* and *integrity.*

The Arts

A direct experience of ordering is learning to center a piece of clay on a potter's wheel, letting the form emerge symmetrically from the moving still point. In music, Bach's *Art of the Fugue* is a masterpiece of pure form. Better known is Pachelbel's *Canon in D.* In painting, Cézanne is the master, discerning reality in terms of the spiritual geometry of cones, squares, spheres, and cylinders, whether the subjects are mountains, still lifes, or persons.

III. DYNAMISM AND THE DIVINE BECOMING: Rhythm and the Restless Voyage

CARNAL SPIRITUALITY

Central to the meaning of flesh is the Spirit that makes it dance and throb in holy rhythm. Sexuality is a powerful expression of this spiritual mode, experienced in the surge of desire, the ache, the longing, the arousal, the waves of moreness, the sensuality of every sense, the choreography of body, the elasticity of time, the rhythm and crescendo, the ebb and the flow. So it can be with every living thing, for all is composed of energy in motion, wrapped in time as becoming. It is little wonder that the poetry of Saint John of the Cross is permeated with sensual imagery, so that concerning God he cries out, "Sick with love I am." Thus, a profound spiritual act is making love to the glory of God, as a liturgy of Incarnation. There emerged in the Middle Ages a "spirituality of love," which held that the sexual union of husband and wife on the Sabbath was "a sacred ritual that participated in the union of the male and female aspects of God." [5]

Another exercise involves giving a variety of shapes to any material, such as clay; or, better yet, helping it give form to itself, with you serving as midwife. Work with a piece of wood, sanding it into a texture worthy of stroking. Take a walk, not to go to any certain place, but for the sheer joy of letting the walk take you. Wash dishes with abandon, sloshing and splashing and reveling in the water and suds. Or doodle, letting the Spirit provide its own dynamic. Get in touch with the gestures of your daily life, and render them more choreographic. Such gestures can become spiritual motions, just as the priest learns to make gracious the uplifting of the chalice, and forming a crucifix with outstretched arms in offering prayer. So can it be with how one does everything—sitting, standing, walking, driving, eating—every action can be done as a work of art.

SPORTS

A ball well hit or a golf swing finely mastered are analogous to a cello masterfully played. Whether vicarious or participatory, sports allow us to partake of an energy, a stamina, a dynamism that can intoxicate. I personally find this true in swimming and jogging. Buoyed up and massaged by the moving water, the swimmer becomes enfolded in rhythm, stroke after stroke, at one with the breathing, heartbeat, and roll of body. In jogging, the settled and settling pace wraps the runner in a liturgy of beat and cadence, flow and rhythm, with the ripple of wind in one's hair. Learning to soar in a sailplane was an unforgettable experience for me. A hot-air balloon can provide a similar thrill. Or for a simpler experience, go fly a kite.

MEDITATION

Words useful for meditating on this mode of spirituality include *restlessness, energy, surge, dance, movement, yearning, rhythm, insatiability, expansiveness, animation, fervor, passion, irresistibility*, and *craving*.

FOCUS

Certain things can mesmerize us, drawing us into their dynamic. The pendulum of my grandfather's clock held such fascination for me as a child. None of us loses the sacred art of fire watching or the delight in "wasted" hours watching the ocean's endless surging. Scripture is filled with such images of movement, with our thirst for God compared to a fountain or to a deer that longs for flowing streams. Once one learns the spirituality of looking, such imagery is available everywhere.

DANCE

In archeology, evidence of sacred dance marks the emergence of spirituality. Psalm 150 climaxes all the psalms with this crescendo: "Praise him with tambourine and dance" (v. 4). And again, "'These are her [Zion's] children and while they dance they will sing: 'In you all find their home'" (Ps. 86:6-7, GRAIL). African American spirituals insist on being sung to clapping and swaying. Experiment with feeling the difference between upbeat and downbeat clapping.

I suspect I will never experience this spiritual mode fully until, like David, I dare to dance naked before the Lord.

I am envious of persons who can dance with utter abandon, for my strict Protestant upbringing neutralized strong feelings of any kind. Consequently, I was forbidden to dance, until I rebelled while in college. But by then, inhibition had done its damage. Only when alone, in the dark of night, do I dare to dance—with God.

SPEAKING IN TONGUES

Glossolalia, or praying in the Spirit, is a passionate relaxing in God, opened by the feeling of being taken over by the Spirit from within. The sounds that emerge are often like those Saint Paul identifies as groaning in travail, much like in childbirth, "with sighs too deep for words" (Rom. 8:26). As at Pentecost, the voices often resemble talking in various foreign languages. One can be primed for this experience by letting oneself make any kind of sound, such as mumbling, and letting one's body beat as if in motion to silent music. Music with a beat is conducive to this kind of motion. By contrasting the frenetic dancing of today's youth with the smooth, fluid movement of ballroom dancing, one gains a feeling for what it might mean to let oneself go into the music—innovating what the Spirit elicits in the moment. Analogous is the abandonment one feels when any emotion becomes overwhelming.

RHYTHMS

One of the important tasks in spiritual direction is establishing a holistic rhythm for one's life. A useful exercise is to keep a time log for a week, recording the dynamics of work/leisure, doing/being, activity/silence, community/solitude, feasting/fasting, and self-realization/self-sacrifice. Strive for the beauty of harmonious rhythm and balance.

LITURGY

Liturgy is the formal celebration of an informing plot, a fundamental rhythm, or a defining gesture, giving meaningful movement to the whole. We bring to such celebrations our best in musical and poetic talent, architecture and vestments, furnishings and sacramentals, interacting for the glory of God. The claim of liturgy on all of life is witnessed to by how it incorporates the materials of our daily life—bread, wine, water, oil, ashes, fire. In liturgy, words are choreographed with such gestures as the individual sign of the cross and in the corporate laying on of hands. Anthropology suggests that the dawn of human consciousness coincided with a need to be nourished by the sacred and symbolic, with a flooding of the senses and a forming of bodily postures. Spiritual renewal today will likely take on similar origins and expressions.

THE ARTS

For expressing this mode in music, one of the most familiar pieces is Ravel's *Boléro*. Also inviting are Liszt's *Hungarian Rhapsody No. 1* and Brahms's *Hungarian Dance No. 5*. In painting, van Gogh is the master, as he strokes and teases and lures everything into movement, from fields to cafés to bedrooms to star-spangled nights.

IV. CONTINGENCY AND THE SUSTAINER: Fragility and the Gift of Life

THE DESERT EXPERIENCE

Without fasting, a daily Thanksgiving would only be fattening. Without a Good Friday, Easter is an exercise in hyperbole. Without emptiness, there can be no fullness, for hands that are full can never receive. In our pampered society, the art of self-discipline has been largely lost. In powerful reaction, twelve-step programs are arising everywhere to enable the discipline necessary for facing addiction, from alcohol to overeating.[6] Most of these programs are clear that unless self-discipline is wrapped spiritually, it will be short-lived. While the desert for early Christians was often literal, today it needs to take on figurative significance. This can entail the vigor of an Outward Bound experience or a serious mountain climb. It can also mean spending time at a monastery where the monks arise at 3:00 A.M. Eating fish on Fridays is a mild way of identifying with the Crucifixion, and fasting on Ash Wednesday a physical way of knowing that "dust you are and to dust you will return" (Gen. 3:19, NIV). The incredible number of so-called miracle diets today bears sad testimony to the need for this spiritual practice, for self-discipline is fast becoming a lost art. Indicative is a recent ad: "Our machines make it possible to exercise without effort."

FASTING AND THE ASCETIC

When one's bodily functions slow through fasting, one is better able to focus. Coupling this discipline with a symbolic identification with the poor, a spirituality of the poor in spirit emerges. Wesley insisted on regular fasting, for reasons dietary and spiritual. Fasting usually involves abstinence from solid food for a specified period, but with sufficient water to prevent dehydration. The Catholic Church expects fasting of some sort on Ash Wednesday, Good Friday, and weekly on Fridays. While this fasting may be total, it can entail a meal of bread and water, or refraining from meat. It is usually accompanied with other spiritual practices, such as prayer, scripture, or Lenten reading.

In our culture, where a child's expression of "I'm hungry" means stopping immediately at the next exit, ascetic practices are essential. Learning to go a little hungry, or thirsty, or unsatisfied, or disappointed, or needing to wait, or to postpone—these are practices for the spiritually disciplined. Athletes, musicians, and dancers know the importance of discipline, for everything worthwhile comes at a cost. Yet when such discipline begins to flow naturally from the love of playing and dancing, the cost becomes the reward. By submitting to the demands of one's craft, one is gifted with the joy of being an artist. The same is true of spirituality.

One can begin with small exercises in self-discipline. Go without a dessert, eat brussels sprouts, put no sugar in your coffee (or put some in if you like it without), forgo a favorite TV show, or leave an interesting letter unopened for a day. Sit without crossing your legs; forgo reading a favorite magazine for an evening; stand when you prefer sitting. Endure a little summer heat or winter cold. Try burnt toast without butter. Swear off snacks. Try being a vegetarian. Interpersonal relations are a ready arena for self-discipline, usually requiring long-suffering. Scripture celebrates the discipline of patiently bearing the infirmities of others. For many of us, the hardest exercise is to relate deliberately to those who bring out the worse in us or tax our patience.

FINITUDE

Alone we came into this world, and alone we will leave it, no matter how many persons surround the bed. Yet society conspires to keep death the best-kept secret by hospitalizing the dying and removing the dead from the family parlor to the "funeral parlor." But it is essential for us to stare death in the face. "I will show you fear in a handful of dust," wrote T. S. Eliot.[7] Christians have traditionally held that one's whole life depends on how one dies one's death. Martin Heidegger insists that the quality of one's existence depends on the way one lives his/her death.[8] To live otherwise is foolish self-deception. Death puts things in perspective, rendering trivial so much of what consumes our lives. Viewed humanly, death is not simply the end of the body. It is the finality of everything we are and have and know. The face of death discloses every moment of living as rooted in dependence, poverty, insignificance, and fragility. For the Christian, each day is to be a rehearsal in dying and rising. Each of us has a rendezvous to keep, and everything depends on the who or the nothingness to whom our final act will be addressed: "Into your hands I commend my spirit."

Exercises that might be helpful here are these:

- Compose your own funeral service.
- Write, and periodically read, your will.

- Meditate on the subject "If I had two months to live."

- Let your imagination reflect on what dying might be like, in terms of where, how, why, with whom, and so forth.

- Newspapers are obsessed with accidents, violence, and death. Read one with an eye to life's contingency, noting how few persons end their lives in the sanctity of their own homes.

- Picture yourself in a casket, and then in the ground. Record your feelings.

- Look honestly at yourself in a mirror. Get in touch with the ways in which you are no longer who you used to be—slower, less functional, less inclined. Discern things that you have probably done for the last time, and things you always wanted to do, but now is too late.

LITURGY OF THE HOURS

Almost from the beginning, many Christian monastic communities divided the twenty-four hours of a day by the Trinity, creating eight segments of time (presently reduced to seven for practical reasons). Each is associated with one or more events in the inclusive pattern of Christian life. For example, the day begins in darkness, awaiting the dawn in silent prayer as on the first day of creation, and at Lauds comes the re-creation of Easter morning. Likewise, at Terce (the third hour after the resurrection), the Pentecost event is celebrated. As a result of Vatican II, the liturgy followed by religious communities and priests has been made available for laity as well—in a four-volume set, or in a shortened one-volume version entitled *Christian Prayer: The Liturgy of the Hours.*[9]

Two of these daily services are particularly important for experiencing the fragility of life. The Trappist monk rises for Vigils in the darkness, around 3:00 A.M. This practice is a response to Jesus' question, "Could you not stay awake with me one hour?" (Matt. 26:40). These dark hours are particularly sacred, with the summer cries of coyotes and the winter howling of frigid winds. This is the time when most persons die, for our hold on life is by the thinnest thread. In the city, these lonely hours are frightening, for we have not yet "taken back the night." In Appalachia, we called a vigil when family members took turns "keeping watch" by the casket through the lonely night.

The second service stressing contingency is *Compline* ("complete"), marking the last hours of the day. Since the monk lives life one day at a time, each night is the final one. Thus, night is the time for making one's peace with the world, and with God. As closure for one's life, what does one need to do—write a note, make a call, speak a word—of regret, forgiveness, love? With this completion in place, one is then prepared to hear the words: "May the all-powerful Lord grant us a restful night and a peaceful death." Sprinkled by water as a recollection of having been baptized into Christ's death and resurrection, one is given the courage to hand back one's life to God. Returning to the cell, the monk enters the "Great Silence" of deathlike sleep, praying: "Into your hands I commend my spirit." Experiencing daily these two special times provides a taste for our fragile dependence on God, whereby to realize that each moment of life is sheer gift.[10]

MEDITATION

Words one might use to focus one's thoughts here include *arbitrariness, dangling, fragile, ominous, desert, contingent, boundary, finitude, dependence, tentativeness, enigma, strangeness, exile, adrift, discontinuity, opaque, inscrutable, night, alone,* and *death.*

ART

The sounds of human contingency are captured well in Barber's *Adagio for Strings,* Fauré's *Requiem,* Victoria's *Requiem,* Bach's *Come, Sweet Death,* and Mahler's Symphony No. 5 (the Adagio movement) and Symphony No. 10 (Adagietto). Human contingency is also expressed in the sound of the blues. In painting, the most famous example related to contingency is Grünewald's *Crucifixion* as part of the Isenheim Altarpiece, where the greenish horror of death's greedy malevolence renders all of life an enigma.

V. COMPANIONSHIP AND INCARNATION:
Friendship and the Guest Appearance

PRAYER AS DISCIPLINE

Etymologically, *prayer* means "asking." In a broader sense, it means dialogue with God, involving expressions of praise, confession, intercession, thanksgiving, and petition. The best analogy for prayer is the ongoing conversation one has with a good friend. Thus, prayer is not an occasional matter but needs to become a habit, rooted first in disciplined obedience and increasingly in the joy of the friendship itself. Recognizing eight steps can be helpful.

1. Become still, preferably in a quiet spot.

2. Remove blockages such as preoccupation, ego centrality, hurts, and jealousies by asking God to remove them.

3. Review the day in dialogue with God.

4. Give thanks for some things; ask forgiveness for others; accept God's forgiveness by forgiving yourself.

5. Share everything that comes to mind, even the smallest things, knowing that God is interested. Picture persons, things, and events. A helpful mental aid is a conscious quadrilateral of concerns:

   a. For the church and its leadership

   b. For the world and particular leaders

   c. For the local area, especially the poor and needy

   d. For the local church, naming by name the hurting and dying

6. Listen, feel, and discern. Apprehend rather than comprehend. God rarely uses words, seeming to prefer communication through yearnings, urgings, desires, magnetized feelings, and hunches.

7. Prepare to live out your prayer. The key determinant of answered prayer is a renewed capacity to love—evidenced in the touch of a hand, a friendly glance, comforting remarks, constructive suggestions, shared joys and sorrows, and the urge to go out of one's way in selfless action. Love is ongoing prayer, resulting in a renewed watchfulness for the hand of God in the commonplace.

8. Express thanks for this special companionship. Amen—"so be it."

PRAYER AS CONTENTION

Prayer as asking involves the dimension of pleading. The Protestant reformers spent hours daily in such prayer with God. Concrete names, situations, temptations, crises, tragedies—all these were seriously lifted up with the firm confidence that God hears and answers prayer. While done verbally, such praying can also entail mental pictures of what one is asking—for example, imaging an ill person as healthy. Prayer of this type involves far more than polite requests. Jesus spoke approvingly of the persistent widow who harassed the judge until he granted her request. Thus, prayer involves contention, meaning an encounter of wills, until one gives way.

A crucial test of human friendship applies to God as well: the ability of the relationship to survive anger, frustration, contention, and even threats. Job, rather than being patient, demanded that God justify his actions. Jesus models in Gethsemane this profundity of prayerful companionship when he returns to God three times, each time beseeching with bloodlike sweat, refusing to take God's no for an answer. So must Christians pray, equipped with a concrete list of names and needs, lifting them before God—prepared, if necessary, to

wave them in God's face. It is a very serious matter to promise someone, "I will pray for you."

PRAYER AS PRACTICING THE PRESENCE

Prayer is not only a discipline; it also must become a way of life.
Brother Lawrence's *The Practice of the Presence of God* portrays this
well. Taking the Incarnation of Christ as his paradigm, Brother
Lawrence shared his duties as monastic cook with Jesus, inviting
him to smell the soup, hear the crack of cut carrots, and taste the
tang of fresh herbs. What more could one want, he asks, than to
keep company with Christ—chattering together, sharing everything, enjoying each other's presence, as the closest of friends? This
companionship involves more than doing things together. There are
times that transcend words, when one wants nothing more than
just to "hang out" with one's Friend.

CONSCIOUSNESS AS DIALOGICAL

The defining mark of self-consciousness is the incessant chattering
between "I" and "me." With practice, this dialogue can become a "praying without ceasing," an ongoing babbling between God and me.

BONDING

Human relationships thrive on signs of commitment, of which the
wedding ring is a classic example. Exchanging objects such as
friendship bracelets or pictures is commonplace among youth as
expressions of bonding. So too as Christians we need symbols of
our lifetime commitment to Christ, much as persons in love share
with each other. Such tokens might be a lapel cross, a rosary in
one's pocket, or wearing special clothing such as the monk's robe.
Nuns wear wedding rings as symbols of Christ as their lover. Thus,
their vow is really a pledge of monogamy.[11]

REMINDERS

Many Jews wear phylacteries, as described in scripture. These are small leather cases containing a scriptural text, worn on the head and/or left arm during prayer, reminding one of the need for faithful obedience. Wearing a cross around one's neck used to have such power. One can resurrect the impact of the cross by imagining wearing a small electric chair, the cross's modern equivalent. I was quite unprepared for how differently I was treated when after my ordination I wore downtown my priest collar rather than street clothing. It had a significant impact on me. Once we take upon ourselves explicit expressions of Christian identity, the meaning of Christianity for many others depends on how we walk, speak, smile, and act. A bumper sticker renders one's driving a witness, for better or worse.

VOCATIVES

Instead of long prayers, Evelyn Underhill encourages "darts of prayer," one-liners, as it were, thrown out to God. Just as lovers whisper sweet nothings to each other, we can do so with God. This includes pet names of endearment. For example, the sound of Mary's name for her son was "Jeshua," and we might also call him by this name.

EXAMINATION OF CONSCIOUSNESS

Jesus Christ is God's disclosure of Incarnation as a way in which the divine intersects with the human. In like manner, the Christian is called to be a continuation of Incarnation. One way to do this is to review each day's schedule with God. In so doing, one can anticipate situations in which one might get "hooked," times of potential weakness or temptation, circumstances likely to evoke defensiveness, and special opportunities for compassion and care. Once prepared, the Christian goes out to face the day with God as companion. Before each engagement that day, one takes a moment to ask for strength to carry out the game plan. In the evening, one does a review in reverse, remembering the day in confession, insight, and thankfulness. One might ask two questions: "Where did I see Christ today?" and "When did I fail to be Christ for someone else?"

This evaluation might result in the need to write a note or make a phone call, and then to settle down in thankful closure by fireside.

GUIDED IMAGERY

Guided imagery is currently popular in the secular world as an aid in accomplishing a goal, enabling healing, or attaining peace of mind. It entails walking into a particular experience by the use of a vivid imagination. Athletes are trained to imagine themselves all the way through an important race, from tying their shoes in the locker room to the victory celebration with friends. Others find respite from a trying day by being guided into walking barefoot through a gentle surf, hearing the gulls overhead, and sitting on a rock as the sun sets in all its glory. Such imagery makes use of all five senses as a way of incorporating one's whole self in the process.

Recent research has identified a number of states that can be served by guided imagery: the feeling state (for changing moods), end state (for enabling a goal), healing state (for strengthening bodily processes), imaginative state (for unloosing the creative process), psychological state (for changing one's self-image), and the spiritual state (for birthing meaning). An example of the latter type might occur in one's imagination as a leader takes a person or group up a mountain road, step-by-step, into an abandoned cabin. On the table is an intriguing box. The person opens it. What one's imagination finds there provides a clue to the Spirit's desire for one's life. Such practices can be self-led as well. Ignatius of Loyola used this technique to fashion what is called an Ignatian Retreat, traditionally one month in length, but presently available in a nine-day version. Here one is assigned a sequence of separate biblical scenes. By using every sense, one is to experience the action from inside each character. ("How must Mary have felt when the angel said . . . ?") One can create one's own such retreat or even a day apart. For example, divide the time allotted into seven equal parts, with a break after each. Enter into the following scriptural themes, using the technique described above.

- Creation: Genesis 1:2–2:3

- Abraham's Sacrifice: Genesis 22:1-14

- Exodus: Exodus 14:15-31

- The Desert Longing: Psalm 42

- The Covenant Renewed: Isaiah 55:1-11

- The Promise Fulfilled: Luke 4:14-30

- The Mission: John 21:1-17

THE IMITATION OF CHRIST

While Protestants favor speaking of Christian life as "following Christ," Catholics prefer the image of "imitating Christ." As Jesus said, "I have set you an example" (John 13:15). Saint Francis is a classic model for such spirituality, taking imitation quite literally. His passion for this was so intense that he experienced a stigmata—he received wounds on his hands and feet like those of Jesus. Imitation entails taking the four Gospels as one's handbook, for they portray Jesus as the "firstborn within a large family" (Rom. 8:29). A classic text for this spirit mode is Thomas à Kempis's *The Imitation of Christ.* In popular piety, Charles Sheldon's *In His Steps* advocates the practice of asking, "What would Jesus think, say, and do in this situation?" One can use novels for this purpose, such as Georges Bernanos's *The Diary of a Country Priest* and Nikos Kazantzakis's *The Last Temptation of Christ.* Among useful motion pictures one might try is *Jesus of Montreal.*

A spiritual director should know scripture well enough to be able to provide passages addressing situations that the directee is going through, encouraging an awareness of Jesus as the "one who in every respect has been tested as we are" (Heb. 4:15). These passages are a start:

- *Abused/Rejected:* Mark 6:3; Luke 4:28-30; 11:53-54; 16:14; 17:25; 18:32-34; 20:20; 21:12-19; 22:33-34, 47-65; 23:1-5; John 15:18-27.

- *Alone:* Matt. 14:13; Mark 1:35; Luke 8:19-21.

- *Anger/Hate:* Matt. 12:34; 23:13-39; Mark 3:1-6; 10:13-16; 11:12-19; Luke 9:51-55; 11:42-54; 13:14-17; 14:26-27.

- *Desire/Affection:* Luke 7:36-50; 22:14-16; John 13:23; 20:11-18; 21:20.

- *Destitute:* Matt. 19:27-30; Luke 9:57-62.

- *Disappointed:* Matt. 11:16-19; Mark 10:17-22; Luke 13:31-35; 17:11-19.

- *Scared/Troubled:* Mark 14:32-42; 15:16-20; Luke 22:40-46; John 12:27; 13:21.

- *Inadequacy:* Luke 18:19.

- *Overwhelmed:* Mark 3:20-21; 6:30-34; 7:24.

- *Sad:* Matt. 26:37-38; Luke 13:33-35; 19:41-42; 22:60-62; John 11:35.

- *Suffering:* Mark 13:9-13; 9:22-27.

- *Tempted:* Matt. 4:1-11; 26:39-46; Luke 17:1.

Other useful passages for spiritual direction might well include the positive dimensions of Jesus' humanity, such as his love of eating and drinking, his joy in the little things, his passion for deep friendships, and his sly sense of humor. A concordance is helpful.

EUCHARIST

From the church's beginning, Jesus was known to the disciples in the breaking of bread. The Eucharist is an ongoing and empowering participation in the Incarnation, Crucifixion, and Resurrection. An increasing number of non-Catholics are attending Masses, available each morning in neighborhood Catholic churches. All persons are invited to participate, although the priest can neither invite non-Catholics to receive Communion nor refuse them. John Wesley encouraged daily participation in the Eucharist. When Holy Communion is regarded simply as an act of remembering a past event, namely the *Last* Supper, it is possible that frequency diminishes its meaning. But Protestants such as Luther, Calvin, and Wesley agree with the Catholic tradition that the Eucharist is a celebration of the *Lord's* Supper, and thus is a joyous and empowering companionship in the present. Thus, to suggest infrequence is like proposing not eating very often for fear we will get tired of food. The Eucharist is an ongoing present event of real Presence, for the one whose name is "God with us" has promised, "I am with you always, to the end of the age" (Matt. 28:20).[12]

Storytelling

In the Christ event, the divine Storyteller makes a guest appearance, thereby becoming the Story within the stories. A helpful spiritual exercise that you might do orally with your director or in writing by yourself is to tell a story in response to each of the following questions:

- Who were you as a child?

- How do you remember one or both of your parents?

- Who are you really?

- Who is God for you?

When you have finished, consider this capstone question: Which is your "story of stories"?

Meditation

Words worth reflecting upon for this spiritual mode include *covenant, Emmanuel, with, Incarnation, for, Abba, Companion, Presence, Eucharist, relationship, contention, Communion, dialogue, Lover, Friend, engagement,* and *wedding*.

ART

Music capable of rehearsing this spirit mode includes Haydn's *The Seven Last Words of Christ on the Cross*, Wagner's "Prelude" to *Parsifal*, and Bach's *Saint Matthew Passion*. In painting, the master is Rembrandt. His Jesus is bathed in a gentle humanness born of profound suffering, with resurrection etched as hint. The importance of his portraits is that the divine has taken up housekeeping among us. Classic is his *Christ at Emmaus*, rendered as the *imitation Christi* in his self-portraits.

MEMORIZATION

My memory is not strong, and yet I still remember Wordsworth's "Daffodils" as the poem we were required to memorize in grade school. And in the haunts of my mind lurks Psalm 19, for which I received a gold star on a memorization chart long ago in Vacation Bible School. Impressive is the medieval practice of every monk memorizing all 150 psalms in Latin, so that by repeating them as he worked, the divine and the secular intersected. I am impressed by persons whose memories are so imprinted by scripture that on their deathbed, even in a semiconscious state, comforting words emerge as if the Spirit is speaking from within. In sad contrast, memorizations of even the Lord's Prayer and the Twenty-third Psalm are no longer common practice.

VI. HOMESICKNESS AND THE PURSUER: Craving and the Hunger for Integrity

RECOLLECTION

Each month many of us try to balance our checkbooks, seeing if we have anything left. We should do the same type of review of our schedule books to see if our doing is balanced with our being, or if our lifestyle is flirting with burnout. This periodic checkup is a way of asking about one's life, "What's the bottom line?" Balancing the checkbook itself can be a spiritual activity, discerning how well one is doing as a steward of resources on behalf of the kingdom.

One exercise is to draw several lines across a piece of paper, labeling the spaces "Physical," "Intellectual," and "Spiritual." Then draw lines down the page over these, labeling the columns "Me," "Family," "Friends," "Strangers," "Causes," and "Church." In each square write two figures: the time spent and the money/resources contributed. Total the columns, reflecting on the meaning of the amounts, frequency, priorities, and rhythms. Do the same with your daily calendar.[13]

Spiritual direction encourages participants to move from such exercises as these to creating a comprehensive rule to which they are willing to be held accountable.[14] Persons should be attentive to the rhythms of work and play, being and doing, silence and sound, type and amount of food and drink, variety and frequency of worship, and ways of being informed and intellectually challenged. Focus should include exercise, possessions, participation in nature, disciplined spiritual practices, culture and beauty, passion for social justice, sabbatical time, sensuality, sexuality, time with family and friends, sharing, and periodic review. Tools for group recollection are also available.[15]

JOURNALING

A diary is a daily record of things done. A journal, in contrast, is an exercise in discernment, reflecting on both one's internal and external life, paying particular attention to one's feelings. A diary might say, "Today I went to the dentist." A journal might say, "On the way to the dentist, I found myself frightened by. . . ." The one is concerned with doings, the other with meanings. Yet journal entries are not essays, conceptualizing one's understanding about something. They are an honest recording of one's life from the inside, the deeper meaning of which is often discerned only upon rereading later. Through journaling, patterns begin to emerge that give negative and positive hints concerning the shape of the whole. Put succinctly, journaling is a primary type of personal self-direction. It can be usefully done in conjunction with one-with-one direction, sharing parts with one's director. I encourage directees to use a loose-leaf notebook for this purpose, drawing a line down the middle of each page. The person writes on the left side, leaving the right side for comments by the director if the person chooses to share that page.

Dividing your journal into sections can expand its usefulness. In addition to the major section for regular entries, a second one can be marked "Month." Take an hour monthly to reflect on your daily entries, writing in this second section your discernment of what really happened that month. Once a year, perhaps on New Year's Eve, meditate upon the twelve monthly entries, placing your discernment in a section marked "Year." Then, after reflecting upon the other yearly entries, record in a fourth section your illuminations—of patterns, breakthroughs, persistent yearnings, stepping-stones, unresolved warnings, and opportunities. Journaling will provide abundant evidence of the One who persistently *pursues*.[16]

DREAMS

The Bible records numerous episodes where God communicates with persons through dreams (for example, Jacob and the ladder to heaven; the wise men warned not to return to Herod). Dreams must be recorded as soon as possible, since the mind's desire to forget them is amazing. Keep pencil and paper by your bed, filling in the details first thing in the morning. Sleep loosens the conscious mind's control over one's storehouse of memory and imagination. Treat a dream as if it is the soul's poem. While the meaning of some dreams is apparent, many are worth sharing with one's director for mutual discernment. Dreams tend to be of two kinds. The first show is courtesy of the memory, specializing in cravings, guilts, and shame, seeking resolution. The playwright for the second type is the imagination, with its offerings ranging from insights to creative possibilities. Whether separate or intertwined, both types provide powerful raw materials for direction.

Healing

Humanness is an interplay of body, mind, and spirit, whose intersection we call soul. Every part of each of us needs healing. The Christian is convinced that God wishes health for everyone, and that disease and death are God's foes as well as ours. This need for wholeness entails three types of healing.

1. *Forgiveness.* All of us harbor deep in our memories acts that, if publicly known, would bring shame and grief. A person cannot be whole without receiving forgiveness for these acts. While it is God who forgives, my experience in direction is that true confession rarely happens without face-to-face soul searching with another person. The twelve-step program structures such confession, requiring each person to spend serious time painfully searching the soul, identifying the hurts he/she has inflicted and has received. Before initiating such an inventory, directors need to decide if they feel able to give absolution in their role. If not, this should be done with a clergyperson who can hear confessions. No words are more healing than those of absolution:

> God, the Father of mercies, through the death and resurrection of his Son has reconciled the world to himself and sent the Holy Spirit among us for the forgiveness of sins; through the ministry of the Church may God give you pardon and peace, and I absolve you from your sins in the name of the Father, and of the Son, and of the Holy Spirit.[17]

The director needs to know the general steps entailed in confession:

- Contrition—expressing sorrow for what one has done

- Confession—concrete sharing of motives and acts

- Satisfaction—discerning and promising ways of undoing the damage

- Absolution—verbally given and received, with a forgiving of oneself

- Thanksgiving—for being made clean, born again

2. *Physical healing.* The need for faith healing is apparent, if for no other reason than that the American Medical Association classifies almost 70 percent of all medical problems as psychosomatic. This does not mean imaginary, but rather that they are rooted in a sickness of the spirit. Since Vatican II, the sacrament of last rites for the dying has been broadened and renamed the "anointing of the sick." It is now available for those facing an operation, the seriously ill, and the elderly. The African American spiritual "There Is a Balm in Gilead" says well its purpose: to revive the discouraged, give insight to the confused, and offer healing love to the sick of soul. As in biblical times, a special "oil of the sick" can be used, and an appropriate prayer speaks of trusting God in all things.

3. *Healing of memories.* I have emphasized the fact that there is no person who has not been scarred. The deepest scars tend to occur early in life when we feel so vulnerable, so small, so alone in a world so large. Blessed are those whose memories are healed soon. Otherwise, as we have seen, memories become increasingly repressed, invisibly haunting our thoughts and actions. While we have seen how this factor is involved in all spiritual direction, one way or another, a director may need to schedule a special session with a person for healing memories. The process leading up to such a session uses the analogy of moving from leaves to branches to trunk to roots to taproot. The director begins to sense the roots, for example, by noting the number of times the person talks about "kindergarten," coupled with "unhappy." The spiritual director asks, "Do you remember being happy as a kid?" The director is digging for the root. "I really was a happy kid." "Then what happened?" We may be near the taproot. "I hate recess. I

really hate it!" "What happened?" "It was a really cold day, and . . . and . . . and. . . ."

We have reached the point where the healing of memories is called for. There may be more stories to tell, but they will no doubt be variations on one theme—about which the person will need to tell the "story of stories." This healing phase requires skill on the part of the spiritual director, as well as sensing whether the directee is emotionally able to pass over the threshold. At any point in the process, the director may need to lighten the sharing, and even be prepared to shift the focus entirely to another topic—or to another time, or to the help of a therapist.

It is one thing to identify the traumatic experience; it is quite another matter to heal memories. I usually do this as a separate session, making clear beforehand what it might be like, thereby letting persons choose whether they wish to engage in it. The process of healing memories is like guided imagery, except the person has given enough of the story for you to use in structuring the experience. The person is invited to reenter the scarring experience, *not as a remembered memory but as a relived present.* Instead of the episode's being framed within the scary world of the child, it is now recontexted in a Christian frame, and that makes the difference. The director walks hand in hand into the experience with the person, acting as a surrogate Christ. The redefined perspective is crucial in order for the person no longer to feel alone, as was dreadfully the case the first time. The director might literally hold the person's hand, or give him or her some symbol that communicates that the person will be reliving the experience enfolded in the unconditional love of God. Reliving this event in the present as an adult frees the person from the ongoing rehearsal of the past as a child. What heals is the powerful contrast between the loneliness of the original experience and the warmth of the redeeming present. At such a time, one can truly discover that the goal of the Pursuer is homecoming.[18]

ENTERING ONE'S SHADOW

The Myers–Briggs Type Indicator is a helpful tool in spiritual direction and is now available for self-scoring.[19] It is based on four Jungian scales: Extroversion/Introversion (E/I); Sensing/Intuition (S/N); Thinking/Feeling (T/F); and Judging/Perceiving (J/P). Each person has a predominant trait on each scale. Grouped together according to respective strengths, these traits compose one's personality type, providing sixteen possibilities. A person's type makes a significant difference in how direction is done, for the Type Indicator helps identify how one is best fed spiritually, what spiritual disciplines may be most useful, and the process by which the person tends to discern and make decisions. The Perceiver learns best by knowing all the options before trying any, while the Judger is inclined to "try one on for size." Thinkers yearn to understand, thriving on an article or book that will advance some aspect of their spiritual quest. The Feeler grows best through sharing with another person or group. Intuitives make abundant use of the imagination in being lured toward spiritual growth, while the Senser prefers not to wander far from what can be explored and experienced with his or her own five senses.

Each scale, in turn, gives clues to one's theology. The Extrovert is most likely to revel in God's creation as the arena of God's ongoing Incarnation, while the Introvert is deeply sensitive to God's personal immanence as the "within" of all that is. The Extrovert's external God of history is in tension with the Introvert's God of the still small voice. Thinkers lead with their minds, fascinated by understanding the breadth and intricacies of God's working, while Feelers are more inclined to know through relationships of intimacy. Intuitives have eyes to behold the potentiality of everything as embraced by divine promise, while for the Senser the concretes of life are sacramentals. And while Judgers thrive on living out the anatomy of their convictions, Perceivers are inclined to search the mystery for hints of tentative meanings. Combinations are helpful clues as well, so that, for example, while the ET thrives in pondering, the EF is open to ecstasy; and while the EN lives life creatively, the ES is touched deeply by the sacramental.

Equally important in direction is that the Myers-Briggs discloses one's "shadow." It appears opposite each person's strongest and thus most developed attribute. And while it signals that part of the person most in need of being redeemed, it also identifies what the person is most likely to avoid and resist. To illustrate this personally, as an ENTJ, my shadow has been the opposite of my thinking (T), which is my feelings (F). In establishing my self-identity through the development of my thinking side with all kinds of university degrees, my feelings were left sadly delinquent. As the shadow that I avoided, they remained unused, hidden, and undisciplined. But lurking there, they could easily get out of control, get projected onto others, and be triggered inappropriately. Spiritual growth for each of us entails the courage and help to enter our shadow. In my case it meant daring to get in touch with my feelings, to risk feeling them deeply, to seek out the roots of my blockage, and finally being freed to feel delightfully alive.

Likewise, in being a strong Extrovert, growth of my underdeveloped introvert side came through participating in a monastic community centered in silence and the rich interior life. Again, opposite my strong intuitive side (that is, imagination) was my underdeveloped sensing side. Growth meant intentionally developing my senses until the smells, touches, and sights of creation have become God's daily gifts. As a Judger, I always make quick decisions, testing them until they become convictions to which I am loyal. Through spiritual direction I have been invited to mature my perceiving side, learning to appreciate the array of options and viable alternatives by which each person is tailor-made by God.

THE ENNEAGRAM

Another way of entering one's shadow is by using the Enneagram. This tool for direction organizes personality types on the basis of one's unsatisfactory way of coping with life. It helps identify a person's spiritual weakness, and how healing is possible. See Appendix 8 for directions in using the Enneagram.[20]

EMPTY PRAYER

Paul speaks of the Spirit's helping us in our weakness to pray with "sighs too deep for words." This can happen because the God "who searches the heart, knows what is the mind of the Spirit" (Rom. 8:26-27). Empty prayer is unlike ordinary prayer in which statements are used, or contemplation in which all activity of the mind is halted. Instead, one permits anything and everything to enter one's mind without filters. Strive for pure listening, pure seeing, and pure feeling, interested only in what may be whispered or what pictures the Spirit might paint on consignment. The objective is to let the Spirit as Pursuer stir up whatever is ripe for redemptive perception.

PONDERING

The spirituality of pondering is related to empty prayer. In contrast to contemplation, in which the mind is seen as a meddling interference, here there is a spiritual honoring of the mind. Daydreaming is claimed as a spiritual activity. Begin with Luther's state of *tentatio*, as a genuine "not knowing." Be intentionally open so that the mind can do the equivalent of surfing. Some of my most fascinating times with God are when I have been pursued into pondering on the meaning of evil, or God's location amidst billions of light-years. These are the times when, as a thinker, I can truly become lost in God.

MEDITATION

Words to consider as focus guides for this dimension of spirituality include *homesickness, yearning, not-quiteness, guilt, wistfulness, regret, haunted, Hound of heaven, shadow, nostalgia, longing, urge, pursuit, search, stalk,* and *providence*.

THE ARTS

Music capable of eliciting this mode includes Dvořák's Slavonic Dance No. 10, Beethoven's *Concerto in D Major for Violin and Orchestra* (Second Movement) and String Quartet No. 15 (Third Movement), and Mahler's Symphony No. 1 (First Movement). In painting, El Greco is the master. His objects are like flickering candle flames, yearning and soaring, with persons reaching out as twisted gyrations of flesh, claimed by a pursuing Spirit. Contemplate his *Christ on the Cross* and *Opening of the Fifth Seal*.

VII. DELIGHT AND THE PROMISER: Ecstasy and the New Innocence

SABBATH PLAY

To be sanctified is to have a new sense of innocence, to which Jesus referred when he spoke of the need to become as a little child. Scripture tells of a very busy God who needed a Sabbath in which to rest and enjoy the works of creating. So it is with us. Without a genuine Sabbath, our work becomes lethal, our moods morose, and our relationships jagged and touchy. Yet our society resists such a rhythm, shaping us into confirmed workaholics.

As a child, my Sabbaths were ruined by being made negative— "Don't do this." "You can't do that!" Only years later did I learn that the negative ("Do not work") is a means to the positive ("You are free to play!"). Augustine calls this idea "holy leisure," and Brother Lawrence refers to it as deliciously "wasting time with God." The Sabbath gives us permission to be useless, to let go of the urge always to be in control.

Activism is legitimate performance carried to an objectionable extreme, as if we are driven to run up the down escalator—in record time. This obsession is more than just "overdoing it." It is rooted in the felt need to justify ourselves by constant motion. Perhaps the only way to change all this is, at first, to schedule mandatory Sabbaths as a duty. When this habit becomes established, we can begin to experience Sabbath as a gift. Alternating work with requisite splashes of Sabbath can transform the compulsive worker into a relaxed, gentle, carefree, compassionate human being. Sunday afternoon is a fine time for lovemaking. Some medieval theologians were so taken by the need of a Sabbath that they believed God actually gave persons in hell their Sundays off. Sickness can be evidence of insufficient Sabbath.

I lost this important part of my spirituality when my last child left home. I forgot how to fly kites, jump in leaves, make snow people, and walk in the rain. Thus, spiritual directors should be lavish in suggesting hot-air balloon rides, taking a child to the zoo, walking barefoot in the park, making sand castles on the beach, giving a nickname to one's car, resurrecting a teddy bear, wearing red socks with matching suspenders, dressing up in garish clothing from a flea market, reading nursery rhymes aloud, reading a Nancy Drew mystery, and perhaps even rereading the Hardy Boys.

PLAYFULNESS

When the Sabbath perspective is internalized, a pervading playfulness is birthed. Sam Keen may have had this in mind when he named the goal of spirituality that of becoming a "foolish lover." A priest unwilling to chew bubble gum in the sacristy is unfit to celebrate the Eucharist. I celebrated a Mickey Mouse Mass recently, giving ears and T-shirts to the children, and stuffed Mickeys to adults who had a hard time smiling. This fanciful and playful world of the childlike is a foretaste of the eighth day of creation, when the kingdom shall be an eternal Sabbath in God.

CLOWNING AND MIME

It is amazing what happens when people don red noses, rubber ears, big shoes, and paint a huge grin on their faces. Behind a mask, our inhibitions are loosened, helping us laugh at ourselves. Learning not to take ourselves so seriously is an important lesson for most directees. Practice by making faces at yourself in a mirror.

SILENT MEALS

Frantic schedules and TV dinners have largely robbed us of the experience of eating as a delight. Plan a meal with an eye to making your plate a colorful collage, appealing to sight, smell, and taste. Eat deliberately, bite by bite, sip by sip. Taste the breadiness of bread, the mashiness of potatoes, the coldness of milk, and the yellowness of peaches. Experience the flavor, the crunch, the color, and the aromas. Let the meal draw together the sun, earth, sky, rain, growers, producers, handlers, cooks—implicitly the whole world.

MASCULINE/FEMININE

Each of us has two sides. The *anima* or feminine side bequeaths us appreciation of beauty, intuition, insight, delicacy, sensitivity, creativity, inspiration, reconciliation, nurture, homecoming, cooperation, healing, ease, and gracefulness of movement. It is our lyric side, in contrast with the *animus* or male side, characterized by a passion for efficiency, analysis, assertiveness, doing, and achieving. Most of us need the assignment of exploring the opposite side of our gender.

POETRY

Lyric poetry is particularly appropriate for this mode of spirituality. Assign some poems by the English romantic poets such as Wordsworth, Shelley, and Keats. As for the modern lyric poets, e. e. cummings is my favorite. Try your hand at writing poetry, frolicking in the thick, moist, lushness of metaphor and imagery. You still haven't caught on if something inside keeps asking, "What good does this do?"

THE SADNESS OF LOSS

Karl Barth once said that resurrection has meaning only for those of us who shed tears at the thought of leaving. A way of exercising our quiet joy in living is to list those experiences we will most miss. I gave this assignment to a person facing imminent death. This is her list:

- Climbing a fire tower to the top, exulting in the world at one's feet

- Smelling and touching the texture of newly turned earth

- Feeling the slippery ooze of sun-warmed mud between your toes

- Listening to such sounds as trickling water and a crackling fire

- Crunching a juicy apple while shuffling through autumn leaves

- Delighting in the giggle of a child being licked by a wiggly puppy

- Splashing in a spring rain, with face turned upward

- Snuggling in a warm bed as a winter storm howls

Meditation

Words evocative of this spiritual mode include *promise, innocence, trust, whimsy, delight, beginnings, mischief, novelty, radiance, humor, fun, lure, enchantment, mellowness, intensity, freshness, glint*—and *Mickey Mouse,* with a hint of *Pluto.*

The Arts

Delightful music of this type must include Haydn's *Toy Symphony, Surprise Symphony,* and *Farewell Symphony.* Of the same sort are Grétry's *Danses Villageoises,* Offenbach's *Gaite Parisienne,* and "Farewell" from Schubert's *Swan Songs.* In painting, Paul Klee is the master, creating a world of whimsy. At his hand, the playful fantasy of ordinary daydreaming takes on an uncanny energy, hinting of Spirit. See, for example, *The Dancer.*

VIII. SACRAMENTALITY AND THE PRESENCE:
The Secular As Sacred

SACRAMENTS AND SACRAMENTALS

Sacraments are events involving words and situations through which God has promised to act. Consequently, these channels of grace are objective, as in the events of Eucharist and baptism. Sacramentals, on the other hand, function subjectively, evoking and reminding us of what is already the case, although we are inclined to forget. For example, holy water, being a sacramental, does not effect anything but reminds us that in baptism we were purchased and branded by Christ. Wearing a cross can be a sacramental, evoking the awareness that we are under the yoke of Christ. Similarly, one might meaningfully bow to a holy place, or walk barefoot on Good Friday. While these are self-conscious and intentional acts, every person has sacramentals, although usually unconsciously. We choose the possessions that surround us, and they, in turn, rehearse our identity. Therefore, the way we furnish our homes and work-spaces deeply influences our attitudes, moods, caring, and openness. We begin to be sensitive to sacramentals when we start speaking of something having "sentimental" value.

A helpful exercise is to make an inventory of those things that actually function in your life as sacramentals. Remember your treasures as a youth, kept in a special cigar box or under the sweaters in the bottom drawer. Look through your wallet and pocketbook for sacramentals. Consider as well your car's glove compartment and trunk, the color of your rooms, the shape and position of your favorite chair and working desk, pictures on the walls, and the CDs you most often listen to. Invite your spiritual director into your home to walk through its space, sharing the impact of what is seen and felt.

When friends gather, they almost always eat and drink something. This is a sacramental act bearing hidden witness to the

Eucharist as the center of the Christian's life. *Eucharist* means "giving thanks," so that the prayer at the beginning of one's meal functions as a mini-Eucharistic prayer. A family's Thanksgiving meal is adorned with sacramentals—of candles and color, with the incense of roast turkey and baked rolls. Trimming the Christmas tree is an exercise in unpacking sacramentals. The graphic contrast between a devouring animal and the gracious beauty of a banquet captures the essence of sanctification. The movie *Babette's Feast* is an invitation to a sacramental life.

Rites of Passage

The traditional sacraments can function as rites of passage. Baptism celebrates birth, confirmation the coming of age, marriage the sacredness of sexuality, and ordination the calling to vocation. But such functioning needs to be broadened, and the number of rites expanded. Augustine suggests that since God functions in countless ways, sacraments are limitless. Actually, if the church does not provide rites for the major passages of life, society will. Presently the secular sacramentals for coming of age begin with acquisition of a driver's license, consummated with a "drinking card" as proof of having arrived. As an exercise, remember the way in which important transitions in your life were marked. Create some short liturgies appropriate for providing a Christian blessing for such occasions, using them with your extended family and friends.

Feelings

We men are notorious for not being in touch with our feelings. As a result, it is difficult to know the feel of one's own selfhood. A useful exercise is to ask oneself at inopportune moments, "What am I feeling right *now*?" Colored squares, posted in key places, can serve as reminders to get in touch with how you feel at the instant you see one. These can serve much like daily offices in the monastery, through which monks are disciplined to feel the emotions of the day's rhythms.

I was amazed when I discovered that each of us has a primary sense in which to revel. This awareness came while listening to an ambience tape. I became enthralled with all kinds of sounds—rain on a roof, the crackle of fire, and the giggle of a child. That night I claimed hearing as my sense, nurturing it like a talent. Now sounds for me are spiritual, whether the wail of coyotes at full moon or a Beethoven string quartet. Find the sense by which you are most blessed. Go to a tea store and relish the smells, or enjoy the taste of gourmet coffees. Do you prefer the sounds of a flute or of a cello? Spend an afternoon at a gallery gazing at paintings, not for the sake of art history, but as an exercise in learning to see. Come to your senses!

NOWNESS

Our culture conditions us to want whatever we don't have. This draws us out of the *now* into the *when*. Yet, as we have noted, Jesus is clear that the residence of the Christian is to be richly and deeply adorned in the present. Take a walk with a friend, promising to speak of nothing but what is immediate to the present. This is hard, for we keep taking ourselves to another *when* or *where*—past or future. This next exercise is not for Baby Boomers. It is for us depression folks who are marked with guilt for anything we do for ourselves. Ponder the biblical story of the woman who anointed the head of Jesus with expensive perfume. Judas, himself a depression kid, was upset, for the money spent on the perfume could have been used for practical purposes. But Jesus responded, "She has done a beautiful thing to me" (Matt. 26:10, RSV). For Saint Paul, the Incarnation continues in each of us: "Do you not know that you are God's temple and that God's Spirit dwells in you?" (1 Cor. 3:16) As an exercise in such sacramentality, seriously ask yourself, How can I treat my body as God's temple? Many of us need to hear Saint Bernard's insistence on treating the body as a friend. Self-indulgent though it will seem for some of us, try a steamy bath by candlelight in a full, foamy tub. Ask yourself these questions: What have I always wanted to do? What haven't I yet dared to do? What have I always wanted to have? These are ways of letting go so as to enter into a sacramental moment. Don't take a swim, but let the swim take you. Do something for the sheer joy of it. Before I die, I may be able to justify a massage.

MEDITATION

Evocative words for this spiritual mode might include *sacred, water, gift, commonplace, earth, sacramental, rare, fire, gratuitous, fondness, domesticity, unique, sanctify, consecrate, air, blessing, Communion, temple, altar, baptism, bell,* and *Eucharist.*

THE ARTS

In music, one might try Gershwin's *An American in Paris*, Copeland's *Appalachian Spring*, Smetana's *The Moldau*, Mussorgsky's *Pictures from an Exhibition*, Beethoven's Symphony No. 6 ("The Pastoral"), and Grofé's *Grand Canyon Suite*. Some of my favorite poets in this mode are Emily Dickinson, Robert Frost, William Carlos Williams, and Edna St. Vincent Millay. Adventuresome persons may try T. S. Eliot and Gerard Manley Hopkins. As for painters, I choose Vermeer, whose diminutive paintings incarnate the domesticity of being, the dignity of the simple, and the sacredness of the commonplace (e.g., *The Milkmaid*).

IX. CALL AND THE DIVINE CREATIVITY: Imagination As Cocreation

CREATIVITY

The God in whose image we are created made human beings after being distinguished as the Creator *par excellence*. Thus, the image that identifies the essence of humans is that of being cocreators with God. We are artists by nature. As an exercise in getting free from the false assumption that art requires special talent and training, establish yourself at a table for half an hour, equipped with thirty cans of food from the pantry. See what you can create. Next time try making something with matchsticks or carving a bar of soap. Try playing in paint, but only after banning paint-by-number kits from your house.

SACRED DAYDREAMING

While attending church, let your imagination roam free. Redesign the sanctuary; improve the bulletin; choose alternative hymns; rework the sermon; and sketch out a new baptistery. Don't let anything remain as it is. Drench it in how it aches to be.

VOCATION

Calvin, as I indicated, makes an important distinction between being a Christian *in* one's vocation and *through* one's vocation. In the first case, one is Christianlike in performing the tasks society prescribes as proper to a particular vocation. Thus, a Christian doctor treats patients with personal respect and care. To be a Christian *through* one's calling, however, means changing the way that vocation is defined. Thus, a doctor might fight free-enterprise medicine by working to establish guaranteed health care for every person— in the meantime establishing a free clinic.

WORK

Benedictines summarize Saint Benedict's Rule as *ora et labora*— prayer intersecting work. To create this intersection, the atmosphere monasteries try to establish is in decided contrast to modern society. Instead of thinking big, efficient, mechanized, and mass-produced, the monastery thrives on what is small, manageable, communal, cooperative, quality-oriented, and artistic. And while monastic work may not always seem very different from work done in the larger society, the difference lies in motive, attitude, and perspective. For the Christian, work is intended to feed the human spirit, so that all work is holy if its goal is to fulfill God's yearning. Thus, even the smallest tasks can be so contexted that they participate in our call to complete creation. For monks, even the scrubbing of toilets can be done to the glory of God. Try applying this concept to your menial tasks.

Work, then, is to be done as a gift to God. But it can also be redemptive for the Christian. It is intentional that monastic work is often hidden, humble, anonymous, and monotonous. The monk is learning to identify with the scriptural *anawim*—the poor and lowly who are most dear to God. Such work teaches simplicity, humility, and a willingness to be unnoticed by the world, for it is enough to be hidden with Christ in God. But today's culture in America teaches many people to resist all this, driven by profit, publicity, ambition, prestige, and notoriety. How difficult it is for us to do humble work, and how hurt we feel if not thanked for acting like Christians. Impressive is the Cuban experiment in having professionals like doctors and judges spend part of their time working side by side with those whom they try to heal or judge with compassion. How deeply needed is the transformation Christianity requires at this point. Our worth depends not on what we accomplish nor on the status we gain by doing it. What matters is being God's friend.

Useful assignments might include these:

- Doing anything for the sake of the doing rather than for the sake of getting it done

- Physical labor for those not in touch with their bodies

- Service work for others in which one remains anonymous

- Helping those from whom there is no likelihood of recompense, recognition, or even thanks

- Surprising people with graciousness, such as paying the toll for the person behind you on the turnpike, or buying a few extra movie tickets to distribute to those in line behind you, or paying the bill for the lonely person sitting at the table in the corner.

LECTIO DIVINA

Meditation means "tasting with one's lips."[21] I first got in touch with this practice by hearing a recording of T. S. Eliot reading his own poetry. *Lectio divina* ("divine or sacred reading") is meditation evoked by spiritual reading, especially scripture. Pray beforehand that God will address you through the reading. Then taste and savor each phrase by reading it aloud, carefully forming each word and physically moving with the cadence of the lines. Von Hügel uses the analogy of letting a lozenge slowly dissolve in one's mouth. The technique involved is to read a particular passage slowly, several times, until a phrase or word emerges with portent. Repeat it, taste it, digest it, and make it part of yourself until you belong to it, for through it God has laid claim to you. Such re-rereading is best done daily at the same friendly time and familiar place, with half an hour being minimum.

Some of us read books in similar fashion, underlining what is worth remembering. Then by rereading the underlines, we write at the bottom of the page the one underlining that somehow says it all. Part of the art of *lectio* is in selecting the right text. The lectionary is a solid source. These daily scripture readings serve as givens that minimize the subjectivity through which we are tempted to filter scripture. Thus, instead of hearing a reinforcement of what we want to hear, the odds are better that we will be addressed by what we need to encounter. Through *lectio* we stand to be addressed and questioned by the Word, which we cannot easily control.

DISCERNMENT OR CLEARNESS SESSIONS

These important spiritual direction tools are described in detail in Appendixes 1 and 2.

PILGRIMAGE

All religions have sacred places to which faithful pilgrims travel. Catholicism has its Rome, Islam its Mecca, and Judaism its Jerusalem. Protestantism seems to be developing one—the Holy

Land. Vacations are the secular equivalents of pilgrimages, but usually they miss the point because they often substitute intense doing for relaxed, meaningful being. Many vacations are frantic marathons to "see it all," producing a host of pictures that friends really don't care to see.

Pilgrimages make contact with the human need to have something to look forward to. As an exercise, deal with such questions as these: Going to what place would be like a dream come true? To bring closure to my life, where would I like to go before I die?

Mini-pilgrimages can be powerful too, as was a return to the Appalachian home of my birth, visiting the family graveyard, and praying in the church where I was baptized. A mosaic in the floor of the medieval cathedral at Chartres, France, is a symbolic pilgrimage in the form of a labyrinth. Diagrams of this labyrinth are available, and canvasses may be purchased for use in actually walking the labyrinth. Churches are painting this labyrinth on their parking lots, youth groups draw it with chalk, and an ingenious friend made one with a lawn mower in a field. The labyrinth is particularly powerful when walked by candlelight.[22]

GROWTH

I still remember the miracle of planting a bean in my very own paper cup and watching it give birth right there on the kindergarten windowsill. To be surrounded by living things is to be fed spiritually. My hermitage is arrayed with plants birthing plants, and pet goldfish grace the pond outside my kitchen window. A fine sacramental practice is sharing life by exchanging plant clippings with friends. A living parable of life's pilgrimage is seeding and harvesting, with reseeding as new beginnings. This human need accounts for our fascination with gardening, even though what is produced rarely covers the expense of the supplies and equipment. Saint Francis understood this sacredness of gardening. When asked what he would do if he learned that he had only one more hour to live, he responded: "I would continue to dig in my garden."

ECOLOGY

As analogy to our faithfulness to Holy Mother Church, the Christian is called to reverence Holy Mother Earth. Yet in both cases we often act as if both church and earth are "its." As an exercise in ecological spirituality, find a piece of abandoned earth, one overtaken by trash, weeds, and neglect. Love that piece of God's creation until it becomes a gift to those who pass by. (The "Adopt a Highway" program is a governmental equivalent.) Keep a plastic bag in your pocket, briefcase, or car, and assume responsibility for picking up trash wherever you are. Have a supply available for friends so that together you might be "scavengers for Christ." Visits to local thrift stores and flea markets do much to instill guilt if one does not develop a "preowned" lifestyle.

STABILITY

Somewhere, for something, and perhaps with someone, each of us will some day be called upon to take a stand. The mobility of modern culture is a distraction and a diversion from such spiritual stability. The accountability that is always part of spiritual direction fosters a posture of steadfastness, of holding one's own ground, of learning to live with oneself with all one's faults, failings, emptiness, and unfulfillment. And it is the support which direction gives that helps a person to stop running, with sufficient courage to be fully present, to be faithful, and to be one's true self.

Jesus' contrast between the house built on sand and the one anchored in rock is apt for a society that no longer encourages or provides stability of place, job, or relationship. Instead, we are tutored to stay only until things get tough or until something more appealing or lucrative comes along. The reward for stability, in my case, has been a hermitage that breeds the friendship of flowers, birds, and animals with which I share this sacred portion of earth. An exterior instability has interior ramifications. In a society where one hardly knows one's neighbors, one remains a stranger to oneself. To combat the demonic forces without and within, one must dare to put down roots in both places. Direction is the commitment to "stick with it" for the long haul. And when we do declare someplace to be home, it is then, ironically, that we can no longer escape our divine homesickness.

MISSION

Christianity is an intensely social religion. To live it, one must drink the cup of discipleship—becoming a slave of all, called "not to be served but to serve" (Matt. 20:28). Blessed are those for whom this way of living becomes so natural that they ask in bewilderment, "Lord, when was it that we saw you hungry and gave you food, or thirsty and gave you something to drink?" And the answer? "Just as you did it to one of the least of these who are members of my family, you did it to me" (Matt. 25:37-40). The only kingdom that we are likely to see on this side of death is the one hinted at in the eyes of the hungry being fed. Christians are to be "pro-life" in the broadest and deepest and fullest sense imaginable—from beginning to end, and every point in between. Where we Christians sin most often and deeply is not in our acting but in our *failure to act*. A test I use to gauge the effectiveness of spiritual direction is the degree to which a person is drawn out of his or her own preoccupations into the needs and lives of others.

NEWSPAPER PRAYER

A prayer exercise designed to evoke this exterior sensitivity is to take a section of the daily newspaper and cut each page into quarters. Shuffle the pieces, draw one at a time, and offer an intercession for whomever or whatever appears there. It is surprising what happens, even if the providence of the draw produces an ad for instant potatoes.

DIVERSITY

Sin resides in the universal human tendency to take who, where, how, and why we are and make them normative for everyone. An important exercise in spiritual direction, then, is to open the parameters of your life by an intentional exposure to diversity, gauged by how strange and uncomfortable you are made to feel. For worship, try a storefront revival. For social class, be the recipient at a soup kitchen. For the human condition, visit a stranger in prison. For culture, order something in a Korean restaurant from a menu that you cannot read. If you lack sufficient courage for any of these exercises, even driving slowly along the side streets of an inner city can be spiritually disturbing.

Another exercise is a response to Jesus' attraction to the rejected of his day, primarily tax collectors and prostitutes. Draw a circle in the middle of a page, and label it "Members of My Community of Love." Write outside the circle the types of persons that you have difficulty including within that circle. Be honest, carefully considering your attitudes toward ethnics, "white trash," communists, witches, gays, and lesbians. You can make this exercise more concrete at a feeling level by asking what types fall outside your comfort level for having one of your children marry or adopt.

Another exercise is to draw a circle and write the kinds of persons whose offenses would render them unacceptable in your church. Would you take the risk of sponsoring them? Does the picture change if you were asked which of these offenses fall outside the limits of God's forgiveness?[23] Would you be willing to become a friend to persons released after serving prison sentences for rape, murder, sabotage, incest, or child molestation? What difference would it make if the circle represented persons you would welcome into your home?

HAGIOLOGY

From the beginning, the church named as saints those deemed to be models of spiritual faithfulness to the Christian vision. Together they give us a sense of being surrounded by "so great a cloud of witnesses" (Heb. 12:1). These witnesses are woven into the church calendar, providing feast days from which Christians are to draw inspiration and spiritual direction. Add and subtract from it so as to make your own hagiology (list of venerated persons), paying attention to your past and present, remembering those who have helped you become who you are. I remember especially a third-grade teacher who affirmed my creativity in painting elephants green.

Meditation

A beginning list of words for this spiritual mode might include *wedding, foretaste, eschatology, cocreation, vision, creativity, process, beatific vision, kingdom, commonwealth, queendom, banquet, garden, judgment, glory, feast,* and *benediction.* At Easter, as the church's climax, the one word that says it all is *alleluia.*

The Arts

In music, try Mahler's *Resurrection Symphony,* Purcell's various trumpet voluntaries, Bach's *Christmas Oratorio,* Wagner's "Good Friday Spell" from *Parsifal,* Beethoven's Symphony No. 9, and Part Two of Handel's *Messiah.* In painting, my favorite is El Greco's *View of Toledo,* where a luminosity of greens washes the landscape in the transcendent glow of vision. "See, I am making all things new" (Rev. 21:5).

The Primal Gesture

The nine spiritual modes and their accompanying exercises are intended to help both director and directee design possible assignments for spiritual direction sessions. But there is one task more. An overarching goal of spiritual direction is to discern one's rhythm of rhythms, one's gesture of gestures, one's experience of experiences, one's story of stories, one's theme of themes, in which one's whole life is to be centered. I can illustrate this best with myself.

Through direction, I have finally discerned that the Eucharist is that primal centering for my pilgrimage. I lose myself in meaning at the altar. It is where I stand to see, and feel, and be. The daily Eucharist at my hermitage is at sunset, in front of a large window looking out over a lake, and beyond it to the endless roll of hills.

This is the time, and this is the place. It is where I lift up into God "the whole of your creation and every speck within it—the creation which you [God] hold in being, the creation into which you incarnate yourself, and the creation through which your Spirit yearns and lures and thrusts all things toward completion—as you become All in all." My daily congregation is comprised of deer, raccoons, and squirrels, and all those who suffer. The choir is a polyphony of birds and crickets, roofed by an azure sky. The bread and wine are offered as "tokens of the works of our hands, the pondering of our minds, and the yearnings of our souls, so that united with Christ's sacrifice we may raise to you this bread of life and this cup of eternal salvation—praising you, blessing you, thanking you, making reparation to you, and interceding for all, especially those most in need of your mercy and nourishment and healing of body, mind, and spirit." All the hurting and dying of the world are lifted up onto the cross, and embraced by the crucified One. The ascent is into life's great Amen. Then, out of the silence, with the cosmos on tiptoes, everything is returned, blessed as the body and blood of Christ. Every speck is a gift by which we "are nourished into faithfulness to your promise—of the new heaven and new earth—that in all things your will might be done."[24]

Eucharist is the primal gesture that choreographs my living. Even my senses sparkle in the vision:

- The *sound* is of pouring and of breaking, wrapped in the whisper of wind.
- The *smell* is the incense of crushed grapes and fresh-baked bread and flowering meadows.
- The *sight* is a memory of drifting grain and lush hillside vineyards in the rhythm of upward motion.
- The *feel* is of fired clay and the altar's rustic wood, embossed with the richness of countless names remembered and prayed for.
- The *taste* is of a cosmos created, redeemed, and sanctified in promise.

My life is a wager that this gesture reflects the way things really are. All of us have such a gesture—an embrace, a climb, a race—a simple act that discloses and rehearses what life is all about. Spiritual direction is a primary way to discern this gesture and then hold it up to the gospel. Faith is commitment to the result—on which one stakes one's life, by which one is fed, and to which one is willing to be held accountable. I suspect that the deeper we search, the more we will discover that our lives are variations on a common theme.

✛

PERSONAL SPIRITUAL DIRECTION
AND APHORISMS FOR THE JOURNEY

Many of us read the books we choose with a marker in hand. What we tend to remember is not so much the book as a whole or perhaps even the author's premise. Instead, we remember the points we underline, especially those with a star in the margin. They grab us, expressing succinctly a truth we do not want to forget, or reminding us of what we had forgotten that we knew. Many of us go back later and collect some of these underlinings in a notebook, labeled something like "Gathered Wisdom." Others of us post a few of these gems on the refrigerator door, the bathroom mirror, by our place at the table—or even on the car dashboard.

It is not difficult, then, to understand Israel's penchant for gleaning aphorisms from her own experience and jottings, incorporating them into sacred scripture. The most apparent result is called Wisdom Literature, classically preserved in such books as Proverbs and Ecclesiastes. But such distilled sayings dot all the scriptural books, whether as liturgy, poetry, song, or prophetic utterances jotted down by a disciple. In the New Testament, Paul's letters freely quote things he remembered—from conversations, scripture, and local traditions. The Gospels are likewise gems of aphorisms, composites of oral traditions, and collections of sayings, the original forms of which we can only surmise. Basically what we have are those utterances of Jesus with such initial power that they became lodged in the memory of the hearers. They were told and retold as oral underlinings until they were finally recorded so they would not be lost.

This process, central to being human, continues today, even in local churches. Many have begun to record the remembrances of their elders so that they will not be lost. And no monastery would be the same without ongoing remembrances of "what Brother James always used to say"—brought yearly to focus with All Souls remembrances in the cemetery. Often a scripture verse is carved into the Communion table, is painted above the chancel, or greets worshipers entering the vestibule. Favorite sayings from Saint Benedict's Rule adorn monastic lintels. Rare is the church school classroom without verses or sayings posted on walls, written on chalkboards, or tacked to bulletin boards. Currently there is a growing interest in calligraphy, with art and craft fairs offering abundant sayings as colorful remembrances to grace one's living space with wisdom.

All this gives ample witness to the important role of personal spiritual direction in human life. *We are what we remember, with commitment a determination born of knowing what we dare not forget.* The human condition being what it is, we do fairly well in our spirituality when we remember. This is why one important role for the spiritual director is to hold others accountable by devices that jog memory into accountability. But, in truth, most spiritual direction sessions are variations on the theme of guilt for having forgotten. The directee asks sheepishly, "Do you remember what it was I agreed to do last session?" Husbands, notorious in their legendary forgetfulness of birthdays and anniversaries, are only tokens of the universal neglect in recalling and thus rehearsing the key meanings that mark defining junctures in our pilgrimage paths. In spirituality, everything depends on remembering and re-remembering. The only Jesus we have is the remembered one, the one sketched from those select words and remembrances with the poignancy to resist time by underlining themselves in the collective memory called the church. So it is with each one of us. The staying power of oral memory and the passages underlined in one's memory are part of the same fabric. We are the composite not only of *what* we remember, but, even more important, of *how* we remember—whether through eyes of anger or of forgiveness.

This helps us understand why *lectio divina* has been so important for Christians and is the primary spiritual discipline for most monks. It is indispensable for recapturing the human practice we are describing. It is a re-rereading in order for sacred words to live again in the present, analogous to how anamnesis is a re-remembering by which Eucharist becomes real Presence. Here we touch the mnemonics of spirituality, the indispensable assists required for our spiritually impaired memory. Communal, corporate, and one-with-one spiritual direction are types where the mnemonics are externally structured. Personal spiritual direction, however, must provide its own structure, or it will fail. Thus, our inevitable tendency to underline when we read is an important expression of our natural inclination to practice self spiritual direction. These "gems" that we underscore function, at least implicitly, as the ingredients we deem worthy of meditation, as instruments of our personal spiritual growth.

This chapter, which provides aphorisms for meditation, is an invitation and a resource for personal spiritual direction. At the heart of this type of direction is serious reading and deliberation about what one reads, out of which emerge aphorisms that choose us for our individualized direction. The remainder of this chapter is a sampling of what such a collection might be like, resulting from my own listening to the Spirit, inspired by persons, readings, and ponderings along the path. They are offered as an exercise in personal spiritual direction. I invite you to sample these aphorisms slowly, reading a few from each section during multiple sittings—underlining as you feel inclined. You might return at another time to star those that deserve special remembrance. A few sayings may even find themselves candidates for the individualized direction that only a refrigerator door can give. But most important, may they encourage the creation of your own "Aphorisms for the Journey." My sampling is arranged loosely by theme.

THE HUMAN CONDITION

- Life gets shorter the longer one lives.
- "In you [God] all find their home" (Psalm 86:7*b*, GRAIL).
- May I not get in the way of what I must be and do.
- Living in the past brings guilt and hurt; living in the future is the root of anxiety and fear; the present is deeply sufficient.
- Beware of those who need to tell the world their name.
- With my divorce, God scrapped the first draft of the design of my life. (Dorothée Sölle)
- The one who grasps loses, but to hold with open hands is to keep.
- Strange though it seems, people usually fail when they are on the verge of success.
- The moment you make anything of your "accomplishments," you die spiritually.
- If you have a heart, you are redeemable.
- There are moments to which one can look back and realize that everything led to that point and everything flows from it. Spiritual direction helps a person prepare for such moments, encourages remembrance of them, and provides supportive accountability for living with the consequences.
- Our crying need is to establish creative distance from our own selves.
- The human predicament is rooted in our unwillingness to affirm that our existence is a gift.
- Every life-plan that focuses on one's self is dangerous, for it makes small ideas and petty adventures the center of the

cosmos. Our hope is in recognizing the absurdity of such a posturing.

- The flesh Saint Paul decries is not the body, but the lifestyle of the secular world.
- We can be at home only in God, in whom we already live and move and have our being.
- Without internal purgation, all of our doing is lethal.
- Depression is the shroud that hides our wounded pride.
- Pride is the arrogance of using God's gifts as though they were our own.
- The last illusion in this life is the belief that anything can resist decay, and thus that death does not have dominion.
- This society so forms us in the squirrel cage of doing that we find satisfaction simply in the squeak of the wheel.
- Rejecting mother and father and sisters and brothers, as Jesus modeled, means to reject the social sources that are determined to assign us an alien identity.
- Tragic is a lost life—as when Ahab became obsessed with a missing leg. Equally tragic is when we become preoccupied with what in the larger scheme is trivial.
- Suicide, which all of us practice in some form, is the insanity of getting back at others by throwing away our own lives.
- For some people, suicide is an attempt to throw back their life-ticket in the face of God—for not existing.
- A tormenting sense of unworthiness is the root of hatred.
- Those of us puzzled by what *original sin* means need only acknowledge our tendency to turn everything to our own advantage.
- The primal sin is "me"ism—the dangerous addiction of *I, me,* and *mine.*
- The human dilemma is not so much our sins as our sinfulness.
- Jealousy is the cause of hurting others—and ourselves.

- While sins are what strain our relationship with God, Sin is what ruptures it.
- The Fall means that we pass on the hurts we receive by perpetuating them.
- Movie stars often turn out badly—until their beauty fades.
- We seem obsessed with filling our emptiness with the graffiti of speech, for noise is a temporary way of escaping the God who waits in the silence.
- For each of us, there will come a midnight hour when we must unmask.
- Sooner or later, each of us will be assigned to the night shift.
- Sin is an identity more than an act.
- Sins are the inevitable result of ambition, the need to control, and the desire to be thought well of.
- Taste the hours of darkness, know silence, do humble service, go a little hungry, taste your own poverty, and then things begin to settle into perspective.
- Your idea of me may be simply a fabrication from materials you have borrowed from others and yourself, reflecting what you think I think of you.
- Our society seems intent on training us for doing, achieving, and performing, while what really matters is being, growing, and loving widely and wildly.
- Experience the night, the loneliness, the silence, the remoteness, the seclusion, the emptiness, the poverty, the futility—indeed the silliness of your life—and you finally learn who you are.
- The truly poor in spirit dwell further in, on down the road, where only mad people dwell and wild owls screech in the night. (Matthew Kelty)
- Although the demons lurking in the shadows of each person's depth have concrete faces, the color chart from which we paint them is marked envy, jealousy, anger, and hate.

- A society almost infantile in its need for something to drink, to chew, to taste, to suck, or to smoke, is scarcely one to encourage important living. (Kelty)
- The Holy Spirit is the principle of unrest that births our unfulfilled longings.
- It is useless to dream of the perfect situation, for there will always be someone before whom our humility is challenged, our patience taxed, and our weaknesses stressed into visibility.
- Relationships are such an inevitable source of suffering that none of us can escape being deeply wounded.
- Without God, anxiety is our only certainty.
- It is a trap to think that the commitment to remain uncommitted makes a person free.
- One best finds the presence and action of the Spirit in the cracks of human life, history, world, and church.
- In being nothing, having nothing, and wanting nothing, one abounds in everything.
- The unfathomable abyss within each soul is where God's struggle with nonbeing comes into focus.
- Human nature resides in the will; the rest is animal.
- Living is exhausting when each morning a person awakes with the feeling of needing to prove that he or she is worth being with.
- We seem born with a deficit account, destined to spend our lives justifying our right to be alive.
- Unless one knows oneself as rooted in God, life is an endless cycle of starting over and over again in order to establish one's identity.
- Things begin to go wrong when we hallow freedom more than compassion.
- Only God has any right to determine our identity.

CONVERSION
(Justification)

- Our need for conversion follows from the fact that our acting is always from the inside out.
- To go up, one must first go down.
- In our society, the lifestyle most ripe for conversion is the one that blinds us with a desire for ceaseless motion, the constant need for achievement, the crude hunger for results, and the insistence upon tangible success—for underneath is the frenzied state of feeling unworthy.
- A mark of true conversion is when a person can rejoice over the gifts and achievements of others.
- Release from being drawn backward by the past gives us freedom in the present to go forward into the future.
- Protestants focus on forgiveness as freeing a person to follow Christ; Catholics focus on the seeds of the Holy Spirit planted in baptism as the power to imitate Christ. Monks focus on contemplation as enabling an intimacy with Christ. As usual, all three are right.
- Pardon and healing are two sides of the same coin.
- Conversion is evidenced in recognizing that our finest sensitivity usually relates to hurts we once received. For example, from feeling unaccepted can be born a compassion to identify with the rejected and marginal.
- The will, as mistress of all our powers, must be well trained, or she will be unable to call us back to ourselves.
- Just as in our first birth, rebirth cannot take place without pain.
- As the South African Truth and Reconciliation Commission bore witness, it is the promise of forgiveness that gives us the courage to confess.
- The cross is the cosmic symbol that human sin entails divine suffering.

- When a person finds himself/herself unable to rise from a fall, that person reaches the point where denying God is unthinkable.
- God's favorite game is "Loser Wins All," where the person with the poorest cards does best.
- Another of God's prized games is called "Lost and Found."
- The loss of ego is the price charged for self-fulfillment.
- There must be a homecoming for prodigals, or else Christianity is a lie.
- In forgiveness, God devours our guilt.
- The only way to transcend the world is through service to it, born of refusing any longer to be its slave.
- To be in but not of the world entails rejecting the world's definition of me and what I need to be about. The contact which proved decisive, the path unexpectedly opened, the other path closed, the thing we felt compelled to say, the letter we felt compelled to write. It is as if a hidden directive power, personal, living, free, was working through circumstances and often against our intention or desire; pressing us in a certain direction, and molding us to a certain design. (Evelyn Underhill)
- Nothing is as useful for testing one's Christian faith as an insult.
- A mark of Christian healing is the abandonment of any need to compete.
- The urgent question today is not so much whether God exists, but whether Christ has the power to transform.
- To seek God is the finest proof of having been found.
- God's most massive action is to wink at my sins.
- Once you realize that God knows everything about you, you are free.
- I envy these words on the tombstone of an unnamed grave: "He did all right."
- What matters is not what others or I think of me, but that I am God's.

GRACE
(Forgiveness and Empowerment)

- Grace remains grace only as long as we lay no claim to it, do not attempt to possess it, and never feel that we deserve it.
- God is the length, breadth, height, and depth of everything.
- Grace is simply an attribute of the God who is graciousness.
- The peace that the world cannot give nor disturb is like the surrender of a sleeping child in a loving parent's arms.
- Grace is an event, never an achievement.
- Since as my Creator I owe God all, in giving Himself as my Redeemer, I doubly owe what nothing can repay. (Bernard of Clairvaux)
- How can the idea of reward make sense when God enables us to be who we really yearned to be all along?
- The reward for loving God is God.
- Weakness is the potentiality for grace.
- Since the Fall is the declaration that all the injuries of the world are interconnected, we are called to take them upon ourselves so as to filter them through God's forgiveness.
- Being made receptive is itself a divine gift.
- In everything that is worthwhile, the initiative is God's.
- Redemption means seeing one's self through God's eyes.
- Grace establishes an impulse to love without constant need for feedback or return.
- Human merits are actually divine gifts.
- The King, full of mercy and goodness, very far from chastising me, embraces me with love, makes me eat at his table, serves me with his own hands, gives me the key to his treasures, converses and delights himself with me incessantly, in a thousand upon thousand ways, treating me in all respects as His favorite. (Brother Lawrence)

- I shall never forget spending months building a six-foot glider, then launching it from the water tower on the hill overlooking my town, in ecstasy over its one-minute flight.
- God lives in us by choice.
- Grace is the amazing gift of being freed from one's self.
- The greatest gift God can give us is the love that we ought to have for God. (François Fénelon)
- The Incarnation is God's promise that "We're in this together."
- Jesus is both physician and lover.
- Evelyn Underhill tells the story of the boy down the road watching her work in her flower garden. She gave him some flowers to take home. Soon he was back. "What do you want now?" she asked. "I don't want anything," he replied. "I just want to be with you."
- We believe in order to attain knowledge; we do not attain knowledge in order to believe. (Augustine)
- In the Christ event, God experiences our return as the prodigal son.
- One can freely give only when one has freely received.
- Practicing the Presence is a matter of showing the Divine Guest around the house of one's mind and the yard of one's living.
- Silence is the posture of listening.
- "You are my Lord; apart from you I have no good thing" (Ps. 16:2, NIV).
- Grace is a free lesson in how to dance with God.

LOVE
(Being Loved and Loving)

- Promising to love "forever" expresses in quantitative terms the meaning of eternity.
- God's unconditional love is the unbearable compliment.
- For better and for worse, we love as we have been loved.

- All sin is reducible to saying no to love.
- True monogamy is the commitment to belong to God alone.
- The greatest happiness in life is the conviction that we are loved—loved for ourselves, or rather, loved in spite of ourselves. (Victor Hugo)
- Perhaps someday, somewhere, I will hug my mother and tease her playfully when she picks at my faults.
- To be loved by the God who knows everything about me is to be freed of all pretenses; from then on, everything else is thankfulness.
- The Christian life does not begin with the command to love, but as a response to having been loved.
- The best analogy for the madness of the Christian's relationship with God is the foolishness of a teenager falling in love for the first time.
- Those who know themselves to be loved cannot do otherwise than to love. (Catherine of Siena)
- God's love brings an indestructible peace and an unearthly serenity, making us immune to gossip, ridicule, persecution, hurt, injury, sickness, and misfortune; these fall from one's soul like water over a stone.
- Loving for its own sake is like participating in great music.
- I am suspicious of any love prompted by hope of gain. (Bernard of Clairvaux)
- God is not loved without reward but without thought of reward.
- Inner holiness is our love of *God* and neighbor; exterior holiness is our love of God and *neighbor*.
- To love a stranger as oneself is to love the stranger within oneself.
- Loving one's enemy is so that the enemy may discover how to love.

- God's name satisfies our thirst, just as a person delights in hearing the name of his or her lover.
- Love is its own sufficient reason for loving.
- Loving other people is much easier when one loses a taste for the lifestyle in which they flourish; otherwise one will harbor secret longings for their success.
- A test of the love that God intends us to show is whether it operates regardless of whether its identity is known.
- A sign of a faithful soul is uneasiness about whether one has responded sufficiently to God's love.
- "I love you" is never a redundant statement.
- Play is the wrestling sport of love.
- Christian love is pure when it is not based upon feelings, just as pure faith is believing without seeing.
- I love because I love, for I am being loved in order to love being loving.
- Where there is love, there is no toil. (Augustine)
- *Eros*, as an act of the emotions, is narrow in scope; *agape*, as an act of the will, has the universe as its scope.
- Since God is immanent within everyone, in loving all people, we love God.
- Love lays claim to others, refusing to let them go until they are loving.
- Love refuses everyone the right to be one's enemy.

SALVATION
(To Render Healthy and Whole)

- The word *salvation* brings together a number of derivations: "salve" (to heal), "salt" (to preserve), "shalom" (to render peaceful), and "silence" (to center).
- Salvation is a process, the center of which is the transformation of motivation through gratitude.

- Since how one remembers past events determines one's present, salvation requires a reconstitution of memory.
- Willingness to be last is possible only when one loses one's appetite for the game of first and last.
- When the Spirit changes one's disposition, even one's appearance is changed.
- Faith is a revolution of the mind in which false consciousness is abandoned.
- Faith is the trust of handing one's self over to God for safekeeping.
- Faith is the risk of having by giving away, loving without feeling, hoping without evidence, and believing without knowing.
- New life begins when, in our empty defenselessness, we fall into the abyss of God's mercy, shattered as our guilt is devoured by love. Then all becomes serene, for now I am permitted to be weak, other sinners appear to be brothers, my hurts blossom into wonder, the defects of others no longer irritate me, and, strange though it seems, I appear to be a kind and gentle friend of all. (André Louf)
- Like Jesus, may we astonish others by being about God's business.
- Everything changes when we can believe that God is on our side.
- God is the soul's bridegroom. (Bernard of Clairvaux)
- I am created to do something or to be something for which no one else is created. . . . God knows me and calls me by name. I can never be thrown away. If I am in sickness, my sickness may serve [God]. If I am in sorrow, my sorrow may serve [God]. My sickness or perplexity or sorrow may be necessary causes of some great end, which is quite beyond us. [God] does nothing in vain. [God] may prolong my life, take away my friends. [God] may throw me among strangers. [God] may make me feel desolate, make my spirits sink, hide

the future from me—still [God] knows what [God] is about.
(John Henry Newman)

- Solitude is a state of mind rather than an absence of others.
- "To be" means that doing and having have become means.
- It is not perfection that one should seek, but God.
- Abandonment in God is a farewell to all you thought you loved, and a giving away of what once seemed so dear, in order to discover that in the eyes of God you are the one who is loved and dear.
- To be healed entails healing within one's own self the wounds festering the world.
- No wonder Bernard of Clairvaux is beloved by Catholics and Protestants alike. He knew anxiety and loneliness as our lot, reason's inability to discover the meaning of life, anguish in the face of death, weakness as a capacity for grace, grace as indispensable for our transformation, body as the soul's companion, sensuality as an expression of divine love, our perennial homesickness for God, the feminine dimensions of the Divine, love as the movement from humility to ecstasy, and our life's pilgrimage as an ascension into God.
- Eternity is the Sabbath of sabbaths.
- What more could one want than to be God's friend?
- Blessed is the transition from defensiveness to the yearning to undo the hurts one has caused others.
- Vows are more the acceptance of a gift than the undertaking of an obligation.
- It is through the Spirit that one recognizes oneself as the Father's daughter, and the spouse and sister of his Son. (Bernard of Clairvaux)
- To will one thing is to know the purity of an undivided heart.
- If our only need is to be filled, used, and made whole by God, then we can no longer really be threatened or hurt.

- Truly to be is to do and let be, without fear of consequences.
- The relationship of God and soul is that of sharing one inheritance, one table, one house, one flesh, and one bed.
- The soul is that growing center where reason, memory, and imagination converge in a commitment called will.
- Saints are like roommates—available for intimate midnight sharing.
- When God declares me to be unique, my obsession with comparing myself with others becomes meaningless, and with it, my feeling of inadequacy.

SANCTIFICATION
(Growth in Grace)

- The Christian is simply someone in the process of becoming restored to being a normal human being.
- Holiness means being a whole person.
- Christians are to be artisans of peace and adventurers in joy.
- A centered person is not hard to sense.
- The ordinary gifts of the Spirit are love, joy, peace, patience, kindness, generosity, faithfulness, gentleness, and self-control (Gal 5:22-23). The presence of these characteristics is the test of whether any extraordinary gifts might be of the Spirit.
- Do not get drawn into the negativity of others, but draw it out of them with a compassionate "nevertheless."
- Since peace is the primal mark of God's presence in one's soul, we cannot lose it—only our awareness of it.
- Adoption by God brings transformation, for no longer am I:
  - –lonely, for I am assured of Christ's companionship.
  - –jealous, for I am the heir of God.
  - –covetous, because I no longer need anything.
  - –angry, because I am forgiven and accepted unconditionally.
  - –sad, for I have been promised eternal happiness.
  - –anxious, for I can rest in the providence of God.
  - –unloved, for God is caressing me.

- Brother Lawrence yearned to do good things for God in such a way that God might not know who did them.
- The purpose of all discipline is freedom.
- Beware of any spirituality that stresses feelings rather than God's action.
- The life of the Christian consists of little else than holy desire. (Augustine)
- The mark of the Christian is peace flowing from a tranquil center.
- Only with Christ is it once and for all; with everything else, it is over and over again.
- Since we can choose the feelings we will allow, nourish, and follow, the trick is wanting to.
- Spirituality is not one characteristic of the Christian life; it *is* the Christian life.
- Remembering is the primary form of faithfulness.
- The Christian is one who, upon waking during the night, has immediate words for God, and first thing in the morning speaks thankfully.
- The Christian has no need to pass beyond the point of longing, hoping, waiting, and anticipating.
- Since the call to holiness involves every sphere of one's life, it is actually the call to sanctify the whole world.
- Faith is a permanent revolution of the mind and heart.

THE CHRISTIAN LIFE

- Christian life seems so simple: to do for God what you commonly do for yourself.
- Put another way, one need only act from a centered soul.
- Everything repeated is habit-forming; so it is with faith.
- To be a Christian is to live on the edge of one's deepest yearnings.
- It is easier to do something than to be someone.

- The one who knows when enough is enough will always have enough.
- Each morning, a new person arises.
- The Christian works not for comfort, but so as not to be a burden.
- Prayer is lifting the agony of the world into God.
- Is it too much for me to hope that, before I die, there shall be about me hints of integrity?
- Be open to interruptions as the knocking of God.
- Never permit a peaceful coexistence between love and selfishness, truth and falsehood, life and death.
- Incarnation is the Christian's model for engagement in the world.
- One must be faithful to the God both within and without.
- Be watchful to catch negative impulses before they develop into a chain of thought, desire, and action.
- What matters is not so much what we do as the spirit with which we do it.
- Nonviolence rarely changes the heart of the oppressor immediately; but it does something immediately to the souls who use nonviolence.
- By saving others but not himself, Jesus models the life of absolute living for others.
- Saint Francis treated any mob confronting him as a mob of kings.
- It is impossible to be half a Christian.
- Smile naturally at strangers so that they know they are not alone.
- The Christian's life-project is to form a second nature out of habits constructed slowly over the course of a lifetime, until the mind of Christ becomes the natural way of living.
- By being rooted steadfastly in God, one can be flexible but not relativistic, committed but not rigid, confronting but not offensive, forgiving but not soft, and witnessing but not manipulative.

- Blessed is the one who is able to recognize the vast difference between pleasure and joy.
- We begin to get the right idea when we are able to boil potatoes to the glory of God.
- What matters is to do the difficult thing, or to give the unpopular message, in the uncongenial place. (Evelyn Underhill)
- Neither sins nor virtues are acts but states, from which acts automatically follow.
- Who sweeps a room as for [God's] laws makes that and th' action fine. (George Herbert)
- Christians dream of what they cannot see, believe what they do not know, and are committed to what they do not understand—with a delightful smile on their faces.
- God sells holiness for a very low price: a piece of bread, a coat of little value, a cup of cold water, and the random change in one's pocket.
- The Christian is incorrigibly pessimistic about the human race, and incurably romantic about God.
- Lyric simplicity, silent wonder, and unfathomable mystery are the daily food of the Christian.
- Tests the Christian would like to pass:
  - Willingness to lay down one's life for Christ.
  - Ability to pick up a pin from the motive of pure love.
  - Contentment in being simply a cell in the body of Christ.
- Spirit is the "within" of all things.
- Sexuality is the joyous intersection of spirit and flesh.
- The presence of God is all around us, in us, among us, in the hills and in the woods, in the blight and in the burden, in the sorrows and in the laughter, so that we can laugh with Christ and shed tears with him. Walk on the waters, and go up to Tabor, in the garden of Olives and at

Cana. With him all the way, all the time. And ours is the
kingdom. (Paul Paulsen)
- God's preference seems to be for speaking through the
  stranger.
- Happy are those who know how to put their whole soul
  into whatever they do—and are.
- Work, well done, is expressive prayer.
- Prayer usually begins as an I/thou dialogue, and, when
  talked out, ends as a union of silence.
- The early desert Christians discovered these key weapons
  for defeating the "demons": fasting, vigils, prayer, and
  scripture, resulting in a contempt for money, absence of
  anger, loss of conceit, love of the poor, generosity to all,
  hospitality for the stranger, calmness in threat, and humility
  in all things; in a phrase, they were loyal to Christ.
- It sounds like very little, but to please God, one needs only
  to live well.
- To be made in God's image is to be creation's cocreator.
- The difference between Christians and secular folks centers
  in their motivation.
- When done for God, work is more valuable than the
  results.
- If the gifts of the Spirit are love, joy, peace, patience,
  kindness, generosity, faithfulness, gentleness, and self-
  control, what more could one want?
- When bewildered by seasons of dryness or depression or
  weariness, simply tell God that you cannot feel her love,
  that you are empty and cold, that you miss her, and that her
  apparent game playing wearies you.
- Thérèse of Lisieux ("The Little Flower") identified her
  "little way" as seeing the small tasks of daily life as having a
  crucial part in the total harmony of the universe, and, so seen,
  needing to be done with love and the most concentrated of

attention, for they are the most important things in one's world.

- Evidence of Christ's presence is that "the blind receive their sight, the lame walk, the lepers are cleansed, the deaf hear, the dead are raised, and the poor have good news brought to them" (Matt. 11:5).
- Train your mouth to say what is in your heart.
- A minister friend, dying of cancer, gave this farewell to his colleagues:

> My illness has been long and painful, the most difficult and challenging experience of my life. I want you to know how much your hugs and kisses, your support and concern, your touches and squeezes, your letters and cards, your calls and visits, and all the other things you have done to help me through this time, have meant to me. Your tremendous support and my faith in Jesus have been my daily strength and peace. I must leave behind now all my diplomas, degrees, plaques, certificates, awards, honors, pins, medals, citations, mementos, and achievements, for I am called to stand empty-handed before my God. It will be the death of Jesus on the cross, and that alone, which will open for me the gates of Paradise.

- Work as if all depends on you; pray as if it all depends on God. (Ignatius of Loyola)
- Gracious and holy God, give us wisdom to perceive you, diligence to seek you, patience to wait for you, eyes to behold you, a heart to meditate on you, and a life to proclaim you, through the power of the spirit of Jesus Christ our Savior. Amen. (Saint Benedict)
- One is committed to "a way of life," while "lifestyle" is the contingent consequence.
- The goal of eternity is perfect ecstasy.
- Treat the body as the soul's good and faithful comrade. (Bernard of Clairvaux)
- There is no ground for ill will if one no longer covets.

- To become as a little child is to begin again to savor the immediacy of the present.
- Since every person is a potential neighbor, there are no strangers.
- In being a person for God, Jesus was a person for others.
- The indelibility forged by ongoing repetition is our only hope of countering the plague of forgetfulness.
- By intersecting *eros* with *agape*, the Christian life becomes marinated in sober inebriation.
- A desert father sold the book that told him to sell all he had on behalf of the poor.
- The gift that brings joy is the freedom to forget oneself.
- When mysticism and revolution embrace, we have the makings of a Christian.
- Concern for how, or when, or how much is to live under the old law of duty.
- Spirituality begins with the transition from talking *about* God to talking *with* God.
- When the appeal of ambition, status, possession, and influence is lost, so is the ability to envy, and thus to have enemies.
- Instead of being proud that his strong city could not be moved, Saint Francis was thankful to God that it had not been dropped. (G. K. Chesterton)
- What matters is the desire to do the most onerous chores to the glory of God.
- Christian friendship includes trees, rocks, the Milky Way, and the frog under the front porch.
- Christian life is best understood not as obedience to God's will, but as faithfulness to God's yearning.
- Worship is the dress rehearsal for acting out daily the sacramental gestures of God.
- Once we realize how little we can get along with, everything becomes different.

- To accumulate is to broaden; to simplify is to deepen.
- Worry is never useful, so anxiety is a bad investment of one's energy.
- Whatever we permit to rob us of the present steals what can never be replaced.
- To be loved by God is to become totally open to the world and others, for one no longer depends on their affection in return.
- Paradise is the experience of an endless yearning that lacks nothing, an inebriation that is sobriety, and a loving that no longer aches.
- The Christian is a person of hyphens, as in being a warrior-monk or a revolutionary-saint.
- A steward is one who can own as if he or she does not.
- The ability to distinguish need from desire is the mark of a redeemed appetite.
- For those watching from outside, the Christian life might appear heroic: as patience in the face of panic, endurance outlasting doubt, silence when misjudged, appreciation of criticism, suppression of ambition, resistance to resentment, and perseverance through the drudgery of uncongenial and unrewarding work. Viewed from within, it is simply God's gift.
- Each of us must try to figure out the question that God is likely to ask on the last day. I gamble that mine will be this: Have you lived deeply, pondered greatly, loved passionately, birthed much beauty, and cared most about those who haven't been able to do any of this?

THE CHURCH

- I am a daughter of the church. (Teresa of Avila)
- In the heart of the church, my mother, I will be love. (Thérèse of Lisieux)

- The church's primal task is to be a training course in the art of loving.
- For both society and individuals, the church is called to eliminate escape, so that finally all must look in a mirror.
- There must always be an *ecclesiola* ("little church") within the *ecclesia* ("big church"), externally as an intimate group, and internally as an embraced soul.
- The church is the body of Christ so that the world can become the fullness of God.
- Our innermost craving is to belong, for which baptism is our certificate of adoption.
- Perhaps God's finest miracle is in making the mildew-smelling church building by the gas station an indispensable cell in the body of Christ.
- The church's greatest failing may be the tendency to make the gospel so complex that not doing it is understandable.
- Church and soul are twin brides.
- There can be no salvation outside the church, for wherever archaeologists find evidence of humans, it is as a communal expression of the spiritual.
- When Christians are knit together organically as a body, it is not difficult to understand that praying for others touches each of us with belonging and healing.
- Wherever there are people, there is work; and where there is work, the Christian is the church humanizing the world.

THE MONASTERY

- Being a monk (male and female) is simply a wholehearted way of being a Christian.
- What makes monks different is not that they are infinitely lonely; the difference is what they do with that loneliness. (Kelty)
- Whenever a monk says he is not finding self-fulfillment in the monastery, he will leave very soon; when a monk's concern is about prayer, no matter how much he may

complain about the difficulty, the monk will stay. (George Hillery Jr.)

- There is much to be learned from the Buddhist's life as a pilgrim—the homeless one, the wanderer, the beggar. He comes to the monastery with only a bamboo hat, straw sandals, and the clothes he wears, with a paper bag hung from his neck in which is a razor, begging bowl, several books, and enough money for his funeral. He is turned away, more than once. But if he perseveres, he is given a three-foot-by-five-foot space in the meditation hall, where he stays and sleeps. There he is to find all that matters.
- Monastic training begins when one feels the burden of one's brothers or sisters.
- Our desert parents regarded the monk's proper dress as whatever garment could be thrown outside for three days without anyone taking it.
- The monastery anticipates a universe remade in God, whose poles are love and praise.
- Silence establishes around a person that zone of peace where God's presence can become irresistible.
- At the crack of dawn, touched by that special moment between dark and light, the monk stands on the frontier between the world that is passing away and the world that is being birthed.
- Realism suggests that deep Christian living may not be for everyone, but it is for those called to be a subversive leaven capable of driving the rest of us up the wall.
- Monastic vows, as a commitment to search for God, are impossible if God has not already found that person.
- Mutual hurting is so inevitable that in the monastery mutual forgiveness is a daily task.
- The purpose of the monastery is to make people lovers.
- The vow of stability is the outward pledge of perseverance, insuring that we will not evade the cross.

- Without vows, the Christian idea of turning worldly values upside down remains a quaint anachronism.
- Being a monk means daily consenting to have one's idols successively smashed.
- To symbolize it all, with bare feet on Ash Wednesday, drink an Advent toast as if it were Christmas Eve.
- The monk withdraws from the world in order to go into training, acknowledging in his soul the immense yearning that runs through every speck of creation.
- While the monastery may be a way of life for some, it can be a spiritual hospital for all.
- When asked what he would do if he saw a brother dozing during communal prayers, Abba Poemen, a desert father, replied, "I would put his head on my knees and let him rest."
- Despite their legendary asceticism, the first Trappist monasteries reserved times each day for what was called useless activity of sheer gratuitousness, thereby providing the detachment by which daily life could regain lightness, charm, and joy.
- The nearness of Christmas can be measured by the degree to which monks become more playful.
- For some, the monastery is for life; for the rest, it is a reminder.

CHAPTER 7

✠

SPIRITUAL DIRECTION
AND CHURCH RENEWAL

SPIRITUAL DIRECTION AS THE NORM
FOR AUTHENTIC PASTORAL MINISTRY

The rediscovery of spiritual direction as a central resource for the pilgrimage of each Christian brings with it the lament that few able spiritual directors exist within the contemporary church. Therefore, the restoration of direction to a central position must go hand in hand with the discovery of a means of training directors within a revised church structure. Training directors and providing direction must become primary activities of every local church, functioning as two sides of the same urgent reality. For this to happen, we need first to address head-on the fear and reluctance of many clergy about spiritual direction. This timidity is understandable because few Protestant pastors have had any seminary training in direction, and only a few have desired it sufficiently to search out available resources. Most Catholic priests, on the other hand, have studied spiritual direction in seminary, yet Vatican II has thrown into question the method by which they received such direction. As a result, few experiential models are available today for clergy.

Some clergy, on the other hand, have been exposed to nondirective counseling, especially as made available through Clinical

Pastoral Education (CPE), usually in a hospital setting. This method, modeled upon secular counseling techniques, has often rendered clergy uneasy about doing spiritual direction at two crucial points. In contrast to nondirective counseling, spiritual direction, as we have seen, is far more intent on formation. And in contrast to the purported neutrality of secular counseling, the Christian director is most often involved in contextual direction. Instead of attempting to function without presupposition, Christian spiritual direction is unabashedly theological in nature. It rests firmly on the axiom that grace, experienced as the free gift of unconditional love, is the restorative ingredient necessary for someone to undergo deep and genuine healing. Consequently, unless pastors come to understand and be tutored in Christian spiritual direction, they will continue to regard themselves, at best, as no more than amateur crisis counselors. As I recall my experience in CPE, the warning throughout was the urgency for us to make professional referrals if a counseling problem entailed more than a surface sorting to help the person make an informed and rational decision. Without decrying the value of either counseling or therapy, I insist that spiritual direction is different. Even when professional counseling or therapy is needed, spiritual direction should still be sought or continued in order to provide a theological context for one's overall pilgrimage.

Consequently, for the church to be renewed through spiritual direction, what is needed is a shift in clergy self-identity. Rather than regarding themselves timidly as unprofessional counselors in a field not their own, clergy need to understand and lay claim to the field in which they have the grounding and capacity—that of *professional spiritual directors.* Clergy need to provide an indispensable context that other professionals are not trained to give—that of "meaning," theologically understood. At the heart of ministry, then, the pastor-priest is a *functional theologian in residence,* exploring and leading others into the mysterious depths of theological/spiritual existence. So much is this the case that even renewing the activities usually associated with ministry depends upon discerning them as indispensable ingredients within spiritual direction. Thus, for example, the primary purpose for preaching the Word and celebrating the sacraments is to ignite the desire to grow in disciplined faith through structures of spiritual direction made normative in each congregation. The primary test of authentic pastoring is the spiritual maturation of one's congregation, individually and corporately, as the body of Christ

Restructuring the Local Congregation

In my book *Worlds within a Congregation: Dealing with Theological Diversity*, I developed a new model for the local church. It is based on the emergence of alternative subcongregations from the five Theological Worlds, which we have already explored in chapter 2. This is done by determining, in turn, how these alternative Worlds provide contrasting ways to carry out spiritual direction through preaching, worship, sacraments, Christian education, administration, and evangelism. In contrast, Wesley tended to organize small groups pragmatically rather than theologically, preferring such factors as age, gender, location, and marital status. My preference is to organize groups theologically, using the "Theological Worlds Inventory," an abbreviated version of which is found in Appendix 5 of this book. Groups can be formed of members reflecting the same World, or they can be a microcosm of the congregation as a whole. However these groups are organized, attention always needs to be paid to the diversity of individuals. Throughout, it is helpful for the leadership to be informed by the proven track records of the Wesleyan groups (Covenant Discipleship), the Cursillo movement (or The Walk to Emmaus® movement), and Alcoholics Anonymous.

The key question regarding church renewal is not so much how to attract persons into sampling what a particular congregation has to offer. (Success at that point is likely to be no nobler than appealing to self-interest, promising in some way to supplement the life someone already has.) The real key is a congregation's answer to this question: What do they expect of persons after they join? At stake in the answer is the quality of the church's existence. In more conservative churches, the answer tends to express a treadmill of ongoing evangelism. The task is to get others outside the congregation to join so that they can seek out others to join, who in turn will seek others. Success tends to be measured by a "doing" external to the congregation's life, measured by the number of persons "brought in." In more liberal churches, on the other hand, the answer centers in giving new persons "something to do." Inclusivity here is a "doing" internal to the congregation's life. Since people like to feel appreciated, useful, and important, inviting individuals to take responsibility for specific tasks is regarded as the best way for assimilation to occur. But whatever the strategy used for making the transition from entering to participating, it is to no avail if it does not lead to inclusivity through being. Put another way, the question needs to be rewritten: Who will persons become after joining? Without this spiritual center, "doing" is little more than maintaining the church's structural mechanics, externally or internally.

This spiritual center as the church's primal and defining task can be expressed in different ways. Discipleship entails moving toward the perfection of loving intent through the means of grace. Spirituality is the name for living out one's salvation as wholeness. However this living is expressed, the primary activities of the church's life need to become a means to this end. Then one begins to experience at soul depth the paradox that Paul understood well: "Work out your own salvation with fear and trembling; for it is God who is at work in you, enabling you both to will and to work for his good pleasure" (Phil. 2:12-13). Thus, everything depends on me, yet not me; all depends on God, but not without me. Or as Ignatius of Loyola expressed the paradox, "Pray as if everything depends on God, and act as if it all depends on you."

Clergy As the Primal Catalyst

Spiritual renewal at the local church level is most likely to succeed if it begins with the pastor-priest. Clergy have the authority best able to author new approaches to ministry at the congregational level. Furthermore, clergypersons might be threatened by a proposal coming full-blown from a layperson. Thus, the laity's initial role might best be in the form of a gentle suggestion, or a sharing of ideas, or a volunteering of time and energy to work with the pastor on a perceived issue or problem. The Cursillo (or The Walk to Emmaus®) movement wisely requires the pastor of a church to attend the weekend experience before it becomes available for any laypersons of that church. Similarly, the first step in refashioning the local church around the dynamics of spiritual direction is for the pastor-priest to receive serious spiritual direction.

This book is designed as a manual to make clear what needs to be involved in such spiritual direction. Acting as a catalyst for reforming the church around spiritual direction will not be easy, for in this process the clergyperson must be open to vulnerability, a trait not generally identified with clergy. Spiritual direction entails the desire to practice theological living. Put another way, the pastor/priest is called to be a "resident theologian" who through sermons, sacraments, teaching, administering, and counseling ignites and nurtures persons toward a maturity of faith. And these activities become most lively and effective when they are birthed from the pastor's own needs, taken seriously. As I have insisted throughout this book, Christian living cannot occur in the absence of supportive accountability. Thus, the spiritually renewed church will be one in which this dynamic operates as the fundamental goal for all its activities. While reading about spiritual direction can be profitable, there is no substitute for learning it by action-reflection training.

THE INITIAL GROUP

After the pastor experiences a period of solid spiritual direction, he or she is ready for the next step: selecting carefully from the congregation a group of eight to ten persons most likely to welcome an invitation to explore what it means to live the Christian faith seriously. Facilitated by the pastor, this group needs to develop trust and depth by sharing faith stories. This is followed by a twofold task: (1) the group needs to help each member discern what personal steps are needed in order to move toward spiritual maturity; (2) the group needs to create a covenant out of these composite needs whereby as a whole they might better function as a healthy cell in the body of Christ. Both of these tasks should be updated as insight and depth emerge through the group process.

To illustrate, one member might discern that the supportive accountability he or she needs is to set aside half an hour for contemplation each day before leaving for work. Another member might discern the need for the group's supportive accountability in mustering sufficient courage to face a tattered marriage. As a corporate covenant, the group might commit itself to pray daily for each other by name, or promise to celebrate the love feast each time the group meets. The goal throughout, then, is the transformation of each person, and, as a group, increased depth in Christian life and living.

The ingredients for transformation include prayer, contemplation, meditation, sacred reading, worship, sacraments, fasting, and deeds of compassion and justice—all under the guidance of the Holy Spirit. Again we hear the insistent refrain: The requirement for such spiritual growth is *supportive accountability*—through one's spiritual brothers and sisters, to one's own committed self-discipline for God. Through this process comes a spiritual expansion of depth and breadth and height through commitment, serving as a foundation for living as if the kingdom of God is already present.

INQUIRER GROUPS FOLLOWED BY
COVENANT GROUPS

The third stage can begin when members of this initial group have attained sufficient spiritual maturity for each person to be assigned as a mentor ("sponsor" or "partner in faith") to each person in an "inquirers group." This group is intended for persons interested in learning more about the Christian faith, without any commitment being necessary at this point. The projected number of weekly exploratory sessions needs to be set in advance, perhaps for three months. The content of these open-ended classes is a sharing of faith stories (or autobiographies) within a context of pledged confidentiality. The focus is on two questions: "Who am I?" and "What do I need at this point in my pilgrimage?" The last scheduled session might best be given closure by the pastor, facilitating a discernment as to which persons have had enough and which ones wish to continue into a second half of the group's life. In this half there occurs a more intimate preparation in anticipation of receiving baptism and/or confirmation. If these sessions are well-organized, relating tradition with experience through one-with-one and group spiritual direction, two things tend to happen: (1) many of the newly confirmed will be eager to continue as a group; (2) many of the mentors, having received spiritual direction in the initial group and provided it in the inquirers group, will be ready to organize and serve as enablers for a group of their own, similar to the one in which their action-reflection training occurred. These persons, at least at the beginning, tend to work more confidently when teamed with another person as cofacilitators. Membership for these new groups can be assigned from names gained through an invitation to the entire church membership. In other situations, it may work best to have the facilitators recruit for their group from among their own friends and acquaintances.

SPIRITUAL DIRECTION LEADERSHIP

Qualities indicating promise for becoming a group leader relate to those characterizing a mature spiritual director—"creative listening, deep caring, open vulnerability, intimacy as 'being with,' openness to alternatives, ability to confront, being theologically informed, being capable of discerning what is behind the apparent, and freedom to encourage others to do things their own way."[1] In addition, the group leader should make strides toward having "a sufficient sense of self-acceptance; security from easy intimidation by anger, silence, or rejection; detachment from excessive ego needs; be at home with and excited about his [or her] own Theological World; understand oneself as a Christian on a pilgrimage; be a person of God; and have one's own spiritual director."[2]

If there is doubt as to whether a particular congregation or group has the willingness and ability to begin at the level we have been describing, an alternative way of beginning would be with some version of "dinners for ten." Each person or couple takes a turn in providing a modest meal and initiating conversation with the intent of getting to know each other as church members. Such a group will socialize at first. But after several sessions, the cofacilitators are usually able to prod the group into deeper sharing by using prepared questions and invitations. These are examples: "Describe a time in your life when God was most real for you." "Share your feelings when you think back to the first church you remember attending." "What Bible verse or book of the Bible speaks most to you?" "If you were to take your faith more seriously, what would you need to do?" After several sessions wrestling with such questions, the pastor (or trained leader) might meet with the group. To be discerned is whether the group has a desire to continue, perhaps no longer centered in a regular meal but in a love feast, thereby symbolizing a willingness to share more deeply around a mutual commitment.

When forming covenant groups, members need to know that they can switch groups at the beginning stage, with no questions asked. As these groups take on a distinctive identity as to type, intensity, and depth, the pastor's task becomes less that of conducting groups and more that of assuming a twofold responsibility. First, the pastor-priest should meet regularly with the group leaders gathered together, perhaps biweekly. These sessions function as the covenant group for leaders, as well as provide ongoing training in spiritual direction by sharing diverse ways of dealing with problems encountered in their groups. Second, the pastor should visit each covenant group occasionally, quietly observing so as to be able to give caring feedback to each leader in private. For example, a particular leader may need help in providing a better balance of piety and social justice in his or her group.

Through personal experience, I have found it best to organize groups for a designated period, perhaps six months. At the end of that time, a verbal self-appraisal is done, perhaps by the pastor. In such a session, the group decides whether it desires to continue as is, or has outlived its usefulness, or would benefit from a "reshuffling" of membership, and/or would be willing to add some new members. I am amazed by the positive power such spiritual direction groups have on their members. Cursillo, for example, encourages groups formed during the weekend experience to continue meeting weekly; these groups are called Reunion Groups. They provide group members with a card containing questions to ask themselves such as, "What have you done since last we met to further your piety, your study, and/or your Christian action?" Another useful question is, "When did you feel closest to Christ during this past week?"

Some of my friends have been meeting weekly for twenty-one years since their Cursillo experience. When I quizzed them about their longevity as a group, the response was simple, straightforward, and identical: "None of us would think of missing these weekly sessions without serious cause; in fact, I plan my week around this gathering." This group, like many others, has gotten to know each other so well that they have settled for a format similar to a Wesleyan class meeting. Their equivalent for "How is your soul?" has become

"How have you been this past week?" Particularly impressive is how many persons whose business takes them out of town will fly back just for the weekly session.

Some groups provide additional structure to the natural rhythm of their meetings by celebrating special times in their lives—such as birthdays, anniversaries, milestones in the group's functioning, the anniversary of a loved one's death, and the dates of baptisms and confirmations. Around such events, a ritual of questions often arises. For example, birthday celebrations can be deepened by asking such questions as, "What was the most important thing that happened to you this past year?" Or, "What would you like to be able to say a year from now when we celebrate your birthday?" Or, "What is your hope for the coming year?

Pastors who are uneasy about trusting the internal dynamic of such groups or are tempted to control them by providing content, would do well to attend a weekly AA meeting. While an outsider might experience such meetings as boringly repetitive, in truth they are the lifeblood of the participants. Members are deeply invested because the issue of each one is the concern of all. I have never heard of an AA group having a problem with membership, attendance, or filling the time. In fact, I know a number of persons who attend multiple AA groups each week. One reason for the vitality of covenant groups is that people love to talk about themselves. And in our society where listening is becoming a lost art, spiritual direction groups provide eager listening. With such tangible support, self-sharing becomes almost inevitable, deepening into confession, and with absolution emerges the craving for a disciplined life.

The task of scheduling such spiritual direction groups often requires imagination, because many members already have schedules that seem full. Possibilities other than the obvious ones include meeting over a meal, staying for an hour after Sunday worship or another church activity, enjoying an early breakfast session together before work, meeting for a midmorning coffee break, or even becoming constituted as a class during the church school hour.

Experience has shown that instead of trying to fit group meetings around individual schedules, it works best for the group to choose a regular weekly time, forcing members to fit the rest of their schedules to accommodate the group meeting.

While I believe that the internal dynamic of such groups can be trusted, it is helpful to note that groups can be organized around topics or functions. For example, traditional Bible study groups offered in most churches can easily be made into "scriptural discernment groups." In such groups, scripture passages (perhaps following the lectionary) are read and reread aloud as *lectio divina*, bringing an openness to being addressed by the Holy Spirit as a guide for daily living. Other groups can be organized for various seasons of the church year, such as providing disciplined spiritual preparation during Advent or Lent. Still other groups can provide action-reflection learning in how to pray, supplemented by a one-with-one apprenticeship. Or still again, groups might coalesce around a missional focus, such as abolition of the death penalty or working with the poor. In these groups, the spiritual dimension soon emerges, for efforts at societal change always bring with them the experience of unending defeat. Today's justice seems destined to become tomorrow's injustice. Thus, the task is never finished, throwing one back upon a foundation not one's own. As Karl Barth put it, ours is not to succeed, but to be faithful; success is in God's hands. Covenant groups can even be arranged around vocational themes, such as gathering persons involved in social welfare, or those involved in homemaking, or those particularly in need of centering in order to render spiritual a job that is boring and mechanical. In all these examples of spiritual direction groups, it is not so important to have answers as it is to manifest a caring attitude.

Renewing Regular Church Activities

Congregational renewal, then, involves two types of direction. First, there is a need for new groups intended to supplement the local church's regular activities. But for a congregation intent upon serious renewal, spiritual direction needs also to be made the informing rationale for all regular church activities. Over the years I have become increasingly skeptical about the ability of traditionally organized church school classes to move beyond information to action. The change that is needed, then, is to make time available for two things: (1) at the beginning of the class, review what members have done as a result of the last class, and (2) near the end of the class, discern concretely what personal and corporate implementations the group members are willing to attempt in the coming week.

The Wesleyan movement is helpful in modeling how attention to the state of one's soul leads inevitably to a "doing" as an expression of its authenticity. The assumption was that a sacred reading of scripture would find its correlation, for example, in visiting persons in prison. Focusing upon the correlation between being and doing can transform church activities into faith events. Thus, church meetings should not occur without tackling in some form the concrete question of who is going to do what, when, and why. The goal of every event should be to enable full Christian life and living—measuring the church's success more by depth than by quantity.

SPIRITUAL DIRECTION GROUPS AS AN ORDER

It is important to recall that the original Wesleyan small groups were intended to function as a sectarian *order* within an inclusive church that proclaims the Word and administers the sacraments. Such an order, with its various levels, was not realistically expected of everyone but only for serious Christians. This distinction between church and order is crucial, for without an order, the church will be little more than an institution based on a least common denominator. And without the church, in turn, small groups are deprived of the preached Word and the sacramental base providing the means of grace. We have seen what happens when an order is deprived of its church base, no longer able to function as an order within the church—it is forced to function as a church. With this dynamic, serious sectarian discipleship is surrendered for the broad-based appeal characterizing a church. By definition, the attraction of a church rests in a broadening of membership requirements, intent on providing "something for everyone."

Consequently, at best, the present resurgence of interest in spiritual direction will occur in sect-like groups that will attract only a limited number of church members. *Degrees of faith are a fact and always will be.* Thus, while we have affirmed spiritual direction as necessary for being a serious Christian, we are forced to acknowledge that only a compromise is realistic—of spiritual direction groups functioning as an order within each church. The early Wesleyan movement, then, provides the most viable model for today's church. *Here the exclusive discipleship of spiritual direction groups functions as an order within the inclusivity of a broadly based sacramental church.*

Wesley was creative in his practicality, for the groups he established were not only based upon external characteristics such as age, gender, and location. They also reflected the diversity of depths characterizing the varied faith pilgrimages of Christians. He quickly learned that serious attention to spiritual growth leads inevitably to a recognition of varied levels and intensities in the spiritual life. Societies gave birth to classes; the more advanced class members were formed into bands; and from bands the most advanced persons could become members of a select society. Spiritual direction, then, is not a monolithic activity from which one graduates or finally "arrives." The ideal, of course, is that all Christians pass from one level to another, in endless growth. But there will be persons at each step for whom that level is a plateau rather than a transition. Thus, it is important that spiritual directors be able to discern when a person is unable to go farther, doing well even to maintain the depth he or she has attained.

Having acknowledged this spiritual spectrum characterizing most congregations, the modern church needs to take Wesley's lead in seeing that no member is exempt from an invitation, luring, or prodding toward a disciplined spiritual life. For this purpose, the names of church members who choose not to be part of the order might well be divided into lists of eight to ten persons. Then from among the members who have received spiritual direction are recruited "caretakers," each responsible for keeping in touch with one list of persons—by phone, e-mail, and visit, at home or at work. The operating assumption is that persons need to know that they are appreciated and missed if they are absent. In this manner, no members of the congregation will be neglected, for whether they know it yet or not, it is impossible to be a Christian alone.

Lay Leadership

While present-day pastors may be able to intermix some spiritual direction with the crisis counseling normally expected of them, the spiritual direction is likely to be quite limited. Furthermore, as the number of clergy continues to decrease, the training of lay leadership will be increasingly necessary. Consequently, Wesley's experience in such training is instructive. By providing corporate spiritual direction, he came to realize that not only is this a powerful tool in each person's pilgrimage, but also it is the ideal method for training persons as spiritual directors. Through action-reflection as apprenticeship, covenant group members are trained in the three major types of spiritual direction. First, they are encouraged and opened to pursue personal direction. Second, they receive the equivalent of one-with-one direction from different persons in the group. Third, they learn the expertise and confidence to direct, and even recruit, a spiritual direction group on their own. By far the best way to learn how to give spiritual direction is first to receive it.

Spirituality and an Elite

In our society, there is a working awareness of the need for various types of "elites." Academically there are escalating levels, from certificates to advanced degrees. Gradation at each level is quite acceptable without any built-in dynamic suggesting that the existence of Ph.D.s intimidates others from getting their GEDs. And yet I experience a resistance in the local church to forming special groups. "Elitism" is the pejorative label given to those who are different from the rest. Yet all around us elites are highly respected. Police forces have their SWAT teams; the military has its crack troops called Green Berets; corporations have their troubleshooters; society has its think tanks; and every phase of the medical profession has its specialists.

The same actually has been true in the church's own life, with its history woven upon the warp of saints and martyrs. And it is with this fabric that our churches need once again to clothe themselves for self-identity. In a society that rapidly exposes the clay feet of its role models, the church must reclaim the mission of birthing those willing and able to move further down the road of spiritual maturity—on behalf of us all.

ANATOMY OF THE HOUSE CHURCH MODEL

In Latin America, the phenomenon of house churches or base communities has provided significant church renewal and expansion. Actually, the idea emerged out of crisis. With the number of priests at a tragically low point, laypersons have been trained to be ministers of the Word. Meetings tend to be in small groups in homes, functioning as households of God. The basic format is spiritual direction done through corporate *lectio divina*. An assigned scripture passage, often coming from the daily lectionary, is read and reread aloud. From this reading emerge words, phrases, or images that can so function as lens that members begin to see their personal and societal life with new eyes. In this way, scripture is able to hold participants accountable for faithfulness in their daily living. The last house church I attended was in Nicaragua on Epiphany Sunday afternoon. Their corporate reading and sharing focused on Herod and the wise men. Before long, a past event had spontaneously become a drama about God, their authorities, and liberators in their own village and country.

This house church model can be used in mainline churches in the United States as a way of offering corporate spiritual direction, each group functioning much as a cell does in a healthy body. My own experience suggests that a love feast or agape meal is a powerful spiritual center for these small groups. This practice is rooted in the frequent meals Jesus shared with his disciples as family. In the early church, these love feasts existed side-by-side with Eucharistic celebrations, but in time only the Eucharist survived. The Moravians reintroduced the love feast in Germany in 1727. Ten years later, Wesley experienced it, instituting it as an important part of society meetings. More recently, the Covenant Discipleship movement has revived this Wesleyan practice. The result is covenant groups that not only provide supportive accountability for following a common covenant and a personal rule, but also the love feast is a powerful symbol of their shared lives. While such a feast can involve a whole meal, the only essentials are bread and water. The parts of this model, echoing the Wesleyan practice, are hymns, prayer, scripture, sharing, and a collection for the poor. The result is that members become bonded in a corporate loyalty, the gifts of each member are identified, and all are equipped through an action-reflection mode of learning by doing.[3]

In reimaging the local church in terms of spiritual direction, it is crucial to keep the goal clearly in mind. Saint Paul is a master at maintaining this primal focus. He confesses, "For to me, living is Christ" (Phil. 1:21). He also claims, "It is no longer I who live, but it is Christ who lives in me" (Gal. 2:20). A renewed church needs to be built upon spiritually directed persons; such persons, in turn, will emerge from a church restructured by and for spiritual direction.

Conclusion:
A Rhapsody

The threefold purpose of this book has been to establish the indispensability of spiritual direction, to help persons give and receive various kinds of direction, and to provide a diverse portrait of Christian spirituality as a context for direction. In situational direction, one evokes and honors the lived "world" of the person's own forging, holding one accountable to the best of that world. In contextual direction, the Christian director helps a person identify the Theological World in which he or she implicitly lives, testing it by the authenticity of the individual's life, and moving him or her to manifest it self-consciously and fully or to move toward conversion. Yet even in situational direction, the director operates implicitly from a Christian context—convinced that healing is possible, that the yearning at the center of each person is for unconditional love, and that ultimately only the grace of God is sufficient for wholeness. And while that view is never to be imposed, it is present in the director's unconditional acceptance of the directee, evidenced by listening discerningly as if he or she is the pearl of great price.

Permit me to close with a rhapsody regarding the wild and wonderful foolishness awaiting anyone who dares to receive and give spiritual direction as a way of tasting the fullness of Christian existence.[1] It involves a life of incredible rhythms, of highs and lows, whether in a concert hall hearing Beethoven's Ninth Symphony or in a Memphis dive trumpeting the blues. Its antinomies include a hunger for community, yet a taste for the silence of aloneness. The yearning is for intimacy, but the embrace occurs on a windswept hill called Golgotha. There is an emptying out of all thought and imagery in order to lose oneself in the Unknown and Unknowable. Yet there is an excitement over the playfulness of imagination and the intensity mind. Christians are claimed by a past that hopes for the future by drinking deeply of the present. They are daring persons for whom belief is etched with faithful doubts. They hold tenaciously to what has been bequeathed, yet they gamble on the new being born.

Christians seek a solidarity with creation, claimed by a spiritual life that recapitulates the Incarnation. The Christian is claimed by Christ's *kenosis* (self-emptying) in order to be grasped by his *pleroma* (fullness). Christian existence is a life of paradox. On the one hand, the Christian strives to live a paschal life, ready at a moment's notice to be slain and offered up, in order to rise again. On the other hand, the Christian is capable of delighting in the body and every sense, in sexuality and sensuality, in the depth and rich breadth of feelings, shaped fancifully by a love of beauty and a compassion for the ugly. Throughout, one's fragile body is embraced as friend, so that the more pious one becomes, the more passionate one's living. One dances in and out of pleasures and temptations, refusing any dualism between the spiritual and the material, between soul and flesh, between inner and outer. The wine of the Eucharist makes common communion with the toast at a fine meal with friends. The chanting in the church finds its echoes in the rhythms of the rock concert. And the kiss of peace has something strangely to do with the touch of a lover.

Yet these joys of life in Christ are tempered by following the Man of Sorrows. Whether in the tragic repetitions of history or the lurking demons in one's own soul, the Christian knows that reality always has a cross at its center. More often than not, one's smile is washed with tears, usually sooner than later. But there are moments in the midst of tragedy when a faint smile is teased into uproarious laughter. There is a strange joy in shouting no to society's tainted claims, and amusement over one's foibles in simply being human. But underneath it all is a serenity born of grace, of having everything because ultimately one has nothing, even though in the eyes of the world this seems like madness. One's Christmases are sacred with a silent holiness, yet Rudolph and abundant "ho, ho, ho's" are evidence of again becoming like a little child. And the tension of Good Friday with Easter births a sober inebriation without parallel.

The question "Who am I?" is forever wrapped in the deeper question of "Whose am I?" In answer, the Christian knows by being known, so strangely loved that only the name God will do. Christianity involves a yoke into which is branded the word *freedom*. Yet it is a costly freedom, tempered in the pain of repentance, and marinated with the courage to endure. Wrapped in Christ's warm mantle of many colors, one is able to enter gladly the prisons of others as if they were one's own. A freed slave, the Christian chooses the bondage of carrying a cross toward the radiance of an empty tomb.

The Christian is happily under orders, in the process of being disciplined so as to be able to love without taking thought, to taste deeply without needing permission, to embrace enemies without need of reward, and to abandon self into God for the sheer mystery of it all. And during those dry desert times, loving out of duty must suffice. Christians are active contemplatives who are profoundly inactive at the center. They hyphenate their living between being and doing, embracing all that both contain. They follow a Christ in whose hand is a whip for money changers, with an angry outcry at the greed of the rich and the callousness of the powerful. Even so, the odds are against ever feeling like a hero. For each victory there are ten defeats, and today's hard-earned justice will inevitably turn sour as tomorrow's injustice. And whatever reward there might be, chances are it will be an ulcer or depression or just plain being misunderstood. Yet their angry master is also the one who has a special love for the village outcasts of this world, and the one who carries so gently the lambs in his bosom.

The Christian's life is one of prayer—knowing the Galilean hills before sunrise, the bloody sweat of Gethsemane nights, the mountaintop transfigurations, and the dry places that only demons call home. Yet even there in the desert searching for water, one vows to smell each cactus in bloom. The Christian greets the orangeness of autumn and the greenness of spring, the summer's gentle rains and the winter's driving snow—equally at home in each, but never fully at home anywhere. The Christian's thirst for knowledge means tasting the latest of everything, while knowing that his or her cup always remains empty. The Christian supports liberation everywhere, insisting that each person have whatever is needed to live fully, while defying as foes all who dare deprive anyone of such fullness.

Fully immersed in this world, Christians belong to no world. Instead, while teased by each hope and every vision, they know them to be only hints of the new heaven and new earth rooted in divine promises. And our yearning to become lost in God only intensifies our tears over the thought of leaving this life. Christian existence is joyful nonsense. In a culture of self-realization, the Christian's call is to renounce self; in the face of noise, silence is the preference; in a world of competition, the Christian's declaration is that the winners will be losers and the losers winners; in a culture whose economy is intent on consumption, the Christian insists on simplicity; in a culture structured by possessions, the insistence is upon detachment; in a culture intent on a high standard of living, the Christian insists upon a high standard of life; and at every point, the Christian exposes the emptiness of fullness for the sake of the gospel's fullness of emptiness.

The Christian is proud to be a fool for Christ. Such a fool is obedient, yet free; under law, yet walking by grace; sinful, yet forgiven; unlovable, yet unconditionally loved; a believer, but with a healthy skepticism; certain, but only by making the ultimate gamble. The Christian claims that God is definitively revealed in Christ, yet is still the Hidden One; knows deeply, but in a cloud of unknowing; believes, but only by faith; and acknowledges that while all things have been made new, everything remains much the same.

Above all, the Christian is a citizen of the church universal. While we delight in the uniqueness of each individual, our deepest joy is to be part of the community that Christ embraces as his own body. Invited to his marriage feast yet to be, we partake of his body and blood. And at these sacred moments, it is enough just to stand around, passing the peace for which the world yearns, being the church adorned as a bride awaiting her divine Lover.

⌒

May the Lord bless us and keep us.
May the Lord radiate with joy because of us
and shine fondly upon us.
May the Lord's face finally be uncovered to us,
and shower us with graciousness.
And may the Lord enfold us always
in the warm embrace of peace.[2]
Amen.

APPENDIXES

✛

PERSONAL DISCERNMENT THROUGH CORPORATE DIRECTION

Sometimes it is important for a person to seek collective spiritual direction in making an important decision. Groups such as the Quakers (Society of Friends) and the Sisters of Loretto have had considerable experience in methods of corporate or communal discernment. The following is a summary of this method, sometimes called a "clearness session," which can be adapted to particular circumstances.

1. *Choosing a discernment group.* This choice can be solely that of the person seeking clearness, but sometimes it is wise to ask others to suggest individuals who might be helpful in one's particular quest. Three to five persons seem to work well. Avoid selecting persons who have strong opinions or possible agenda regarding the outcome of the discernment. Seek persons who listen well, who tend to ask probing questions and to make suggestions rather than to express opinions, whose dispositions are supportive and caring, who know you reasonably well, and whom you can trust.

2. *Facilitator and planning.* The person asked to facilitate the session should understand the group discernment process, be skilled in keeping the group focused, be upbeat in mood, and know how to evoke responses. The person seeking discernment should meet with the facilitator in advance, making sure that he or she understands the seeker's needs, hopes, potential blockages, and areas of uneasiness. Together they can prepare in advance so that the primary question can be presented clearly. The meeting place should feel intimate, with a seating arrangement conducive to conversation.

3. *Beginning the session.* Prepare the room in advance. The seeker and facilitator should arrive early, greeting friends, introducing any strangers, and helping everyone feel relaxed. The facilitator should begin with prayer, asking for the guidance of the Spirit. Depending on the group members, it is sometimes wise to take five minutes for the group to put to rest any preoccupations remaining from activities prior to arrival. Quiet music sets an appropriate atmosphere for becoming centered. Early on, the facilitator should state briefly and succinctly the reason for the gathering. If members do not know each other well, it is often helpful to have a few statements from each, indicating the nature of one's relationship to the seeker. These words should be affirming, supportive, and encouraging. It is important that these preparatory features be short and to the point; otherwise they can distract from the focus of the meeting.

4. *Ground rules.* The facilitator makes clear the ground rules for the session:

- The session must be completely confidential, with no exceptions.

- The process begins with careful listening, followed by questions for clarification.

- Questions are then asked for the purpose of gaining additional information and/or probing more deeply.

- Finally, individuals share discernment they have gained, and the group helps the seeker move toward what needs to happen after the session.

Throughout the discernment process, the group needs to understand that they are not seeking what they think, or want, or even think best, but they are seeking discernment as to what God is about in the person's life.

5. *The presentation*. The seeker begins by stating in one or two sentences what is being asked. For example, "I need discernment about the direction my calling needs to take at this juncture in my life." Or, "I need help in knowing how to respond to a difficult situation." The seeker then spells out the question, sharing with the group everything that seems relevant to the issue. The facilitator needs to see that there are minimal interruptions during this sharing, until the basic anatomy of the question is fairly well sketched out. The group should encourage the person "just to talk," "empty it all out," "even if it doesn't make sense."

6. *Dialogue*. When the person has said all that he or she feels necessary, the facilitator invites group members to ask questions for clarification. Then a conversation follows, sharing feelings, perceptions, hunches, uneasinesses, and encouragements— much like one's sharing with a close friend. To be avoided is giving advice, such as "What you ought to do is . . ." "Oughts" and "shoulds" are not helpful. More helpful are statements such as: "I wonder if . . . ?" or "Could it be that . . . ?" or "Have you ever thought about . . . ?" or "I could see you . . ." or "How would you feel if . . . ?" Depending on the nature of the issue, the person might need expressions of confidence that he or she is capable of resolving the issue.

7. *Finalization*. The facilitator needs to make sure that every group member is heard, as well as sense when the conversation has reached the end of its usefulness. At this point, it is wise to ask the person directly, "Has this been helpful?" If the response is "Yes, but . . . ," the facilitator directs more conversation toward the

uneasiness or confusion. If "Yes," the person is invited to share what he or she has learned or has had clarified, and where things are now.

8. *New steps.* The facilitator then tries to help the person discern, with possible help from the group, what might happen after this session: "I think I need a few days to mull over what we've said." Or, "What I need to do now is. . . ." Or, "Would you be willing to come back together in a week to review with me what I've come up with?"

9. *Closure.* The facilitator closes the session affirmatively, with the promise of ongoing support. End with a prayer of thanksgiving.

$$\maltese$$

GROUP DISCERNMENT THROUGH CORPORATE DIRECTION

C hurch meetings and conferences have been largely taken over by *Robert's Rules of Order*. Decisions are the result of parliamentary procedures, resulting in the will of the majority. In decided contrast is decision making through corporate spiritual direction. The first Christian record of this process being used was the Jerusalem Conference, described in the Book of Acts. The important issue at stake was the relationship of Christianity to Jewish practice. Even more important was asking the right question. The question was not about what each individual wanted, or even what each person thought was best. Instead, the question was, "What is God's will in this matter?" This involved listening to each other, after which the entire assembly "kept silence" (Acts 15:12). During this Spirit listening the conclusion became clear: "It has seemed good to the Holy Spirit and to us . . ." (15:28). While God speaks to individuals, the unique power of the church is its magisterium—

the power to discern the counsel of God through the consensual deliberations of the church as a whole. At one end of the Christian spectrum are the Quakers, who discern in silence the illumination of the Inner Light. At the other end, the Roman Catholic Church is so excited by this promise of the Spirit that it declares the result infallible ("not deceived"). This occurs when the pontiff (meaning "pathfinder" by being a "bridge") speaks *for* the church, not *to* the church. In other words, faithful discernment occurs through the church for the church. Perhaps the best proof of the Holy Spirit is the degree to which the Ecumenical Councils in the church's history, although often a motley political conglomeration, were nevertheless the instruments through which the Spirit bequeathed us the major beliefs of Christendom (e.g., Nicaea, Chalcedon).

Discernment means midwifing that which the Holy Spirit yearns to bring into being. My first experience of group discernment happened in the 1960s when my local church called an emergency meeting after an African American couple attended worship that morning. For the first hour, the meeting was nasty, with anger, racist slurs, and passionate defensiveness. Things were clearly moving toward the predetermined racist "solution." Finally one elderly woman stood. "Well, we sure made it plain what *we* want. But the real question is what does *God* want, and I think that is even plainer!" There was an endless minute of silence. Then someone called for prayer, and within half an hour the group physically embraced, sang a hymn, and without even thinking of a vote, the discernment of open membership had occurred.

Many of us feel irrelevant to the decision-making process in many church meetings and conferences. Sitting through vote after vote of "receiving," "referring," and "concurring" is boring. Rubber-stamp is too kind a label. Many times I have been part of choosing delegates and electing bishops. I know all about the dynamics of voting for those in power positions, or for those to whom we owe a favor. In contrast to such political maneuvering, corporate discernment asks, "Which persons are truly open to the Spirit, have sufficient spiritual maturity to discern for the church, and thus are being called by God through us at this particular point in our corporate history?" To reformulate the question is to insist on an alternative method.

Group discernment is called for in the major sectors of the church's life—whether this is in establishing social justice priorities or creating a theology of budgets. Rephrasing the question can be threatening, for it forces us to transcend committees and commissions which by nature vote to maintain control and increase appropriations. Additionally, the voting method allows determination to be independent of implementation, whereas discernment and implementation cannot be separated. A Wesleyan hymn puts all this well:

> Jesus, we look to thee, Thy promised presence claim;
> Thou in the midst of us shalt be,
> assembled in thy name: . . .
> Present we know thou are, but O, thyself reveal!
> Now, Lord, let every bounding heart the mighty comfort feel.[1]

Appropriating the genius of their early leaders, the Jesuits have been helpful in developing a corporate process of spiritual direction for discerning God's will on important issues. The process can be described as having four stages:

1. *Individual preparation.* Each person is expected, through prayer, meditation, and self-examination, to:
   a. Become indifferent to everything else but God's will in regard to the issue to be placed before the group.
   b. Commit himself/herself to accept and support whatever discernment comes through the group.
   c. Honestly get in touch with his or her prejudgments, letting go of them by acknowledging that he/she does not yet know God's will in this matter.
   d. Become informed about the alternatives, reading and seeking insight through conversation with others. Remain open; listening should be one's posture.

e. Discern which Christian principles seem to be relevant (e.g., preferential option for the poor, inclusivity, the church as the body of Christ, etc.).

2. *Communal dialogue.*
   a. Provide an environmental context that is conducive to the process. Often this means thinking in terms of circles rather than rows, or of a leadership center rather than a raised podium. Short worship is often wise, but prayer invoking the Holy Spirit is imperative.
   b. Establish ground rules that make difficult any reversion to the voting method, indicating clearly to all the process to be followed. Be certain that the facilitator understands the discernment process thoroughly, making certain that there will be no debate. Debate assumes that one knows in advance what is best, that conflict is a necessary process for making decisions, and that the conclusion will result in a win/lose situation.
   c. In contrast, open dialogue is the method to be followed, implying that the answer is not yet decided, that all persons are important in the discernment process, that the answer will emerge, and that we are all in the process, to succeed or to fail, together.
   d. Depending on the size of the group, it may be helpful to break into smaller groups, perhaps of eight to ten persons.
   e. The facilitator should see that the dynamic is lively and non-repetitive, for a point well made need be stated only once.
   f. Consider only one issue at a time, establishing any subissues that can make the main issue more manageable. Whatever is then posed, the responsibility of the whole group is to surface all the pros that together can be detected. When finished to the satisfaction of the group, all the cons are corporately detected. The intent is clarification, not evaluation.
   g. Choose scribes, both for small groups and large, in advance. These should be persons skilled not only in distilling the var-

ious points made, but in discerning patterns, clarifying options, and recognizing unexpressed consequences. At different points, the scribe should provide feedback to the group in order to ascertain accuracy and clarity. Sometimes it is helpful to have a "process observer," especially when this method is new to the group.

h. Take prayer breaks, giving members time apart to ponder, or call for a short period of collective silence before the discussion continues. It is important that there be no caucusing, as is traditional, with all sharing to be done in the groups, not with individuals during breaks. Keep reminding everyone that the task is *corporate* discernment.

3. *Decision.*

a. When all that needs to be said has been said once, the facilitator invites anyone who feels moved to speak to suggest what might be the sense of the group. Inappropriate would be such comments as, "What I think we ought to do is. . . ." Appropriate would be such comments as, "What I think I hear the group saying is . . ." or "It seems that perhaps we are moving toward consensus on. . . ." Such comments are a testing of the water. It is amazing how members seem to know immediately when someone has spoken for them and when "that isn't quite it." The facilitator has to discern when something approaching consensus seems to be emerging. After stating so, and watching for verbal and nonverbal signs, the facilitator then asks, "Can all of us live with this discernment?" If there are some who cannot, the process continues. If this continuation still does not lead to consensus, the facilitator needs to discern when it may be time to ask those who are in disagreement if they are willing to step aside on behalf of the group. That is, do they truly feel heard so that there is no reason remaining for blocking the decision? The scribe then reads what has been recorded as a "consensus of the group." This statement may need some minor adjustments, but the group will know when the decision has been made.

b. Appropriately, closure is consistent with the way the process began, with worship as an act of joy, or at least with a prayer of thanksgiving.

4. *Post-Session.*

True discernment is best known after the fact, when the group adjourns and lives with the decision for a while. If the issue is major, it is helpful to provide an opportunity at a subsequent time for the group to indicate if there is ongoing satisfaction. If the discerning group is large, it is wise that any uneasiness a person might have be reported to one's small group for reconsideration, if deemed appropriate. It would be inappropriate for one person to try to make his or her uneasiness major by writing a letter to all or making a declaration to the large group.

✠

SAMPLE RULE

While rules can focus on particular issues or disciplines, each person should develop a rule that deals with the spectrum of his or her living. Making such a rule begins best by discerning the implicit "rule" on the basis of which one already lives. As creatures of habit, we are methodical in almost everything that we do. Since many of us are oblivious to this fact, spiritual direction is often needed not only for an honest identification of one's life structure, but also to probe behind it to the spiritual base of which one's habits are an expression. Beginning with such clarity, one is then able to create an explicit rule that can be lived out from within, rather than lived by imposition from without. Dimensions with which a rule might well deal include these:

1. *Daily spiritual disciplines:* for example, what Protestants call devotions, what Catholics do in using the breviary, and what monks participate in as the daily office. This can include disciplines such as the prayer of centering and intercessory prayer.

2. *Sacred reading:* for example, using the daily lectionary for *lectio divina*.

3. *Disciplined study:* for example, a program in spiritual reading that includes such classics as *The Practice of the Presence of God*, *The Cloud of Unknowing*, and *The Imitation of Christ*.

4. *Church participation:* for example, corporate worship, with special attention to the Eucharist.

5. *Social justice ministry:* for example, involvement with symptoms of poverty, such as providing tutoring; and dealing with causes of injustice, such as lobbying for changed legislation.

6. *Financial intentionality:* for example, moving toward a tithe; focusing upon a "prophetic" project, such as abolition of the death penalty or Habitat for Humanity.

7. *Time inventory:* for example, periodic review of how one uses one's time so as to encourage a creative rhythm of being/doing, work/leisure, family/self, friends/alone time, service/self-affirmation, and engagement/silence.

8. *Lifestyle:* for example, periodic examination of one's possessions, such as home, car, clothing, furniture, dishes, etc., moving toward a sense of stewardship, simplicity, low consumption, energy efficiency, and shared use.

9. *Environment:* for example, intentionality in surrounding oneself with the materials and shapes of earthly beauty, in contrast to what is plastic, commercial, and/or ornate.

10. *Body stewardship:* for example, regular exercise, healthy diet, prudent use of drugs and stimulants.

11. *Being informed:* for example, daily knowledge of world, national, and local happenings, examined from contrasting perspectives.

12. *Spiritual direction:* for example, find a spiritual director whom one trusts to provide the unconditional support and rigorous accountability that is needed but often avoided.

13. *Retreat:* for example, schedule a monthly time alone for recollection, and a longer yearly time apart, such as at a monastery.

14. *God:* Commitment must be to seek God for God's own sake, purifying one's motives so that faith is not for the sake of acquiring anything, but in order to be faithful.

✛

RULE AND THE WESLEYAN COVENANT

M y experience is that spiritual growth goes hand in hand with the ability to make and keep promises. That ability, in turn, is greatly enabled by making these promises liturgically. This makes clear that the real director is the Holy Spirit, and the ability to be faithful depends upon one's openness to the Spirit's workings. An important contribution to the liturgy of spiritual direction is the Wesleyan Covenant for Watch Night or New Year. It is particularly appropriate for establishing one's rule as that to which one commits oneself and to which one is willing to be held accountable. I have adapted the covenant here for use as such a liturgy.

> Eternal Creator, I invoke your presence as witness to the covenant I now make with you through this rule. I ask that you will support me and hold me accountable to this promise, content with the place and work to which you appoint me. May I want nothing more than you as my reward.
>
> Christ, you call us to many tasks. Some are easy, others difficult; some bring honor, others reproach; some are suitable to our

inclinations and interests, while others are contrary to both. In some we may please you and please ourselves; in others, we cannot please you except by denying ourselves. Whatever our task, if we are to have the strength to be faithful, it is you who must strengthen us.

Holy Spirit, be with me as I now take upon myself with joy this yoke of obedience, committed out of love for you, to seek and to do only your will. Therefore, I shall no longer be my own, but yours. Put me to what you will, rank me with whom you will. Put me to doing, put me to suffering. Let me be employed for you or laid aside for you, exalted for you or brought low for you. Let me be full, let me be empty. Let me have all things, let me have nothing. I freely and heartily yield all things to your pleasure and disposal. And now, O glorious and blessed God, Father, Son, and Holy Spirit, you are mine and I am yours. So be it. May this covenant that I have made on earth be ratified as well in heaven.

Amen.[1]

APPENDIX 5

A THEOLOGICAL WORLDS INVENTORY
(abbreviated)

Instructions: In each of these questions, place a 1 in the box beside the phrase or word that best completes the sentence for you. Then place a 2 in the box that expresses best your second preference. Trust your first inclination.

LIFE

1. Life for me is a:
   - ☐ Mysterious pilgrimage
   - ☐ Basic right
   - ☐ Quest for self-fulfillment
   - ☐ Rebirth
   - ☐ Courageous act

2. To have meaning, life entails:
   - ☐ Unveiling the mystery
   - ☐ Winning a victory
   - ☐ Being whole
   - ☐ Removing guilt
   - ☐ Living faithfully one's duty

3. Which set of worst/best describes the dynamic of living?

☐ Separation/reunion

☐ Conflict/vindication

☐ Emptiness/fulfillment

☐ Condemnation/forgiveness

☐ Suffering/endurance

THE HUMAN CONDITION

4. I experience the negative human condition most often as:

☐ Feeling alienated

☐ Being treated unjustly

☐ Being rendered invisible

☐ Feeling guilty

☐ Experiencing pain

5. Words describing how it feels to experience this condition are these:

☐ Wanderer-orphan-stranger

☐ Enslaved-oppressed

☐ Self-doubting-impotent-aching

☐ Selfish-devious

☐ Wounded-victim-undone

SIN

6. Sin is:

☐ Closing one's eyes to the Mystery

☐ Compromising too soon

☐ Misdirected good

☐ A condition defining us even before we act badly

☐ Part of life's struggles

7. Often the effects of sin are:

☐ Separation

☐ Indifference
☐ Unrealized potential
☐ Perversity
☐ Weakening

REDEMPTION

8. Conversion is from:
   ☐ Alienation to homecoming
   ☐ Oppression to liberation
   ☐ Nothingness to self-identity
   ☐ Guilt to pardon
   ☐ Suffering to integrity

9. Redemption for me comes from experiencing Jesus as:
   ☐ Illuminator
   ☐ Liberator
   ☐ Nurturer
   ☐ Savior
   ☐ Comrade

10. The gospel invites me to:
    ☐ Lose myself in God
    ☐ Give myself for a cause
    ☐ Learn to love myself
    ☐ Deny myself for others
    ☐ Remain faithful to the end

11. Freedom means:
    ☐ Going home
    ☐ No one being hungry
    ☐ Losing self-doubt in becoming who I am
    ☐ A chance to start over
    ☐ To outlast

12. Faith is trusting in:
- ☐ The Mystery
- ☐ The future
- ☐ Myself
- ☐ A new beginning
- ☐ The inevitable

13. What tends to give me hope:
- ☐ Experiences that hint at the meaning of the whole
- ☐ Changes in this world that will make it better
- ☐ Support that encourages me to become who I am
- ☐ Trust in God's gracious forgiveness
- ☐ Divine companionship to see it through together

14. An image that appeals to me is:
- ☐ The ocean
- ☐ Tomorrow
- ☐ A room of my own
- ☐ Spring housecleaning
- ☐ A day off

15. I tend to view death as:
- ☐ Opening to another world
- ☐ A foe to be resisted
- ☐ Part of life's rhythm
- ☐ Something I deserve
- ☐ A reality to be faced steadfastly

16. An ideal Christian would be a:
- ☐ Mystic
- ☐ Visionary
- ☐ Saint

- ☐ Witness
- ☐ Martyr

17. Christian existence centers in:
    - ☐ Spiritual oneness
    - ☐ A common cause
    - ☐ Focused growth
    - ☐ New birth
    - ☐ Strength to persevere

DOCTRINE

18. God is the one who:
    - ☐ Brings deeper harmony
    - ☐ Takes sides
    - ☐ Lures forth possibilities
    - ☐ Atones for us
    - ☐ Experiences our hurts and needs with us

19. God is the one who:
    - ☐ Draws us into union
    - ☐ Promises a new heaven and earth
    - ☐ Adopts us as family
    - ☐ Forgives us personally
    - ☐ Identifies with us

20. Who is Jesus?
    - ☐ Disclosure of what we have not recognized
    - ☐ Foretaste of what is promised to be
    - ☐ The definitive human word about who God is
    - ☐ God's definitive word about who we are
    - ☐ Our suffering companion

21. Jesus is best understood as:
    - ☐ Illuminator–evoker
    - ☐ Pioneer–prophet
    - ☐ Threshold–model
    - ☐ Savior–Lord
    - ☐ Friend–sympathizer

22. I am drawn by picturing Jesus as:
    - ☐ Alone with God in the mountains in prayer
    - ☐ Casting out the money changers
    - ☐ With the woman at the well
    - ☐ Overcoming temptation in the desert
    - ☐ Agonizing in Gethsemane

23. Who is Christ?
    - ☐ Revealer
    - ☐ Messiah
    - ☐ Teacher–example
    - ☐ Redeemer
    - ☐ Suffering Servant

EVANGELISM

24. I regard evangelism as effective if it brings someone to:
    - ☐ Sense the priority of being over doing
    - ☐ Encounter the plight of the oppressed
    - ☐ Be awakened to try
    - ☐ Belief
    - ☐ Find the courage to continue on

∾

WORLD 1   WORLD 2   WORLD 3   WORLD 4   WORLD 5

SCORING

The answers under each of the previous 24 questions are arranged in the order of the five Worlds. Thus, under each question, World 1 is the first option, followed by Worlds 2, 3, 4, and 5. Tally how many 1's appear in the first option of each question, and record that number in the box for World 1 immediately above. Do the same for the second option, recording the total under World 2, and so forth, until you have done all five options. Then go back and do the same for the options you have marked with a 2, indicating in each of the boxes above the distribution of your second choices. The World in which your first choices cluster will indicate your primary World, and where your second choices cluster will suggest your secondary World.

None of us lives in only one World, but for most of us there is one that is home base. Ideal is the ability to enter empathetically into each of the other Worlds, while having a welcoming place to which we can return for renewal. The more evenly distributed the answers, the more likely it is that one has not yet come to a committed spiritual base, and is still searching for home. Second and third preferences provide creative dimensions to one's primary World.

Since individuals are often unaware of their own theological-spiritual identity, this inventory will likely be helpful in spiritual direction. Likewise, it serves as a basis for knowing what disciplines and tools might be best for deepening a person's identity. It can also help those whose orientation is unduly narrow or closed to become broadened and more open in perspective. This inventory is also helpful personally to those who are giving spiritual direction. Directors need to be aware of their own spiritual orientation, as a caution against projecting their own World and theological preferences onto those they are directing.[1]

$$\maltese$$

THE TWELVE-STEP PROGRAM
AS A SPIRITUAL DIRECTION MODEL

Perhaps no recent program in spiritual direction has had more impact than the twelve-step approach developed by Bill Wilson for alcoholics. It has proven itself effective not only for alcoholics, however, but also for working with those experiencing personal and/or societal rejection for behavior springing from other conditions over which they feel powerless to control. In fact, this covers more than the spectrum of recognized addictions, from drugs to obesity. Those committed to this spiritual direction approach insist on its usefulness for everyone, since all persons are addicted to their own version of shortcomings. This program combines the corporate spiritual direction of the meeting itself with one-with-one spiritual direction, available through a personal sponsor who can be reached anytime, day or night, for particularized support, accountability, and modeling of what is possible. This spiritual direction of "tough love" is rooted solidly in Theological World 4, that of

Condemnation and Forgiveness. Its inspiration is the Oxford movement, intent on fostering the spiritual renewal of the Church of England.

There is good reason to believe that the present widespread use of this twelve-step program of spiritual direction outside the church is the result of the church's forfeiture of spiritual direction within the church. I remember as a child in a small Appalachian coal-mining town hearing the preaching of tent revivalists. And one night, as Billy Sunday made his altar call, my uncle, the consummate alcoholic, came forward—crying, falling on his knees in confession, and being changed for life through the ongoing support and accountability of the little church on the corner of Argyle and Main Streets.

The premise of the twelve-step program is clear. Without spiritual direction, the alcoholic can never recover. Thus, what is needed is a path of spiritual growth that provides for clear, step-by-step spiritual direction. For this, there are twelve designated steps, reflecting a five-part spiritual dynamic.

The first three steps are a "surrender": I can't; God can; so let God do it. **Step 1**, the absolute beginning point, is a deflation of ego, meaning the collapse of self-centeredness, rooted in the conclusion that the self is powerless to control the self. **Step 2** is the acknowledgment of a Power greater than oneself. In **Step 3**, one turns one's life over to that Power. An antiphon from Week 2 of the breviary says it all: "Surrender to God, and he will do everything for you."

While some Christians may believe that they are beyond this initial phase, residents of World 4 hold that in Christian self-deception we find harbored some of the worst examples of addiction, especially indicated by the popular label of workaholic. Luther's absolute dictum at the heart of the Protestant Reformation is a recovery of Saint Paul's confession: "I do not understand my own actions. For I do not do what I want, but I do the very thing I hate" (Rom. 7:15). One way or another, we all seem driven to justify our own lives, against the inner gnawing of our low self-image, attempting to quiet the fact that whoever really knows me will not like me—including myself. This approach to spiritual direction holds that the alcoholic only shares in more graphic terms the human condition claiming us all. Thus, acknowledgment of this human condition as individually expressed is the necessary starting place.

Step 4, with the help of one's spiritual director, is the difficult task of making a painful and thorough inventory of all that one has done to hurt and abuse others. **Step 5**, even more painful, is the confession of all this sordid life to another human being. Clergy are being trained to help with this event of "washing clean" and giving complete forgiveness. For some this entails the experience of sharing without being condemned. For others, this step is a graphic example of Catholic confession at its best, complete with absolution:

> God, the Father of mercies, through the death and resurrection of his Son has reconciled the world to himself; and sent the Holy Spirit among us for the forgiveness of sins; through the ministry of the Church may God give you pardon and peace, and I absolve you from your sins, in the name of the Father, and of the Son, and of the Holy Spirit. Amen.

The first phase, then, is *surrender,* and the second is *confession* of one's life thus far. The next phases can be labeled *housekeeping, maintenance,* and *mission.* The housekeeping of **Step 6** is in identifying the character defects that underlie one's questionable behavior, of which alcohol misuse is an expression. This is followed by **Step 7**, again the acknowledgment of our inability and, thus, the need to "let go and let God." The theological root throughout the twelve-step program is that God can and will do what we will not and cannot do. The process is a spiral that becomes increasingly concrete. In Catholic confession, forgiveness gives rise to satisfaction, meaning to undo, as much as possible, the ill effects of the sin one has confessed. This is the case as well in the twelve-step process. In

Step 8, one makes a list of those whom one has harmed, a list to which one is expected to add, for awareness increases as "letting go" deepens. **Step 9**, very sensitively expressed, is to make amends where possible, but never in a way that hurts or harms others. That is, while blurting things out may help one feel "cleaner," healing should never be irresponsible. Otherwise, the healing process can be more hurtful than the condition one is attempting to undo. Love is both the motive and the goal, and taking responsibility for oneself is the means. The dynamic is personal willingness to let God take one's failings away.

The next two steps can be classified as "maintenance." **Step 10** is a continuation of the daily inventory of the harm one has caused others and self, as in the earlier housekeeping, admitting where one is wrong. As Jesus' parable illustrated, a house cleansed of a demon can become an emptiness that even more demons may discover and move into. **Step 11** entails the use of prayer, meditation, and other spiritual practices to deepen and strengthen one's relationship with God.

The final phase, **Step 12**, is the mission of knowing that the goal of healing entails helping others heal. That is, through spiritual direction one learns how to become a spiritual director. Once an individual has been spiritually awakened, his or her calling becomes to awaken others spiritually. Particularly helpful is the underlying dictum that when all else fails, work with another alcoholic, trying together to remain sober. Here is the awareness that the spiritual director needs always to be, to use Nouwen's phrase, a "wounded healer." Only those who know themselves as being in need of spiritual direction can make trustworthy directors for others. As the African American spiritual puts it, "Not my brother, nor my sister, but it's me, O Lord, standing in the need of prayer."

✛

MYERS-BRIGGS TYPE INDICATOR

The Myers-Briggs Type Indicator (MBTI) is widely used for various purposes. It no longer needs to be administered professionally but is available in a number of forms. Materials for qualified users, as well as a Form G Self-Scorable Edition, are available through Psychological Publications, Inc., 5300 Hollywood Blvd., Los Angeles, CA 90027. An abbreviated version appears in David Keirsey and Marilyn Bates, *Please Understand Me: An Essay on Temperament Styles* (Del Mar, Calif.: Promethean Books, 1978). The MBTI Inventory is also available on the Internet.

Helpful materials for understanding and using this typology are Gordon Lawrence, *People Types and Tiger Stripes* (Gainesville, Fla.: Center for Applications of Psychological Types, 1982); Isabel Briggs Myers and Peter Myers, *Gifts Differing* (Palo Alto, Calif.: Consulting Psychologists Press, 1980; and Isabel Briggs Myers, *Introduction to Type* (Palo Alto, Calif.: Consulting Psychologists Press, 1998). My effort at applying the MBTI theologically and spiritually appears in

"Myers–Briggs Type Indicator: A Psychological Tool for Approaching Theology and Spirituality," *Weavings*, 6:3 (May/June 1991): 32–43.

The MBTI is not a diagnostic tool, but a descriptive one, locating the person in the midst of sixteen contrasting personality types. These are based on four Jungian scales:

1. *Extrovert–Introvert.* This refers to the home base where the person is centered and to which one returns for recentering—either through relating to others (E) or through quiet solitariness (I).

2. *Thinking–Feeling.* This distinction indicates how a person weighs data for making decisions—whether through objective analysis and rational conclusion (T), or subjectively through shared emotions as to what "feels right" (F).

3. *Intuitive–Sensing.* Here the difference is between one's preferred source of data—whether through imagining the possibilities (N) or through empirical facts (S).

4. *Judging–Perceiving.* This scale refers to how one knows what one knows—whether by making quick decisions to be verified through their lived implications (J), or more tentatively through assimilating relevant data (P).

One's personality type depends on the weight of each scale, as well as the sequence in which the scales interact. It is not always necessary to understand the complexity of all sixteen types for them to be useful in spiritual direction. Let me illustrate this personally. For years I believed I was bereft of any spirituality because the only model I had was my parents, who were introverts (I). Their piety of prayerful silence only elicited from me thoughts of mischief. Only much later did I discover, much on my own and by chance, that there could be such a thing as an extrovert spirituality (E). Likewise, as a youth, I felt alienated from my small church youth group because the meetings were primarily a sharing of feelings (F). Only at Yale did I learn that I had a mind, and that thinking was a valid way of celebrating the God of creation (T). Also, as a youth I was never impressed by those who claimed to base their faith on physical things like miracles, or tangible appearances of Jesus, or apparitions of Mary, or hearing voices (S). Only in college, claimed by great poetry, did I understand that for me the truth of Christianity rested in its capacity to grasp my imagination with creative vision (N). Further, when a group of my teenage friends and I planned to go somewhere to eat, I would become frustrated by how much time they would spend discussing where to go (P). My favorite line was: "I don't care where we go, but let's go somewhere! If we don't like it, we can go somewhere else!"—spoken as a true "judging" (J) personality to my "perceiving" friends.

Later, the MBTI made clear that these same ways of functioning determined how I taught, which followed directly from the way I learned best. This was through action-reflection, or doing and evaluating. Thus, while some of my colleagues might lecture, for example, on death and resurrection, I would take my class to the morgue, assign them to nameless cadavers and instruct each student to prepare a funeral service for his/her newfound "friend." And while other colleagues might lecture on poverty and social justice, I had students live on the streets for twenty-four hours without money. In discovering about myself and how I function, I learned concurrently about the contrasting ways others learn. Then it was that I recognized spiritual direction as one of the best ways of learning, for it is built on diverse means for accomplishing diverse things in each of us, who collectively are quite diverse.

THE ENNEAGRAM

The Enneagram, from the Greek word *enneas* for "nine," can be helpful in identifying each person's inevitable "addiction." While the Myers-Briggs Type Indicator indicates the positive dimensions of one's personality, the Enneagram indicates the negative dimensions, the compulsions that coping ingrains into each person's personality as its basic driving force. Consistent with Christian theology, the Enneagram insists that there is in each of us a "paralysis" or hindrance to becoming our authentic selves. This is a defense mechanism by which we attempt unsuccessfully to cope with our life situations. *Sin* is the appropriate term, for it results from the self attempting to achieve security and meaning by its own efforts. Spiritual direction is likely to be sought when this "hidden sin," or dark side of one's personality, will not be quieted. Through direction an individual can be helped to see what it is that he/she attempts to avoid, to which the coping is a reaction. This is usually not difficult for the director to discern, but it is usually difficult for the person to acknowledge, for we tend to take pride in seeing our coping as an accomplishment.

The director should not succumb to the temptation of making direction simply an alternative way to cope, which the Enneagram might encourage. What is needed is healing, dealing with the concrete *why* of one's avoidance, with appropriate spiritual disciplines serving as invitations to the Spirit's action. Even if this cause is overly raw, some changes can still be managed by dealing with the symptoms.

This is the typology of persons which for me the Enneagram provides:

1. The **Perfectionist** tries, as a way of coping with anger, to be acceptable by doing everything "right." Negatively, Perfectionists can be excessively critical and impatient. Positively, they can be careful, direct, and sacrificial. The healing goal is *serenity,* attainable through redemption as unconditional acceptance by perceiving Jesus as a failure from the human point of view.

2. The **Altruist** tries, as a way of coping with neediness, to be appreciated by being helpful. Negatively, Altruists can manipulate, being unaware of their hidden motives. Positively, they can be sensitive and hospitable. The healing goal is *humility,* attainable through grace as a free gift to the needy and undeserving.

3. The **Achiever** tries, as a way of coping with the fear of failure, to be of worth by being successful. Negatively, this workaholic type can be demanding and impersonal. Positively, Achievers can be efficient, enthusiastic, and visionary. The healing goal is learning how to *be* through experiencing love as a "nevertheless" rather than as a "because," so that success rests in God's hands, calling the Achiever instead to be faithful.

4. The **Feeler** tries, as a way of coping with consternation over being ordinary, to be special by the depth of his or her emotions. Negatively, this type can be theatrical, complaining, and unhappy. Positively, they can be compassionate and creative. The healing goal is *composure or calmness,* made possible by experiencing one's self as the one for whom Christ left the ninety and nine.

5. The **Thinker** tries, as a way of coping with the feeling of emptiness, to be full of knowledge. Negatively, this type can be distant, noncommittal, and not in touch with their feelings. Positively, they can be informed, reflective, and discerning. The healing goal is *engagement,* made possible by experiencing God through the Christ who gave himself unto death.

6. The **Conservative** tries, as a way of coping with the fear of his/her inner inclinations, to be secure by insisting that everything be done according to rules and duties. Negatively, these types can be dogmatic, insecure, and "super-responsible." Positively, they are reliable, prudent, and loyal. The healing goal is *courage,* possible through being affirmed as a covenant partner in the width and depth of God's providential vision.

7. The **Optimist** tries, as a way of coping with pain, to disregard what is not affirmative. Negatively, this type can be superficial, through avoidance and loquaciousness. Positively, they can be cheerful, friendly, and happy. The healing goal is *realistic commitment,* sensed through God's activity in Jesus Christ as incarnational in the totality of human living.

8. The **Powerful** tries, as a way of coping with weakness, to control everything. Negatively, this type can manipulate and intimidate. Positively, they can be courageous and productive. The healing goal is *empathy,* enabled by experiencing Jesus as the Suffering Servant and the Sacrificial Lamb.

9. The **Passive** tries, as a way of coping with fear of conflict, to reduce tension by always "making peace." Negatively, this type can procrastinate, react, and seem colorless. Positively, they can be impartial listeners who are nonthreatening, and can be agents of reconciliation by taking issues on themselves. The healing goal is *diligence,* made possible through the God who takes sides.

✛

TDF PERSONALITY INTERPRETATION

David Farr developed a simple and yet surprisingly useful approach to understanding the process by which diverse personality types come to action.[1] All of us use three functions, but their different sequences result in contrasting ways in which persons behave, learn, and interact with others. These functions are:

1. *Thinking:* the mode for organizing and using data.

2. *Deciding:* the mode for evaluating data (for example, acceptability, relevance, significance) for rendering a judgment.

3. *Feeling:* the mode for experiencing the impact of something, as in the "feel" of one's self, others, or things.

Each of us has one of these three modes as a favorite, one that is much less developed, and one that is between these two in terms of development and use. In coming to action, the sequence is from the preferred to the second, and finally the least preferred. A person's primary mode is identifiable by the relative amount of time he or she spends on coming to action. Based on one's favorite mode, we can speak of three primary personality types:

1. *Thinkers.* Their strength resides in their data and ideas; they are logical, systematic, orderly, rational, analytical, organized, and articulate; and they plan in advance. Their potential weaknesses are not being in touch with their feelings; being more interested in understanding than in doing; and being tedious, indecisive, uncommitted, and needlessly complex.

2. *Deciders.* The strength of these persons is their many opinions and their ability to make efficient evaluations and judgments; they are committed, clear, energetic, persuasive, and task-oriented. Their potential weaknesses are in being opinionated, judgmental, oversimplifying, and taking action without sufficient data.

3. *Feelers.* Their strength resides in their rich experience; they are intuitive, sensitive, and caring. Their potential weaknesses are in being subjective, impulsive, moody, ill-informed, easily persuaded, and vacillating.

These personality dominants are filled out by the sequence of the remaining two modes which one follows in coming to action. This results in six diverse personality types: TDF, TFD, DFT, DTF, FDT, FTD. We can illustrate how this works by considering two of these types as examples.

TFDs initially face the environment by thinking (that is, analyzing, organizing, interpreting). They respond with feeling (for example, excitement, fear, anxiety). From the weight of this "feeling impact" of the data, they either make a decision or return to the thinking mode for more data. Here, as in all types, the first and second modes, being most familiar and used, tend to circle until the impact is sufficient to pressure the third mode into action. Thus, when someone has difficulty coming to an action, it is usually because of hesitancy to exercise the third mode, which is the most undeveloped.

In contrast is the DFT personality type. These persons are eager to try something—an opinion, judgment, almost anything. What follows is the feeling that this decision affects, which is the way in which these persons try the decision "on for size." The result is the magnetizing of their feelings. This sequence of D and F cycles until it is strong enough to nudge the thinking processes sufficiently to work on how to do the action. In this way one's strong energy and enthusiasm become oriented toward a "how" of action.

This typological understanding is useful in spiritual direction particularly in three ways. First, often a person is "hung up," unable to come to action about some important aspect of his/her life. This is likely to be because the third mode needs to be encouraged and held accountable; otherwise, the first two modes will keep processing in a circular impasse. I can illustrate this with my own case as a DFT. As a D, I easily become involved in a number of ideas and am able to feel deeply about them (F). Yet until the T (thinking) is disciplined and held accountable to thinking through how to put some of these ideas into operation, I am inclined to plunge into something else, leaving "balls in the air," so to speak.

Second, knowing one's favorite mode helps identify those disciplines most likely to be helpful in encouraging the directee toward a mature spirituality. Thus, TFDs, for example, will do best by being given something to read so as to become informed, weighing from this information that which feels right or possible. The danger, of course, is that they may feel that they will never know enough to be able to decide to do any of what they read. DFTs, in contrast, learn best by an action–reflection mode. Instead of reading about contemplation, they would thrive, for example, on spending a weekend in a monastery, where contemplation is the way of life. The danger here, of course, is that such a person will delight just in "monastery hopping."

Third, understanding this process helps the director be patient, yet firm when necessary, if the directee is having difficulty coming to action.

Other interesting factors can emerge from this understanding. The Thinker prefers personal spiritual direction; the Decider prefers communal direction; the Feeler prefers a one-with-one direction. The Thinker is primarily interested in the past, thriving on learning about spiritual traditions. The Decider is future-oriented, concerned for possibilities of change. The Feeler is interested mostly in the present, for what is immediately available to experience. The Thinker has a preference for seeing; the Decider for doing; and the Feeler for hearing. Thinkers tend to be more conservative, being problem-oriented. Deciders are optimists, appreciating opportunities in regard to which they are risk takers. Feelers are more realistic, celebrating the now.

In direction, it is helpful to know that the TDF desires to be complete, the TFD to be perfect, the FDT to be involved, the FTD to be pleasing, the DFT to be urgent, and the DTF to be strong. A person is likely to have most interpersonal difficulty when relating with the opposite personality, so that a TFD is most likely to find bewildering the DFT, for these seem to do everything backwards. One can function best in a group setting with those whose sequence is in the same direction, even though persons may enter the process at different points. Thus, one direction is TFDTFDTFD, while the opposite is DFTDFTDFT.

Thinkers exercise power through the use of information, and thus are most themselves when they are "in the know." Deciders exercise power through brokering advantages by networking, and thus are most themselves when they are in the middle of things. Feelers experience power through relationships, and thus are most themselves when they are well-related. When trouble arises, it is usually because the Thinker is being limited or deprived of the flow of data. The Decider experiences problems when deprived of linkages. The Feeler is undone when relationships are undercut or infected.

✛

FAMILY SYSTEMS

R ecent research on families tends to focus on the anatomy of alcoholic or dysfunctional families. Yet the evidence is considerable that the birth order of members of all families tends to establish certain characteristics in each person. Based on my own experience as the father of five children, I have found it useful as a spiritual director to give attention to possible implications of family structure for the person being directed.

1. *The first child.* The firstborn tends to be ultraresponsible, whether as the custodian of the dysfunctional family name or as the center of attention as the only child. Often this child can be characterized as a workaholic, claimed by doing and uneasy about being, fearful of never quite measuring up.

2. *The second child* often feels a need to be different from his/her older brother or sister, whether that means acting positively or negatively, depending on the characteristics of the prior sibling.

3. *The third child* is often characterized by the need to be totally outside the competitive dynamic of the first two siblings. Depending upon whether he or she has extrovert or introvert characteristics, this child will tend to be the opposite, fleeing the home in activity, or nestling in the cocoon of his/her own room. Sometimes the third child's role will be that of the "black sheep" or the family clown.

4. *Additional children*. These tend to be characterized by the dynamic established by the first three children, often feeling like outsiders, or pressured unwillingly into taking sides as a way of coping.

For more information on the impact of birth order on one's personality, see Edwin H. Friedman, *Generation to Generation* (New York: Guilford Press, 1985), and Michael E. Kerr and Murray Bowen, *Family Evaluation* (New York: W. W. Norton, 1988).

THE JO-HARI WINDOW

The Jo-Hari Window is a useful tool for spiritual direction. The following is an adaptation and expansion of an idea first suggested in 1955 by Joe Luft and Harry Ingham at the Western Training Laboratory in Group Development. The Jo-Hari Window is comprised of four quadrants.

Illustration 1

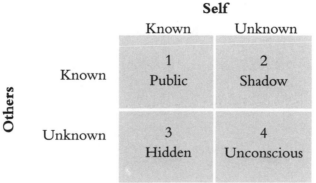

Area 1 represents the Public Self—the self known to the person and to others. (See Illustration 1.) The size of that area indicates the degree to which that person feels free. If small, the person is unaware and closed. (See Illustration 2.) If large, the person is not unduly intimidated either by others or haunted by unknown aspects of the self. (See Illustration 3.)

Area 2 represents the Shadow Self, which is unknown to the person but recognized by others. An example might be a person in whom anger continues to be inappropriately triggered, while the person passes this off as justified or as the way everyone acts. Thus, such persons are unaware of imposing themselves on others.

Illustration 2 **The Shadow Self**

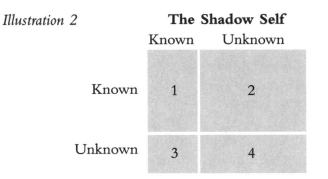

Area 3 is the Hidden Self, which, while known to the person, is kept hidden from others. This person is self-aware but closed, being insecure and cautious in relating to others. Illustrative might be persons who avoid intimacy out of shame over their past life.

Illustration 3 **The Hidden Self**

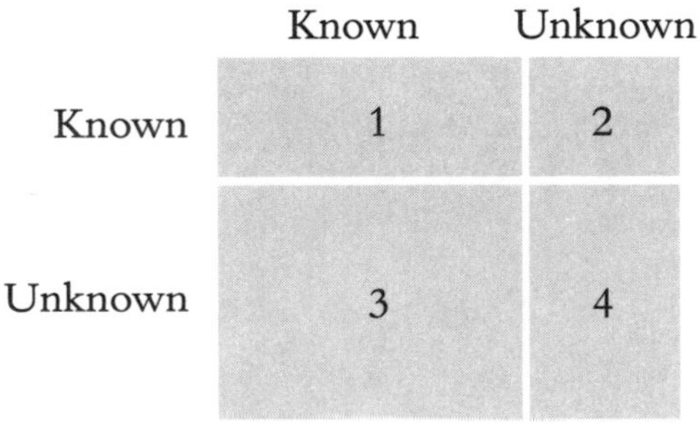

	Known	Unknown
Known	1	2
Unknown	3	4

Area 4 is the Unconscious Self, which is the area unknown both to the person and to others. The unconscious arena is where each person, especially during the earliest years of life, represses situations and memories that are too painful to cope with. These never fully disappear. If the pain and heaviness of repression are weighty, memories will keep surfacing, reappearing in the symbolism of dreams, as unknown anxiety, or as destructive projection.

Illustration 4

The Unconscious/Closed Self

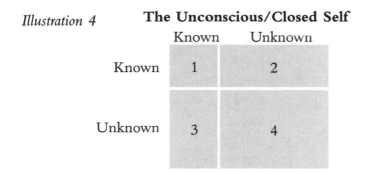

Illustration 4 indicates the enormity of the unknown in threatening certain persons. On the other hand, ingredients of the unconscious can be sublimated so that their energies are directed into positive channels. Thus, through spiritual direction, or therapy if necessary, the unconscious can become a reservoir of creativity and depth. Tapping this reservoir becomes possible when persons are given the loving support that enables them to become vulnerable, with courage sufficient to face whatever "demons" are closeted there. To the degree that the Public Self expands progressively into this closeted unconscious, the area carved out can be meaningfully referred to as one's soul.

Illustration 5

Public Self with Soul

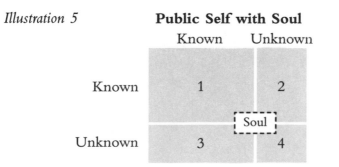

The soul is that potential depth at the center of each person—as a rich reservoir of imaginatively available symbolism, imagery, and memory. This is the center of one's true self. To illustrate, there are persons for whom the term *superficial* seems appropriate, as evidenced by conversations that are continually peripheral. They go nowhere, for there seems to be nowhere to go. There is little to discuss beyond the weather and last night's slapstick TV. There are other persons, however, about whom one senses a wisdom, a depth, a wealth of experience, a center forged deeply by life. Educated or uneducated, such persons seem to possess a sacred place within themselves, where they have pondered. We sense that somehow they *know,* whatever that might mean. And no matter how much they might share, there always seems to be more, at a depth that cannot be emptied. And so, rather than try, one is sometimes content simply to be in their presence. Such soul depth is the goal of spiritual direction. (See Illustration 5.)

✚

PRACTICING FOR THE NOW
WITH THE ONCE WAS

Many persons have a hard time savoring and relishing the now. They can sometimes be helped by evoking fond memories of the once was, for example, when they saw life through the eyes of a child. For those of us who are older, the following is an exercise in "Remembering When."

Remember . . . ?
- Playing hide-and-seek at dusk
- Sitting on the porch on a hot summer night
- Playing Red Light, Green Light; Capture the Flag; jacks; kickball; dodgeball; Mother, May I
- Running through the sprinkler
- Catching lightning bugs in a Mason jar with holes in the lid
- Sliding down a snowy hill on a piece of cardboard

- Enjoying homemade cookies and cold milk at Grandma's
- Surveying the whole world from a treetop
- Cops and Robbers, Cowboys and Indians, Skin the Cat
- Penny tops that spun forever and penny balsa wood airplanes that looped
- Laughing until you ached and ran out of breath
- Jumping on the bed, and pillow fights
- Eating a chocolate ice-cream cone on a warm evening
- Getting a cherry Coke at the drug store if you "behaved"
- Catching snowflakes on your tongue
- Sliding on the snowy sidewalk until it was slippery
- When keeping a special secret was what made friends
- When finding a nickel made your week
- When Judgment Day meant being sent to the principal's office
- When decisions were made by playing "One potato, two potato, three potato, four"
- When healing depended upon having cuts and bruises kissed
- When snow was a miracle rather than a hardship
- When luxury meant having school called off
- When sleds were the fastest vehicles imaginable
- When having to go to bed was the ultimate punishment
- When wearing a hat was a parental indignity
- When coveting meant clutching one penny in front of the candy case at the drug store
- When the neighbors' garbage cans were the tabernacles of untold treasures
- When coming of age happened the day Dad stopped the car and asked, "Do you want to drive?"
- When water of any kind was the ultimate fascination
- When the bean actually "hatched" in the paper cup on the kindergarten windowsill
- When rain backed up in the alley rivaled Hoover Dam

- When your first "house" was called a hideout
- When a box of sparklers on Fourth of July evening was the ultimate spectacle
- When a loaf of bread rarely made it home without getting squashed
- When getting a bike was the ultimate liberation
- When old underwear was destined to become kite tails
- When girls (or boys) became scary overnight
- When coming of age for a young man meant getting knickers and boots with a pocket knife on the side
- When balsa wood was the ultimate building material
- When baseball was played with a broomstick and a rubber ball
- When you could create any game with a few empty tin cans
- When "pick up" was a totally innocent phrase
- When refrigerators were orange crates in the window
- When scooters were two-by-fours with skate wheels
- When waxed paper was invented for sliding boards
- When what friends had in their lunch sacks was always more interesting than yours
- When "oly-oly-oxen-free" made perfect sense
- When war was a card game, and water balloons were the most lethal weapons
- When detergent had free dishes inside, and Cracker Jacks gave real prizes
- When losing a nickel allowance was the worst tragedy
- When every dog was a mutt
- When resurrection meant seeing your old clothes in the new throw rug
- When sitting on the curb by the telephone pole was the center of the universe

NOTES

CHAPTER 1
Spiritual Direction: Its Types, Purposes, and Models

1. Karl Barth, *Dogmatics in Outline*, trans. G. T. Thomson (London: SCM Press, 1949), 35.

2. Thomas C. Oden, *Care of Souls in the Classic Tradition*, ed. Don S. Browning (Philadelphia, Pa.: Fortress Press, 1984), 18.

3. William O. Paulsell, *Letters from a Hermit: with Letters from Matthew Kelty, O.C.S.O.* (Springfield, Ill.: Templegate Publishers, 1978), 61.

4. For development of and liturgy for such contracting, see W. Paul Jones, "Friendship and Circles of Commitment," *Weavings*, 7:3 (May/June 1992): 35–40.

5. See the "Twelve-Step Program As a Spiritual Direction Model," Appendix 6 of this book.

6. See Lovett Hayes Weems Jr., *The Gospel According to Wesley: A Summary of John Wesley's Message* (Nashville: Discipleship Resources, 1982), 29.

7. *The Book of Discipline of The United Methodist Church—2000* (Nashville: The United Methodist Publishing House, 2000), 49.

8. This distinction is analogous to the one between situation ethics and contextual ethics. Compare, for example, Joseph F. Fletcher, *Situation Ethics: The New Morality* (Philadelphia, Pa.: Westminster Press, 1966) and Paul Louis Lehmann, *Ethics in a Christian Context* (New York: Harper & Row, 1963).

9. José Ortega y Gasset, *Man and People*, trans. Willard R. Trask (New York: W. W. Norton and Company, 1957), 99.

10. Alice Miller, *The Drama of the Gifted Child*, trans. Ruth Ward (New York: Basic Books, 1981). See W. Paul Jones, "Suffering into Wholeness: Vulnerability and the Imprisoned Child Within," *Quarterly Review*, 15:3 (Fall 1995): 275–85.

11. Dietrich Bonhoeffer, *Life Together*, trans. John W. Doberstein (New York: Harper & Row, 1954), 119.

12. Sandra M. Schneiders, "The Contemporary Ministry of Spiritual Direction," *Chicago Studies* 15:1 (Spring 1976): 119.

13. Søren Kierkegaard, *Stages on Life's Way*, trans. Walter Lowrie (Princeton, N.J.: Princeton University Press, 1940).

14. Jim Fowler and Sam Keen, *Life Maps: Conversations on the Journey of Faith*, ed. Jerome Berryman (Waco, Tex.: Word Books, 1978), 118 ff.

15. Matthew Kelty, *Sermons in a Monastery: Chapter Talks*, ed. William O. Paulsell (Kalamazoo, Mich.: Cistercian Publications, 1983), 7, 17.

16. Dag Hammarskjöld, *Markings*, trans. Leif Sjöberg and W. H. Auden (New York: Alfred A. Knopf, 1965), 205.

17. See, for example, *Monos* 2:6 (November–December 1999).

CHAPTER 2
Spiritual Diversity:
The Tailor-made Nature of Spiritual Direction

1. See H. Richard Niebuhr, "Christ the Transformer of Culture" in *Christ and Culture* (New York: Harper & Row, 1951), 190–229.

2. David B. Barrett, ed., *World Christian Encyclopedia: A Comparative Study of Churches and Religions in the Modern World AD 1900–2000* (New York: Oxford University Press, 1982).

3. See W. Paul Jones, *A Season in the Desert: Making Time Holy* (Brewster, Mass.: Paraclete Press, 2000), 91.

4. These options will be developed later into "Theological Worlds."

5. I describe this healing process in detail in W. Paul Jones, *Teaching the Dead Bird to Sing: Living the Hermit Life Without and Within* (Brewster, Mass.: Paraclete Press, 2002).

6. W. Paul Jones, *Worlds within a Congregation: Dealing with Theological Diversity* (Nashville: Abingdon Press, 2000). This book resulted from research into how residents of each World are best fed—in terms of learning styles, sacraments, and worship; what special gifts each World brings to the life of the church; and how persons in each World are best reached in terms of preaching, evangelism and pastoral care.

7. See W. Paul Jones, *Theological Worlds: Understanding the Alternative Rhythms of Christian Belief* (Nashville: Abingdon Press, 1989) for a fuller

description of each world, illustrating each with resources from literature, mythology, painting, and music.

8. Bernard of Clairvaux, "On Loving God," in *Bernard of Clairvaux: Selected Works* (New York: Paulist Press, 1987), 199.

9. This is an abridgment and a paraphrase of André Louf, *Tuning In to Grace: The Quest for God*, trans. John Vriend (Kalamazoo, Mich.: Cistercian Publications, 1992), 76–77.

10. See W. Paul Jones, *A Season in the Desert,* "Prayers to Honor Each Other's Stories," Appendix 6.

CHAPTER 3
Communal Spiritual Direction:
The Wesleyan Movement As Model

1. Diadochus of Photice, "On Spiritual Perfection," in *The Liturgy of the Hours,* 3 (New York: Catholic Book Publishing Co., 1975):101.

2. A sermon by Saint Caesarius of Arles, in *The Liturgy of the Hours* 4:1548.

3. See *The United Methodist Hymnal* (Nashville: The United Methodist Publishing House, 1989), Nos. 337, 378, 374, 536.

4. James Nelson, "United Methodist Heritage," section I, paper C, of the *Spiritual Formation Resource Packet* (Nashville: The United Methodist Board of Higher Education and Ministry, 1982), 2.

5. *The Book of Discipline of The United Methodist Church—1980* (Nashville: The United Methodist Publishing House, 1980), 73.

6. James Nelson, "United Methodist Heritage," 2.

7. Ibid.

8. See Ernst Troeltsch, *The Social Teaching of the Christian Churches*, vol. 1, trans. Olive Wyon (New York: The Macmillan Co., 1931), 331 ff.

9. See *The Book of Discipline—2000,* 49–50.

10. Ibid., 72.

11. Ibid.

12. See James A. Coriden, Thomas J. Green, and Donald E. Heintschel, eds., *The Code of Canon Law: A Text and Commentary* (New York: Paulist Press, 1985), 1 ff.

13. *The Works of John Wesley*, 5 (Grand Rapids, Mich.: Zondervan Publishing House, n.d.): 187.

14. See W. Paul Jones, *A Table in the Desert: Making Space Holy* (Brewster, Mass.: Paraclete Press, 2001), "Lectio Divina," Appendix 3.

15. *Book of Discipline—2000*, Article XVII, 63.

16. Ibid.

17. Ibid., question 16, 204.

18 "Jesus, United by Thy Grace," No. 561, *The United Methodist Hymnal.*

19. *Book of Discipline—2000*, 73.

20. See *The Works of John Wesley*, 5:296.

21. *Handbook for Today's Catholic* (Liguori, Mo.: Liguori Publications, 1994), 57.

22. Weems, *The Gospel According to Wesley*, 41.

23. Cited in John Ryan, *Alleged Socialism of the Church Fathers* (St. Louis, Mo.: B. Herder Book Co., 1913), 9.

24. *The World Almanac and Book of Facts 2002* (New York: World Almanac Books, 2002), 487.

25. Ibid., 40.

26. United Nations Web site: www.un.org

27. Bread for the World Web site: www.bread.org

28. Ibid.

29. *USA Today*, 14 December 2000.

30. www.un.org

31. Environment News Service Web site: ens.lycos.com

32. www.korpios.org

33. *Forbes*, 18 March 2002 (found at www.forbes.com).

34. *Time*, 29 June 1998 (found at www.time.com).

35. *Forbes*, 18 March 2002 (found at www.forbes.com).

36. Summary findings of Bureau of Justice Prison Statistics: www.ojp.usdoj.gov

37. Nelson, "United Methodist Heritage," 5.

CHAPTER 4
The Art of One-with-one Spiritual Direction

1. For more information about confidentiality, see the Guidelines for Ethical Conduct of Spiritual Directors International at www.sdiworld.org or write to SDI at 1329 Seventh Avenue, San Francisco, CA 94122-2507.

2. T. S. Eliot, "The Hollow Men," in *The Complete Poems and Plays* (New York: Harcourt, Brace and Co., 1952), 56.

3. See W. Paul Jones, *A Season in the Desert*, "Sentence Completion Inventory," Appendix 4.

4. See these other tools for spiritual direction: W. Paul Jones, *A Season in the Desert*, "Image Association Inventory," Appendix 5; and in this book: "TDF Personality Interpretation," Appendix 9; "Family Systems," Appendix 10; "The Jo-hari Window," Appendix 11.

5. See, for example, Eckhart Tolle, *The Power of Now: A Guide to Spiritual Enlightenment* (Novato, Calif.: New World Library, 1999).

6. Mary M. Funk, *Thoughts Matter: The Practice of the Spiritual Life* (New York: Continuum International Publishing Group, 1999).

7. Rudolf Bultmann et al., *Kerygma and Myth: A Theological Debate*, ed. Hans Werner Bartsch (New York: Harper Torchbooks, 1961), 32.

8. From "Heaven and Earth, and Sea and Air." Words by Joachim Neander, 1650–1680. Translated by Catherine Winkworth, 1827–1878, altered.

CHAPTER 5
Dimensions, Exercises, and
Resources for Spiritual Direction

1. For a details on some of these exercises and others, see W. Paul Jones, *Trumpet at Full Moon: An Introduction to Christian Spirituality As Diverse Practice* (Louisville, Ky.: Westminster/John Knox Press, 1992).

2. T. S. Eliot, "The Dry Salvages," *Four Quartets*, in *The Complete Poems and Plays*, 136.

3. See W. Paul Jones, *A Table in the Desert*, "Two Short Prayers (for the moments before sleep, and the moments after awakening)," Appendix 1.

4. See "Practicing for the Now with the Once Was," Appendix 12 of this book.

5. *Bernard of Clairvaux: Selected Works*, 6.

6. See the "Twelve-Step Program As a Spiritual Direction Model," Appendix 6 of this book.

7. T. S. Eliot, "The Waste Land," in *The Complete Poems and Plays*, 38.

8. Martin Heidegger, *Being and Time*, trans. John Macquarrie and Edward Robinson (New York: Harper & Row, 1962), 279 ff.

9. *Christian Prayer: The Liturgy of the Hours* (New York: Catholic Book Publishing Co., 1976).

10. See W. Paul Jones, *A Season in the Desert*, "A Daily Office (for Vigils, Lauds, Sext, Vespers, Compline)," Appendix 2; and "Two-Week Schedule for Daily Use of Psalms," Appendix 3.

11. See W. Paul Jones, "Friendship and Circles of Commitment," *Weavings*, 7:3 (May/June 1999): 35–40.

12. To deepen one's understanding of the Eucharist, one might meditate upon the relevant scriptural passages. See W. Paul Jones, *A Table in the Desert*, Appendix 6. Also see W. Paul Jones, "Eucharist As Promissorial Act: A Roman Catholic/Protestant Reconciliation?" *Quarterly Review* 20:3 (Fall 2000): 305–12.

13. See "A Sample List of What to Remember Daily," in W. Paul Jones, *A Table in the Desert*, Appendix 4.

14. See "Sample Rule," Appendix 3, and "Rule and the Wesleyan Covenant," Appendix 4, both in this book. Also see W. Paul Jones, *A Table in the Desert*, "A Sample Rule," Appendix 5.

15. See W. Paul Jones, *A Season in the Desert*, "Recollection Exercise for Spiritual Direction," Appendix 1.

16. See W. Paul Jones, *A Table in the Desert*, "Journaling: An Introduction," Appendix 2.

17. From *The Rites of the Catholic Church* (New York: Pueblo Publishing Company, 1976, 1983), 382–83.

18. For more detailed instructions, see W. Paul Jones, *Trumpet at Full Moon*, 113–117. Also see Matthew Linn and Dennis Linn, *Healing of Memories* (New York: Paulist Press, 1974) and *Healing Life's Hurts: Healing Memories through Five Stages of Forgiveness* (New York: Paulist Press, 1978).

19. See "Myers–Briggs Type Indicator," Appendix 7 of this book.

20. There are currently some self-scoring Enneagram Inventories available, such as: "The Enneagram Inventory," Lifewings, P.O. Box 460688, San Antonio, TX 78246-0688. As an introduction, see Maria Beesing,

Robert J. Nogosek, and Patrick H. O'Leary, *The Enneagram: A Journey of Self Discovery* (Denville, N.J.: Dimension Books, 1984).

21. See W. Paul Jones, *A Table in the Desert*, "Lectio Divina," Appendix 3.

22. Available through Veriditas, 1100 California St., San Francisco, CA 94108.

23. See W. Paul Jones, "Beyond the Mercy of God?," *Weavings*, 15:5 (September/October 2000): 30–39.

24. This prayer is my expression of the meaning of Trinitarian spirituality.

CHAPTER 7
Spiritual Direction and Church Renewal

1. See Jones, *Worlds within a Congregation*, 217 ff.

2. Ibid.

3. *The United Methodist Book of Worship* (Nashville: The United Methodist Publishing House, 1992), 581–84.

CONCLUSION
A RHAPSODY

1. What follows draws inspiration, in part, from the pamphlet *Voyage, Vision, Venture: A Report of the Task Force on Spiritual Development* (Dayton, Ohio: American Association of Theological Schools, 1972).

2. My free translation of Numbers 6:24-26.

APPENDIX 2

1. From "Jesus, We Look to Thee" by Charles Wesley, 1707–1788.

APPENDIX 4

1. Based on "A Covenant Prayer in the Wesleyan Tradition," No. 607, *The United Methodist Hymnal*.

APPENDIX 5

1. The full "Theological Worlds Inventory," complete with descriptions, indications of strength and weaknesses, and suggestions for multiple use with congregations, can be found in W. Paul Jones, *Worlds within a Congregation: Dealing with Theological Diversity* (Nashville: Abingdon Press,

2000), Chapter 4. A fuller description of the five Theological Worlds appears in W. Paul Jones, *Theological Worlds: Understanding the Alternative Rhythms of Christian Beliefs* (Nashville: Abingdon Press, 1989). The reader is given permission to reproduce the abbreviated form in the present book, or the full version, for use in spiritual direction.

APPENDIX 9

1. More information is available from TDF Publishing, 3248 North Hoyne Ave., Chicago, IL 60618, or on the Internet at www.tdfpublishing.com.

This page is an extension of the copyright page.

"Spirit of the Living God" by Daniel Iverson. Copyright © 1935 Birdwing Music (ASCAP). International Copyright Secured. All Rights Reserved. Used by permission of EMI Christian Music Group, Brentwood, TN.

"A Theological Worlds Inventory" adapted from *Worlds within a Congregation: Dealing with Diversity* by W. Paul Jones. Copyright © 2000 by Abingdon Press. Adapted by permission.

The English translation of the Words of Absolution from *Rite of Penance* © 1974, International Committee on English in the Liturgy, Inc. All rights reserved.

Psalm 86:6*b*-7 from *The Psalms: A New Translation*. Copyright © 1963 Ladies of the Grail (England). Used by permission of GIA Publications, Inc., exclusive agent. All rights reserved.

ABOUT THE AUTHOR

Born into a family of United Methodists, W. Paul Jones became a Family Brother of the Trappist Order in 1989 and took his life vows in 1992. His pilgrimage led him to Catholicism because he found in Trappist spirituality a powerful parallel to the Wesleyan movement. As he sees it, the spiritual renewal of Catholicism is amazingly close to the spiritual renewal John Wesley attempted in the Church of England. Paul describes himself as having a Protestant mind and a Catholic heart.

Paul alternates life as a Trappist monk in the Ozark Mountains with life as a hermit in the foothills. His present social justice work centers on the rural poor and prisoners on death row. Paul is the author of eleven books, including *Teaching the Dead Bird to Sing: The Hermit Within and Without*, *A Table in the Desert: Making Space Holy*, and *A Season in the Desert: Making Time Holy*.

Dᴏɴ'ᴛ ᴍɪss ᴛʜᴇsᴇ ᴛɪᴛʟᴇs
ꜰʀᴏᴍ Uᴘᴘᴇʀ Rᴏᴏᴍ Bᴏᴏᴋs

Fᴇᴇᴅ Mʏ Sʜᴇᴘʜᴇʀᴅs
Spiritual Healing and Renewal
for Those in Christian Leadership

ʙʏ Fʟᴏʀᴀ Sʟᴏssᴏɴ Wᴜᴇʟʟɴᴇʀ

The vocation of Christian leadership can be overwhelmingly demanding, potentially wounding, and stressful. This book takes seriously the struggles and burnout of those in caregiving ministries, while affirming that God deeply cares about the well-being and sustenance of leaders within Christian communities as they feed the sheep in many diverse ways.

Writing both from her personal experience and her many years as a spiritual counselor and retreat leader, Flora Wuellner affirms the urgency of this deep need within Christian leaders to be bonded through Christ to the heart of God. Wuellner offers reflection questions and guided meditations that employ many of the reader's senses to draw them into this sustaining relationship.

ISBN 0-8358-0845-9
192 pages | Hardcover

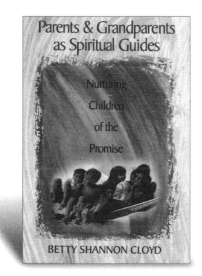

PARENTS AND
GRANDPARENTS AS
SPIRITUAL GUIDES
Nurturing Children
of the Promise

BY BETTY SHANNON CLOYD

"Today we are increasingly disconnected from one another and especially from the lives of children around us. . . . As a result, the lack of a community of caring people in the lives of children creates a tremendous crisis in the whole arena of family life," says Betty Shannon Cloyd.

The focus of *Parents and Grandparents As Spiritual Guides* is to urge parents, grandparents, and other responsible adults to reclaim the primary role of spiritually guiding children in the context of the Christian faith. Just as we care for our children physically, emotionally, and mentally, we must also care for them spiritually. Cloyd asserts that the family and the church should be in a sacred partnership, yoked together in the blessed privilege of providing a spiritual foundation for children. This book gives practical, easy-to-understand instruction for anyone who wishes to act as a mentor or spiritual guide for a child.

ISBN 0-8358-0923-4
168 pages | Paperback

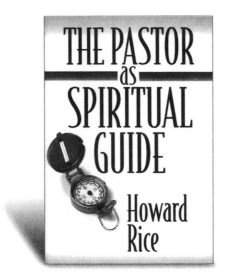

THE PASTOR AS
SPIRITUAL GUIDE

BY HOWARD RICE

This book is for clergypersons and others in Christian leadership
roles who want

- to discover a fresh approach to pastoral ministry
- to learn spiritual self-care skills to avoid burnout
- to approach their work with more imagination and
  understanding of spiritual guidance
- to measure ministerial "success" in new ways

ISBN 0-8358-0846-7
208 pages | Paperback